EDDIE McGEE'S COMPLETE BOOK OF SURVIVAL

EDDIE McGEE

STANLEY PAUL
London Melbourne Auckland Johannesburg

Stanley Paul and Co. Ltd

An imprint of Century Hutchinson Ltd

Brookmount House, 62–65 Chandos Place
Covent Garden, London WC2N 4NW

Century Hutchinson Australia (Pty) Ltd
PO Box 496, 16–22 Church Street, Hawthorn, Melbourne, Victoria 3122

Century Hutchinson New Zealand Limited
191 Archers Road, PO Box 40-086, Glenfield, Auckland 10

Century Hutchinson South Africa (Pty) Ltd
PO Box 337, Bergvlei 2012, South Africa

First published 1988

Typeset in Monophoto Rockwell Light by
Vision Typesetting, Manchester

Printed and bound in Great Britain by
Scotprint Ltd, Musselburgh

British Library Cataloguing in Publication Data

McGee, Eddie
Eddie McGee's complete book of survival.
1. Survival – Manuals
I. Title
613.6'9

ISBN 0 09 172450 3

The techniques described in this book have been tried and tested by the author, mostly in survival situations. However some are illegal in some countries including Britain and accordingly should *not* be used in such countries. No responsibility for prosecutions that may result from use or misuse of these techniques can be borne by the author or the publishers.

Contents

About the Author

Eddie McGee is recognized as one of the world's leading authorities on survival. A former paratroop sergeant major, he ran the military survival wing before setting up his own National School of Survival based in North Yorkshire.

During his army career Eddie took an active part as a survival adviser on many expeditions such as the Great Zaire and Operation Drake as well as undertaking his own solo trip across the Sahara and the straits of Indonesia and Malaya. A qualified diver and world authority on tracking, in 1982 he received the Queen's highest police award for bravery after tracking down a triple police killer. Since leaving the services Eddie McGee is in great demand as a lecturer and technical adviser to many outward bound organizations and each year takes a group of disabled children on their own expedition as far afield as Kenya and Morocco.

Introduction

I have at my outdoors training centre many books on the subject of survival. Some are extremely good and give lots of useful advice; on the other hand some are blatant copies of other books. My experience, on reading the latter, tells me that the authors have neither been in a real survival situation nor attempted to practise some of the skills they so flippantly write about.

No one is immune to accidents: they happen all the time, and to anyone. Some may only be minor and these we are able to deal with easily, often in the comfort and safety of our own homes. But if we were to be suddenly confronted with a major accident or catastrophe – call it what you will – how many of us could deal so easily with it then? Well, the answer is you can if you want to and hopefully after reading this book you'll have the confidence and knowledge to survive in any situation, no matter how isolated.

It's not easy trying to light a fire by rubbing two sticks together, especially when you're cold, wet and hungry. In fact it's almost impossible. I know, I've done it! Nor is it easy trying to build a snow shelter when your hands and feet are so cold you can hardly feel them (I've done that as well). If you really want to test your survival skills to the full, try bobbing around at sea in a small dinghy for a few days without any food or water. You'll soon begin to realize what true survival is all about.

Many years ago when I was a young paratrooper in the army I was selected to train for a very specialized role. To enable me to get close enough to carry out my task I would have to endure many cold, wet, tedious days of stalking and waiting in bogs, marshes, snow holes and caves. During training my instructor drilled into me how important it was to work with Mother Nature. 'McGee,' he would say, 'you have to learn to eat, sleep, think, hunt, kill and shit like an animal if you want to survive. If you don't you will die; it's as simple as that.'

Time and time again I'd repeat those words of wisdom as I went about my task, and how right he was for had I not followed his teaching I wouldn't be alive today. I've grovelled lower than a snake, lived like a sewer rat and eaten anything that moves to survive. To this day I've never forgotten his words and wherever I travel in the world I always prepare myself physically and mentally first.

Many times I've deliberately set myself specific survival tasks to test my physical and mental attitude. I've walked alone across great deserts and through almost impenetrable jungles and savannahs just to prove that I'm capable of doing it. More than once I've survived in snow holes and caves high in the mountains just to experience the difficulties of near freezing conditions. Once I travelled down an uncharted river in a canoe for a thousand miles to see if I could do it alone.

Throughout the book I've tried to explain and simplify many of the survival skills that helped keep me alive and hopefully after reading it you too will be better prepared should you ever find yourself in such a situation. Don't think you won't be able to stay alive because you've not had these experiences. There is much you can learn just by reading this book and by being ready to apply what you have learned. You've already taken the first major step to survival simply by having it in your hand.

But, to add a note of caution, as I warn you on page 73, the trapping of animals and birds is illegal in most countries so don't do it. Respect the countryside.

Remember, this book is to teach *everyone* basic survival skills, it is *not* just aimed at the professional explorer or camper.

Finally, you will notice throughout the book that I continually draw your attention to certain aspects of survival often prefixed by the words WARNING, CAUTION or REMEMBER in order to emphasize specific points. Above all, from the moment you realize that you're in a life or death situation – THINK SURVIVAL!

Acknowledgements

My grateful thanks to:

My wife Vera, who I see from time to time, and my sons Eddie and Perry, whose help has kept me free and at large on the streets.

And to all my friends, pupils and colleagues out there in the Survival World with whom I've shared many happy hours beneath the stars.

CHAPTER 1

Survival Psychology

When injury, death or capture confronts someone who is not in familiar, supportive conditions, survival will usually depend upon a realistic appraisal of the facts, and taking the right action to deal with the situation. It may be rapid evasion, or it may be determination and confidence to sit it out patiently. Strength, aggression and heroism are not always the best approach to a crisis. The strongest are not always the best at staying alive.

Man is without doubt the world's most efficient survivor, often facing almost impossible odds. Humans have, time and time again, managed to drag themselves back from the brink of death by their natural inborn survival instincts and abilities to improvise in any terrain, but we do not always make the most of our instincts. Our psychological responses to an emergency or crisis often prevent us from taking the right action. The mind and the emotions can destroy all chance of survival, just as they can help the survivor win through.

Each of us has been confronted with basic domestic 'survival' situations: illness, problems at work, a family bereavement, a car accident and so on. Fortunately most of us are able to cope with these situations quite well; even when confronted with a major crisis we still manage to carry on.

With the development of modern travel we find ourselves increasingly facing serious survival situations for which we are not prepared. Within minutes we can be flying across deserts, oceans, mountain ranges or jungles, many so inhospitable to man that to survive unprepared in any of them is almost an impossibility. Yet if we have learned to cope both mentally and physically in our concrete jungles, there is no reason why we should not be capable of coping in the wild.

So it would be foolish to assume that nothing adverse could ever happen to you simply because you do not go out of your way to confront danger. Let us consider an example of an unlooked-for survival situation.

Civilian aircraft on popular routes between major cities do crash into jungles or deserts. Ships and ferries do collide at sea, people do get lost in hills and mountains and cars sometimes break down in countryside that can, with a change of weather, become extremely hostile. It doesn't matter what situation you are in, there are certain basic points that apply to all of them. The most important is simply that unless there is any obvious physical injury, it will probably be your mental approach to the situation that will determine whether you live or die. Fear, panic, mental fatigue can all undermine you. Fear of the unknown . . . suddenly being pitched out of the warm comfort of an air conditioned cabin and seconds later finding yourself sitting alone on the rotting floor of a dark, heat-choking jungle . . . panic will be almost uncontrollable, but control it you must. It is essential to distinguish between fear and panic (see page 13). Fear is a natural instinct and if not controlled can become as dangerous to you as the crash itself. But if you cope with it, use it, it can help you.

So, I'm on the ground. How did it happen? Where am I? Does anyone know I'm here? How will I survive? These fears and many others will be rushing around in your mind. Everything will be confused. The sooner you are able to control these thoughts, the sooner you will be able to look after yourself.

Assume that the pilot has let the authorities know about the crash. Take stock of the terrain around you, and of the accident. It is very unlikely that you will be devoured by wild animals, or clubbed to death by savage natives. On the contrary, wild life and local inhabitants could help you stay alive, as you will discover later in the book. Once you have control of your fears and have accepted the facts of your situation, it is now up to you. Settle down, develop a routine and get on with the business of survival.

Mental and physical stress reinforce each other. In any survival situation both will affect your chances. It is therefore important to be able to recognize mental and physical fatigue, as well as other basic enemies to life – injury, cold, heat, wind, wet, fear, shock, panic, thirst, hunger, pain, disease, self pity, loneliness, boredom and non-preparation.

Attitude

Common sense, confidence and thoughtfulness are all important factors in survival. You cannot avoid danger by pretending it's not there, but your attitude towards survival, including the way you are using this book now, can become a crucial factor in whether you will make a good survivor or not. A willingness to think about the possibility of disaster striking – particularly if you are going trekking through some mountains, or on a wilderness trail, or even holidaying near a remote desert or on a tropical island – is a good sign. If you are an 'armchair traveller', content to wander in your imagination, to enjoy fictional adventures rather than real ones, you will approach the subject differently. Actual survival is serious; it's a matter of life and death.

The essence of being able to survive in any terrain is adaptability; not to pit yourself against the environment, but to use it to help you live. You are more likely to be able to adapt to your circumstances if you have prepared yourself. I'd like therefore to look at what I call 'pre-training'.

Pre-training

Not only to the would-be survivor, but also to everyone who travels, the importance of pre-training and familiarisation cannot be emphasized too strongly; it is of paramount importance. Knowing beforehand how to deal with a potentially dangerous situation is a terrific morale booster, and never more welcome than in a life-or-death predicament. Having the knowledge and ability to cope gives a lift to the confidence. When your confidence falls the level of stress will be higher, and the likelihood of panic greater. When your confidence is high and you have all your emotions and fears under control, you are well on your way to making it.

Before being sent into battle around the world modern soldiers are taught to exist in all types of terrain, from the extreme regions of the Arctic, hot dusty deserts and steaming jungles, to moorlands, mountains and seas.

Hundreds of years ago the Japanese Emperors recruited the services of an elite band of warriors called Samurai to keep law and order. These warriors were dedicated fighting mercenaries who, to enable themselves to survive, practised the art of hand-to-hand fighting (later these skills became known as martial arts) and lived off the land. Before a man could present himself as a warrior he first had to undergo many years of intensive training, using both his mental and physical powers. To condition himself to living off the land he would spend weeks, even months, in the most inhospitable of terrains, learning how to survive. Later, when accepted into the elite Samurai guard, he would put these skills into practice as he moved around the country carrying out his duties. As well as developing his fighting skills to a fine art, he also developed his stamina both mentally and physically. The Samurai realized that to survive any battle it was just as important to gain control of the mind (its fears and emotions), as it was to develop physically. We may not think of being in a survival situation as though it were a battle against death, but we should. Present day airline pilots and crew practise survival skills regularly; so too do the people who sail ocean liners around the world. Very few of us actually practise survival skills that could save other people's lives, as do doctors and nurses and those trained in first aid. But the ordinary man or woman in the street is not exempt. We learn, from a very early age, various aspects of everyday survival including safety around the home, medical care of the family and what food or clothing are needed etc.

It is important, however, to realize that there is no substitute for experience, and experience can only be gained by being in a survival situation. Since the last thing most of us want to do is place ourselves in danger, we have to do the next best thing and that is to prepare ourselves for any eventuality that could arise. We need to be able to deal with situations outside our home or working environment, to deal with emergencies affecting others as well as ourselves.

Pre-training is simply common sense. For example, if you're going abroad for a holiday, read up on the country, not only its night life and the golden beaches, but read about the interior, how the people live, where the country is in relation to other countries. It's also worth identifying who you should contact in an emergency: not all countries have a 999 police emergency system on the telephone, in many cases the emergency will not arise near a telephone. Just because you think you won't be venturing far off the beaten track, that you'll be staying near the tourist centres, you may think this is a waste of time, but don't wait until you *are* off the beaten track before deciding to look into the possible dangers.

Most people do know their limitations and try to avoid the unexpected, but arguments, fights, and even accidents do happen on holiday. After all, it's not your fault if the aircraft has been hijacked or that the car broke down miles from anywhere during a freak snow storm. Or that a stupid driver said he would be back to collect you and hasn't returned or that you'll have to start walking or hitch a ride, because you don't have any money and it's beginning to rain. Things like this have happened to hundreds of people all over the world, and one of these people could be you!

Even in a comparatively safe survival situation, stress can so easily build up. You may have to deal with things that you thought, sitting in the safety of your house, you would be able to handle. But then there comes the fear of being alone, of not knowing where you are; feelings of inadequacy, frustration and annoyance at yourself for getting into the situation in the first place. Add to this the possibility of being tired, hungry, cold, scared and if you're honest with yourself, perhaps a little panicky, and you are in a survival stress situation. A few minutes ago you felt safe and secure, and now . . . ?

The first thing you should do when you find yourself in this situation is simply to sit down and take stock. You may begin to feel panic. If you need to, have a good cry. A good cry never hurt anyone; it's one of nature's safety valves and allows us to release our feelings and emotions. If you feel like it, try shouting. Stand up and curse everyone and everything around you – this also releases tension.

Once you have this out of your system empty out your pockets, handbag or briefcase and set whatever you have on the ground in front of you. This again will occupy your mind and give you something to think about. All of this helps relieve the stress. Having done this, see what you can make of the items displayed before you: matches to light a fire, a cigarette to control your nerves, a handkerchief to bandage that small cut on your arm. Soon you'll be fully in control of your emotions, then you can begin to form a plan.

What to do

Firstly *Inspection*: inspect yourself and equipment. See to any injuries immediately such as scratches, cuts etc.
Then *Protection*: if you're certain that you're going to have to spend the night there, set about building yourself some sort of shelter. Keep yourself warm and dry.
Now *Location*: try to discover where you are and how best you can help anyone who is trying to rescue you.
Finally, *Water and Food*: concentrate on finding fresh water and food.

Know yourself

You don't need to be an expert to be able to understand the basic psychological aspects of survival, but you must start by knowing your own weaknesses (and strengths); for instance, if you're terrified of spiders, heights, the dark, water or confined spaces. These and suchlike fears can present you with obstacles that you must overcome in any survival situation. They may not present an obstacle to the person next to you, yet physically you both face the same problem.

There are a number of basic elements which come up time and time again in survival situations and we must look briefly at these:

1 Mental fatigue

This includes self-pity, loneliness and awareness of your lack of preparation. Fatigue, whether mental or physical, is debilitating. It can result in lethargy and carelessness when you most need to be alert.

Determination, confidence and a positive attitude are all part of avoiding mental fatigue. Fear can be used to keep yourself on your toes to help you fight the slippery slope to despair. Lack of hope is the mind's way of giving up the struggle. Remember that if you really have the will to live, to survive, then you can beat mental fatigue. Lack of sleep will ultimately lower your mental resources and only sleep will make up for it. So, pace yourself physically as well as mentally. If you want to be at your best under the circumstances you should hope for the best and prepare for the worst. If you only prepare for the best, disappointment will eat into your store of confidence. Mental fatigue will win. Don't let it – you can fight it. Self-pity and loneliness can be held at bay by being constructive and active.

2 Physical fatigue and injury

We will deal with specific injuries and ways of coping with them later in the book. For the moment I want to discuss the psychological implications of physical fatigue and injury. Obviously if you (or someone else) are injured you must deal with it as quickly and efficiently as you can. An injured person can find the will to fight on if others are confident and decisive in dealing with the injuries. Keep a careful watch on your body. Note its reactions under the stress of your situation. Pain is an indication that something is wrong. If moving a limb really hurts don't ignore the pain, or think you should just be brave about it. Identify the cause if possible; if not, try to ease the pain – don't let it get you down.

Heavy limbs, aching joints, painful muscles (were you fit before your trip?) can all affect the way you feel and think about your predicament. If you are so exhausted that you are overcome with the desire to sleep, find a safe spot and take all possible precautions. Fight the fatigue until you have done this.

Everyone has a different tolerance level where pain is concerned: some people are simply better at withstanding it than others. Do not assume that because *you* can cope well with a particular type of pain, someone else is simply being feeble when he says he can't. Even though he may be at the limit of his ability to deal with it, leadership and inspiration is more likely to get him into a better state of mind than simply shouting at him.

Torture is a deliberate method of breaking an individual; a survival situation in the wild can result in torture from nature every bit as effective as the most brutal that man has to offer. There is no doubt that many individuals, both soldiers in action and civilians in the wilderness, have overcome extraordinary physical suffering by sheer strength of mind. Fitness of body is equally important, so you will be at an advantage if you have looked after your body. Fitness is therefore very desirable both for your body's sake and for your state of mind when setting off on what could become a hazardous journey.

3 Fear and panic

We know that fear is a natural emotion and that it can easily be brought on through lack of confidence in one's ability to survive or through not knowing basic survival skills. Fear causes anxiety, and anxiety causes panic. Even unfamiliar surroundings can bring on fear and induce stress. No one is immune to fear, we all suffer from it. Some can cope with most of their fears quite easily whilst others are not so fortunate. Excessive fears can lead to mental breakdown. If someone who is usually stable and confident is suddenly thrust into a real emergency this can stretch mental stamina to breaking point, especially if there has been no previous training or warning.

Try to distinguish between fear and panic. You can be in control of yourself while feeling fear; panic usually involves lack of control. Fear is the normal reaction to danger. It can cause the body to increase the adrenalin in the system and also increase the pulse rate so that the body is better prepared instantly to fight or respond to the danger. Panic usually results in over-hasty, unthought-out actions, which greatly increase the danger. Examine the causes of your fear. Often they will be groundless and you will conserve valuable energy by not allowing the fear to lead to panic. If you feel an overwhelming sense of panic, stop everything, breathe deeply, look around and take stock, keep breathing deeply. Is it really as bad as it looks? Since panic can lead to excessive hastiness and therefore carelessness, slow down. Remember, the dangers may in fact be harmless and the panic caused by misreading the situation can become a killer.

4 Shock

Shock often accompanies an injury. Excessive shock will not only induce fear but will also throw the body into a state which quickly uses up vital energy reserves. A victim suffering from shock may have the following symptoms: bouts of shivering or trembling, convulsions, often sweating profusely even when the temperature is perhaps below freezing, pallor, thirst and possibly coma. Shock is a potential killer and should be as carefully monitored as any physical injury. It isn't something that one can 'control'. If, however, survival depends on you keeping moving, weigh up the situation and determine whether or not you can afford to rest. Decisions like this are never easy, but being prepared, even if you have only read about such situations, should lead you to make the right choice.

5 Cold, wet and wind

It is commonly accepted amongst survival experts that our lack of ability to deal with cold and wet causes a great deal of stress and anxiety, apart from the physical deterioration we may suffer. We have become so used to living in our modern world, wearing the right kind of clothes to suit the climate and the occasion, that the ability to use the natural foliage around us has almost disappeared. Yet in most survival situations, nature can provide the means and materials to help fight off the cold and wet and keep us alive.

Every year thousands of people die, even with the right protective clothing, because they've failed to realize how lethal cold and wet can be, especially when there is also wind. On its own wind isn't usually a killer, but the danger can be increased enormously when all three conditions prevail. Hypothermia then becomes a definite danger to life and should never be underestimated. Cold is debilitating and getting warm again becomes the only thing you can concentrate on. As your body begins to feel numb, so your mind and determination slow up until you are no longer in control. Survival is then very difficult, and as far as your life is concerned, keeping warm and dry is your top priority.

Cold is such a major survival hazard that we must look at the two basic types – wet cold and dry cold.

Wet cold This is the kind you endure when pitched into a freezing river or ocean, or when stranded out on the moors soaked by incessant rain. As with pain, individuals have different tolerances. Some can remain afloat for hours in near-freezing temperatures after being washed overboard while others have died in a matter of minutes, so low has been their resistance to the water temperature – shock is usually a factor here.

Standing out in the open, drenched by driving rain, can be just as lethal as being submerged in freezing waters, particularly when there is wind. The body tries desperately to conserve vital heat, which in turn is being continually 'blown' away by the wind. When this happens the body quickly chills and within minutes the inner core, the body's last remaining reserve of energy, begins to fade and then we quickly lapse into a coma and death. A large number of 'outdoor casualties' each year are people caught out by wind chill. On a pleasant sunny day it's possible for them to walk in the hills not realizing that the higher they climb the colder it gets. With nothing on other than a thin summer dress or a loose fitting shirt and cotton trousers, the walker becomes a potential victim of hypothermia as the wind rapidly reduces the body temperature.

Dry cold This is when the body loses heat and vital energy and the inner core supply is drawn away. The victim becomes so numb with cold that he can no longer summon enough energy reserve to combat it. That is when people usually die of hypothermia. Death through dry cold is usually a much, much slower process than through wet cold. Often the victims, mostly elderly though certainly they are not the only ones, don't even notice the cold creeping over them. Huddled around a sparse fire or curled up in the corner with only the flimsiest of clothes to protect them, they eventually lose consciousness and die. With proper insulation and the right kind of clothing it is possible to stay alive even at temperatures well below freezing.

But as we know from soldiers and scientists who have had to endure long periods in sub-zero conditions, even the right clothing may not be enough. When all three of the potential killers occur – cold, wind and wet, hypothermia is still a very likely outcome. It is as well to remember that in any of the conditions mentioned a good sixty per cent of your body heat is lost due to evaporation from the hands, feet, head and face if they aren't covered. Later on in the book we will look at ways of surviving extreme cold.

6 Heat

Heatstroke is caused by overheating the body core, usually by exercise in a hot, humid environment. Irritability, headache and confusion develop and, unless treated by resting and finding shade, may progress to coma and death. However, in cases where people have died in deserts or during heatwaves, the sun has only been a contributing factor. The more usual cause of death is dehydration, but as any desert survivor will tell you, the cause of dehydration is the sun and the heat.

Obviously if you're caught up in a forest fire or a raging inferno in a building, the heat will kill you, although even then the cause of death can be smoke rather than the temperature. For outdoor survivors we are really talking about the heat of the sun. There are cases of people being lost at sea, adrift in small boats, who have suffered long periods of exposure to the sun's rays and have managed to survive. People have been horrifically burnt in fires and lived to talk about it. The human body is a walking miracle and providing you treat it correctly, keeping yourself fit, well fed and properly clothed, it will endure most environmental hazards.

A basic knowledge of how to handle survival situations in the desert should make it possible for you to prevent the worst effects of heat and dehydration.

In the same way that certain parts of the body must be covered up to give you any chance of survival in the cold, it may be necessary to expose the face, hands and so on to prevent the body from becoming overheated.

Patience can be a virtue in a desert survival situation: you may feel desperately anxious to travel in the direction you think will bring you to safety, but being able to discipline yourself so that you sleep and shelter first in whatever shade is available during the day, and travel at night, may make the difference between life and death.

7 Thirst and hunger

The drinking of liquids, especially water, is vital to sustain life no matter what the temperature outside. When hot we sweat more and therefore require more liquid to prevent dehydration. In colder climates we tend to sweat less, but nevertheless still require a daily input of liquid. The only remedy for dehydration is water. As with heat, your attitude towards thirst and hunger can prevent you from panicking, from taking careless and hasty steps which will themselves cause more danger to you than your lack of food or water. Some knowledge of the body's physiology will help you to discipline the way you use the scarce resources that may be at your disposal. 'Know your body' is as valuable a maxim in a survival situation as 'know your enemy' is in war.

It has been claimed by some people that the human body can survive for up to six days without water. A classic example of this is the Indian Fakirs. After placing themselves in a deep trance they are capable of sitting or lying down in one position for days without moving a muscle, but after being examined by medical experts it was noted that in many cases the Fakirs had in fact suffered extreme dehydration.

During my army days I was taught that the longest a person can go without water in a temperate region such as Europe is four days. After that the body begins to demand moisture and the craving can become so intense that the victim loses all sense of reason and time.

In the desert the length of time one can go without water is reduced considerably, very often down to a single day. To starve the body of moisture is both stupid and dangerous. If there is water available, drink it! Keep your reserves topped up. If you've been without water for a long time, drink it very sparingly, by sipping at first. Do not gulp a great deal of water very quickly when you have been dehydrated. Avoid impure water if possible, however thirsty you feel. Don't let your desperation overcome your common sense and caution.

Chewing pebbles does not alleviate your thirst, it pre-occupies you and uses up precious energy.

Hunger in the initial stages of survival is not nearly as serious as going without water. Obviously if there is food around then eat it. Keep up your energy reserves, but if there is no food available you don't need to worry, at least for a few days, even if you feel weak or shaky. If you haven't suffered a great deal of energy loss it is possible to go without food for two to three weeks, living off your body fat. The exact length of time depends on the terrain you are in at the time and your physical condition. In the hot weather we tend to eat less anyway. As the body loses heat and energy in cold, we need to keep that vital energy reserve stocked up, so we need to eat more. Once again, it is foolish and dangerous to starve yourself of food especially when it is available. Think calmly about eating – chew food thoroughly and make it work for you.

Conclusions

The will to live, the determination to succeed and survive is almost as important as food, water, warmth and avoidance of injury and illness. Your frame of mind can make the difference between life and death. How each person gets the most out of his mental resources will depend on the individual. The fact that you may never have done what you are setting out to do doesn't mean you will fail.

At the beginning of this chapter I mentioned how important it is to keep both mental and physical stress under control. If you can, try a little spiritual guidance, even if you aren't religious. More than once when I have found myself in a tricky situation, I've turned to prayer for help. Any soldier or explorer worth his salt will tell you the same. The feeling of spiritual 'help' can be a great healer in itself. While having to sit for ages on the bank of a river, deep inside swamp infested jungle, I have taken out a small Bible and just read a bit: once when I was crossing one of the great deserts on my own at night, I read chapters aloud. The comfort I got in the solitude and silence was a terrific morale booster.

By whatever means – deep breathing, slow-counting, resting, reading a Bible, building a shelter or leaving a marker trail – try and become calm. Get on top of your environment and you'll have a better chance of survival.

Your ability to keep calm and in control will help others around you. It may be that someone in your party died and a little religious and spiritual guidance is needed. If you are the eldest or leader you will be expected to deal with the situation.

As soldiers who had to fight behind the enemy line in a small group, we naturally became very close and when a death occurred, no matter where we were and how risky it was to our mission, we always ensured that the proper burial and prayer service was carried out. For that reason I have included The Lord's Prayer, Psalm 23 (the Lord is my shepherd) and prayers for burial on land and at sea. Morbid as it may seem, a simple service is often seen as a morale booster too. Those around you feel that the best that can be done has been done.

THE LORD'S PRAYER

Our Father which art in heaven: hallowed be thy name: thy kingdom come: thy will be done: on earth as it is in heaven: give us this day our daily bread and forgive us our trespasses as we forgive them that trespass against us: and lead us not into temptation: but deliver us from evil, for thine is the kingdom, the power and the glory forever and ever.
Amen

The Lord's Prayer may be said by anyone at any time, as a daily/evening prayer, before or after a service.

PSALM 23

The Lord is my shepherd; I shall not want.
He maketh me to lie down in green pastures: he leadeth me beside the still waters.
He restoreth my soul: he leadeth me in the paths of righteousness for his name's sake.
Yea, though I walk through the valley of the shadow of death, I will fear no evil: for thou art with me; thy rod and thy staff they comfort me.
Thou preparest a table before me in the presence of mine enemies: thou anointest my head with oil; my cup runneth over.
Surely goodness and mercy shall follow me all the days of my life: and I will dwell in the house of the Lord forever.
Amen

THE BURIAL PRAYER

Forasmuch as it hath pleased Almighty God of His great mercy to take unto Himself the soul of our dear brother/sister here departed, we therefore commit his/her body to the ground; earth to earth – ashes to ashes – dust to dust; In the sure and certain hope of the resurrection to eternal life through our Lord Jesus Christ.
Amen

The Burial Prayer may be said as a member of the funeral party drops handfuls of earth on the body.

BURIAL AT SEA

Forasmuch as it hath pleased Almighty God of His great mercy to take unto Himself the soul of our dear brother/sister here departed, we therefore commit his/her body to his/her resting place in the deep.

The burial prayer may be said as a member of the funeral party drops handfuls of flowers on the body as it is cast into the sea.

CHAPTER 2

Navigation

Astral navigation

With one hand firmly clasping a steaming mug of cocoa and the other a thick cheese sandwich, I settled down snugly beneath the dry warm bracken little realizing, as I stared up into the clear star-lit sky, that I was about to discover the wonders of astral navigation.

On this occasion I'd gone along with my Dad to help check the nets of his pheasant traps on the remote Yorkshire moors. The night air was thick and heavy with the earthy smell of dry bracken and heather. Tonight would be a good night for poaching. As I sat there looking up into the sky I asked Dad why was it that if you looked at the stars for a long time some of them appeared to move whilst others remained still. Dad smiled, shuffled his feet and gently knocked his pipe on the toe of his boot and stamped out the ash. He removed an apple from his lunch box. 'See this apple?' he said. 'Imagine this is the earth.' He took his torch, lit it and set it into the ground with the light shining upwards. 'This is the sun. The sun remains still in the sky whilst the earth and other planets move around it like this.' Dad made a wide circle around the torch beam. 'As the earth spins it rotates on an axis, a sort of invisible rod.' Dad took a pencil from his top pocket and pushed it through the centre of the apple. 'Each earth rotation takes twenty-four hours. This gives us our day and night. To circle around the sun the earth takes three hundred and sixty-five days, one year. As it rotates it tilts on its axis, sometimes towards the sun, sometimes away. When tilting towards the sun it gets hotter, away from the sun it gets cooler. This is where we get our seasons.

'As the earth continues to orbit, each time it tilts it takes us nearer or away from visible stars, so they appear to be either climbing higher in the sky or lower.'

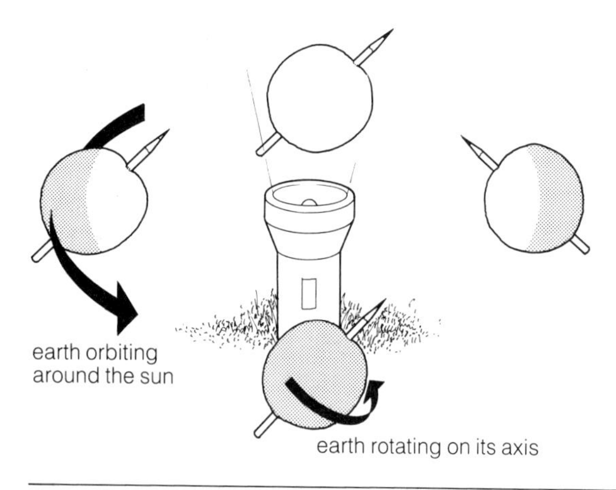

I never forgot that evening. In just a few short minutes Dad managed to explain more to me about the earth and stars than any teacher ever did. From that night onwards I was hooked on star navigation and for hour upon hour I'd sit outside in our garden just looking up into the sky in wonderment.

Interestingly enough, very little has changed in the millions of years since the earth was formed, so the way we see the stars today is very much as our ancestors saw them. We do, of course, have instruments like the compass with which to take bearings and the telescope to study and survey the stars, and more recently we have actually sent man into space to have a much closer look. But when it comes to simple survival navigation we still use the same groups of stars, and in many cases the same techniques to guide us, as were used by our ancestors. Of course, knowing as we do how the earth rotates around the sun and how it is continually spinning, we are able to make a much more accurate reading, even by using a couple of stakes driven into the ground.

In the sky there are many groups of stars (constellations) that are familiar to most of us, such as the Ploughs (Ursa Major and Ursa Minor), Orion's Belt, Cassiopeia and of course the North Star, all easily visible to anyone living in the Northern hemisphere, and all except Orion's Belt visible all year round. Oddly enough, to the naked eye each has seven stars in its group. This makes them easier to recognize. In the Southern hemisphere probably the first group of stars easily recognized is the Southern Cross.

Because the earth is continually spinning all stars seem to move from east to west in great arcs. To the survivor this is a useful direction finder. First choose a star, then drive two stakes into the ground.

The tops of the stakes should line up with the star and be level with each other. As you sit and watch the star will either dip, fall or move to the left or right. Whatever it does, the following information can be gleaned from it:

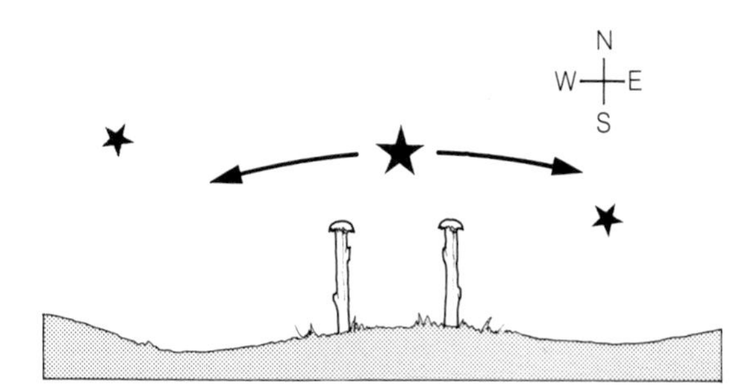

When a star appears to be

- *Falling before you, you are looking approximately* west
- *Climbing before you, you are looking approximately* east

When a star appears to be

- *Looping flatly to your right, you are looking* south
- *Looping flatly to your left, you are looking* north

As a good survivor it is important for you to be able to familiarise yourself with astral navigation from all regions of the world and you can do this simply by paying a visit to your local library and reading about it or by visiting your nearest planetarium. Other than that you will have to do what I did – get out there and travel.

Marking your trail

The Aborigine is recognized as the nearest living link with primitive man and even today you can still find many Aborigines using the same basic primitive skills passed down by their ancestors – such as astral navigation. When he wants to travel safely in a straight line across the bush or desert, he does so by following the stars at night or, in cloudy daylight, a series of fires or markers. The fires he lights on top of hills and as he walks he lights other fires in line. A very simple, very basic, but extremely accurate way of navigation.

In many of the world's deserts a similar method is employed, but instead of lighting fires, poles and/or flags are used, or even piles of stones.

This centuries-old method of navigation is so accurate that it is almost faultless. No matter how much the earth spins and turns, once you have set out your markers you can only go in a straight line. During the day or by the light of the moon you are guided by the shadows and shapes of the poles. On a moonless or overcast night you simply use the light of fires alongside the poles as a guide.

Sometimes the same poles are set out in the form of a compass.

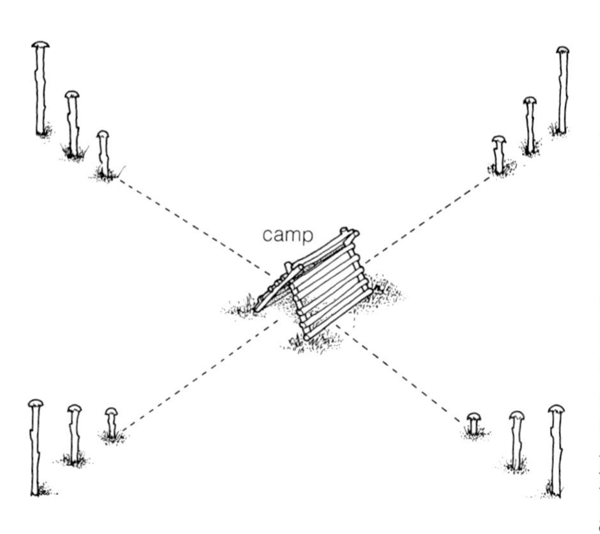

With the smallest pole to the centre and the tallest on the outer ring, from whatever direction the nomads approach the camp, they will always be able to see the tallest pole first and even if there is a thick mist or sandstorm they know that by standing with their stomachs to the tallest pole and looking towards the next one they are accurately lined up in the direction of their camp. Should they misjudge and walk past the camp, all they have to do is to find similar poles on the other side and repeat the march in.

When the Aborigines travel in groups, if it is too dark to navigate by the stars or to see their poles, they either carry a long pole or use a length of rope as a guide. For this they travel in threes or fours. The pole or rope is held tightly by the man at the front of the line and the man at the rear. Those in the middle simply walk alongside or hold the guideline gently. Any deviation from the route by the first man is immediately felt by the others and they can call out to warn him. Ingenious, yes. Effective, very.

In jungles a method is used similar to the upright poles: three cuts are made into a tree trunk, two in the direction of camp, and one – the outward direction mark, which is the largest – on the other side of the trunk. This means it is more easily visible when travellers are searching for it on the return journey. Once the mark is found you can feel around the trunk of the tree until you have located the other two marks. Simple, but again extremely effective, especially if you have to travel at night.

I have used all these methods many times, especially when training on the moors or in the mountains. As I said, piles of stones or even heaped snow can act as markers; you can even set out flags by hanging them on trees. It's a skill that you must go out and practise. An interesting exercise is to place the marker sticks at night using a known star as a guide, wait a couple of days and on a clear night, using the same star, set out another series of poles. You will be amazed how much the star seems to have moved off your original line of direction. Remember to take into account the movement of the earth as well as your own movement, as described on page 18.

Try to be innovative: if you are not going to burn anything as your 'marker', use whatever comes to hand, even piled up brushwood will do. Anything that you can see easily from a distance and that you don't want to take with you.

Terrain clues

Soldiers are taught to observe the SHAPE, COLOUR, SHADOW, SMELL, SPACE, MOVEMENT and NOISE of the terrain they move across.

Shape It is important to know the type of terrain you are in, and to work out its difficulties before walking out. Make a mental note: is it rugged, flat etc? Remember the shape and contours. Can you be seen by your rescuers? How much will you blend in with the environment?

Colour Burn rubber or old oil to give black smoke in arctic conditions. Burn fresh foliage or grass for white grey smoke against green fields and woods. Fresh green grass and rich soil indicate areas of intense growth and animal life; harsh bracken or dry earth indicate sparse growth and probably cold bleak mountainous regions. The colour of the land will tell you the difficulties of travel and navigation. River, jungle and desert foliage indicate just what kind of terrain you have to survive in.

Shadow Since clouds mostly form over land, shadows that they cast indicate land or icebergs nearby. Shadows also indicate vegetation, mountains or man-made industry.

Smell Make a point of remembering terrain smells of salt, water, vegetation, smoke fumes, and even animal droppings.

Space Make a mental note of the gaps between mountains, ridges, trees, rivers, buildings and hedges.

Movement Notice signs of animal migration such as tracks, flights of birds etc., ships, passing aircraft routes, flow of rivers, cloud formations.

Noise Observe very carefully any of the following sounds and their direction: wind, storms, mechanical and animal noises, explosions or thunder.

All of these must be considered when attempting to use basic navigation to reach safety. The interesting thing is that most of us do consider these without actually thinking about it. Navigation isn't just about going from A to B; it's about movement across land, sea and air accurately and safely. Poles have to be found, fires lit, tinder gathered, distance worked out and so on. Remember, when you're tired, cold, wet and hungry you will make mistakes. When you make mistakes you are more likely to die – it's as simple as that.

Signs and signals

People who have found themselves in survival situations in the past and with whom I've spoken have used other ingenious devices to blaze trails – old tyres hung from trees, coats or shirts set on scarecrows, hubcaps or car doors used as markers, and reflectors or old mirrors hung to catch the last shimmer of the setting sun.

One may also use inner tubes set alight to give off dense smoke, oil spillage or spelling out S.O.S. in the sand – even piles of stones, shrubs or grass. The choice is yours.

Eskimos regularly use little lamps made from seal or whale blubber as guide markers, and during the last war partisans and troops regularly used 'desert burners', which were nothing more than a couple of old tins half filled with sand and oil. Even people surviving on remote desert islands have improvised using coconut oil or palm leaves with which to signal and mark trails, and if you travel to the Far East even now you will find hundreds of local fishermen using the very same coconut oil lamps.

Another primitive example of basic navigation is observation of plants and animals. Certain species of plants point in specific directions. The common sunflower, for instance, is so-called not because it has a large flower head that looks like the sun, but because it moves around and follows the sun's rays. During the night sunflowers tend to swing back and pick up the sun's rays as it reappears in the east the next morning. If you want to see an excellent example of this you should go to the sunflower fields of France, where there are row upon row of flowers all turned towards the sun. Many trees use the tops of their branches to do the same thing, pine trees in particular. Next time you come across a forest of pines, note how the topmost branch bends towards the sun and, like the sunflower, it too swings back during the evening to await the new dawn.

Some ways of marking a trail

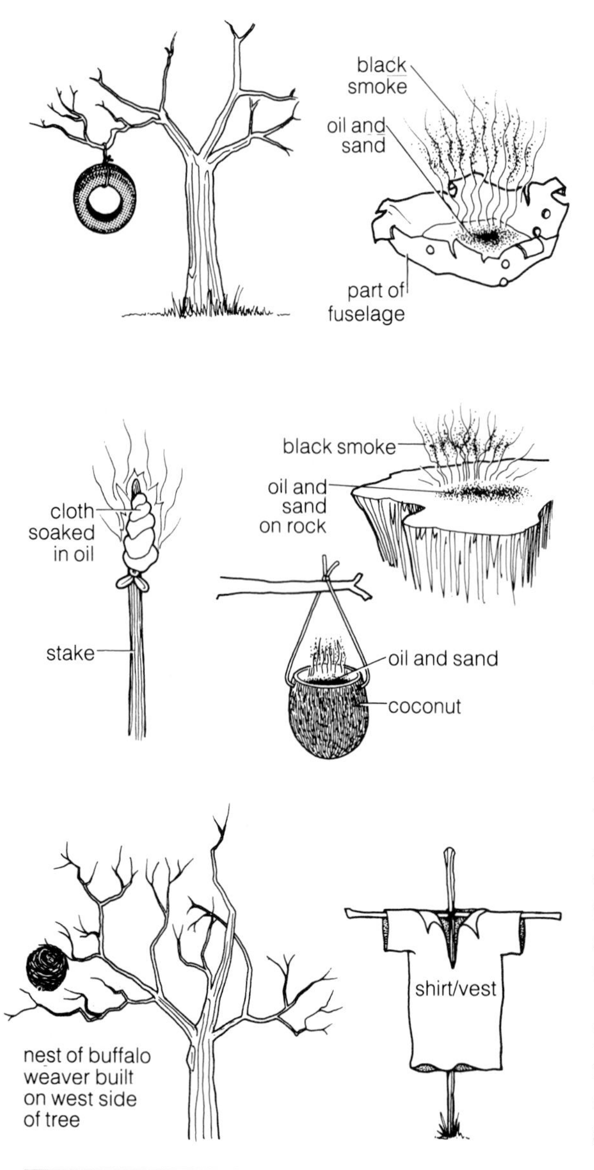

Although many species of birds act like a compass and at certain times of the year point themselves south or north, the flora in general will be of greater help. But to be sure, if possible, you must do your homework and read up on the habits of animals, birds and plants in the region where you intend to travel, so you can use your observations to help you in your attempt to survive.

Deep in a forest where trees grow close together, they tend to grow straight up with branches spread fairly evenly around the trunk, but where trees have lots of space around them you'll find that the bulk of the branches will be on the south side if you're in the northern hemisphere and on the north side if you're in the southern hemisphere. This is because the tree is reaching out towards the sun, just like the sunflower. Also the trunk of the tree on the opposite side to most of the branches tends to be much tougher.

To stabilize the tree and counterbalance the weight of the branches, the roots on the side with most branches tend to run out close to the surface of the ground whilst those on the less dense side appear to go straight down into the ground. To the survivor this provides an abundance of direction finding information.

North American Indians were great believers in using the trees and plants for their navigation. It's worth noting though that trees close to the equator are not nearly as helpful, as they grow more evenly.

The desert compass

The stick and shadow method is another primitive but very accurate means of navigation. Choose a flat piece of ground about a metre square. In the centre press a small stick, about 12 inches long, firmly into the ground.

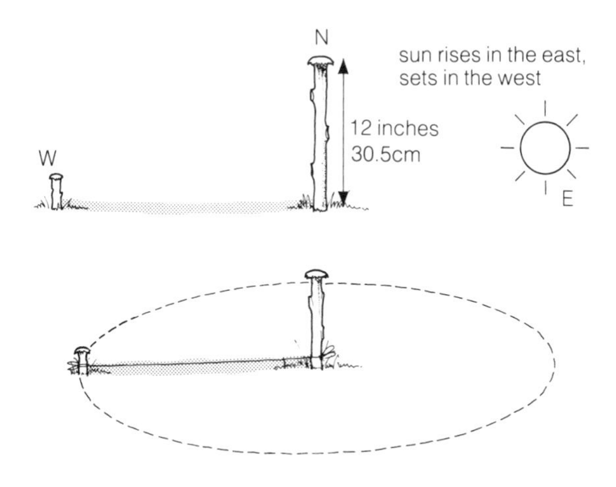

As the sun strikes the stick it will cast a shadow. At the end of the shadow place a smaller stick, then using a bit of twine or grass affix this to the centre stick and draw a full circle using the smaller marking stick as the perimeter.

You have now made a primitive sundial. As the sun rises and sets, so the shadows will shorten and lengthen. Using other marker sticks place these at the ends of the shadows and very soon you will have completed your sundial, for telling the time, and your compass, for giving direction.

In the northern hemisphere at midday the shadow from the stick should be short and pointing northwards. Remember, the sun rises in the east and sets in the west. In the southern hemisphere the shadow from the stick will be pointing south at midday. On the equator the shadow will be almost directly below the stick and could be either north or south, depending on how close, north or south, to the true equator line you are.

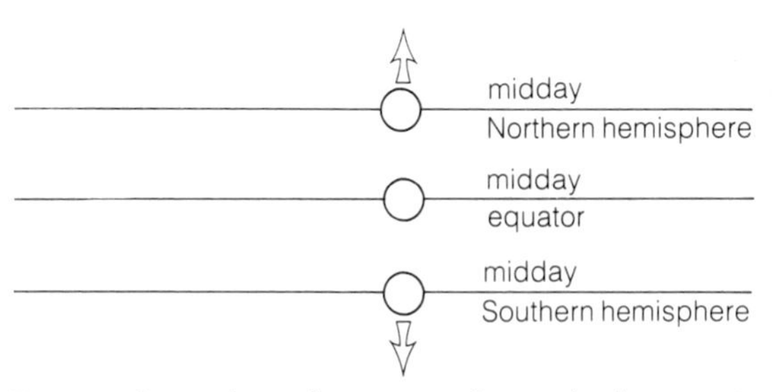

Remember that the sun takes six hours to travel through a ninety-degree angle no matter where you are, north or south of the equator. As the sun rises the shadows will tend to grow shorter, so that alone will tell you if it's morning or afternoon. As the sun sets the shadows become longer. Even on cloudy and overcast days it's still possible to distinguish some sort of shadow. If you intend to stay in the area for some time, leave your sun dial in position and learn how to use it.

A simple method of maintaining a reasonable line of direction is to keep the sun on your right shoulder up until midday when travelling north. After midday keep it to your left. This method won't give you a pin-point accuracy, but it will take you in the right direction. When you're walking south just reverse the sun on the shoulder position.

It's advisable when using these methods to keep looking back and checking that the sun is on your shoulder and not on your back. If, at the end of the day, when you stop to rest, you place a small marker stick pointing in the direction you were travelling, come morning you should be able to resume your walking line, but the shadow will now be on the other shoulder.

I personally never travel anywhere in the world without a compass and one of the simplest and finest is the Silva compass (overleaf). There are many variations on the market, but for my money the Silva compass is the best. It's simple to use, extremely accurate and can be adjusted to any region.

The Silva compass

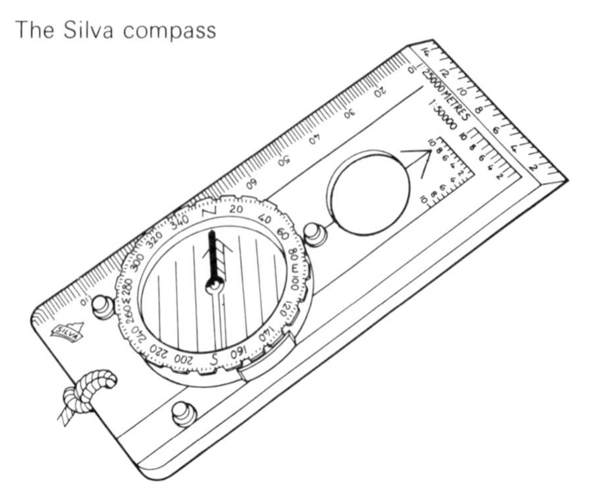

The moon

It is possible to tell what direction you are travelling in simply by looking at the moon. For instance, when the EARTH, MOON and SUN are in a direct line the shaded side is facing EARTH. When the EARTH is in a line between the SUN and MOON, the MOON is visible from EARTH as a complete circle. When the MOON is viewed from EARTH as it enters into its first and last quarters it is seen as a semi-circle.

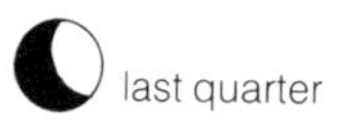

A. If the moon rises BEFORE the sun sets the illuminated side will be seen on earth in the WEST.

B. If the moon rises AFTER the sun sets the illuminated side will be on the EAST.

C. If the moon rises at the SAME TIME as the sun sets we see a FULL MOON.

D. A rough guide to finding NORTH/SOUTH using the moon can be had simply by drawing a straight line from the two points of the crescent.

A useful way of finding an approximate north/south direction

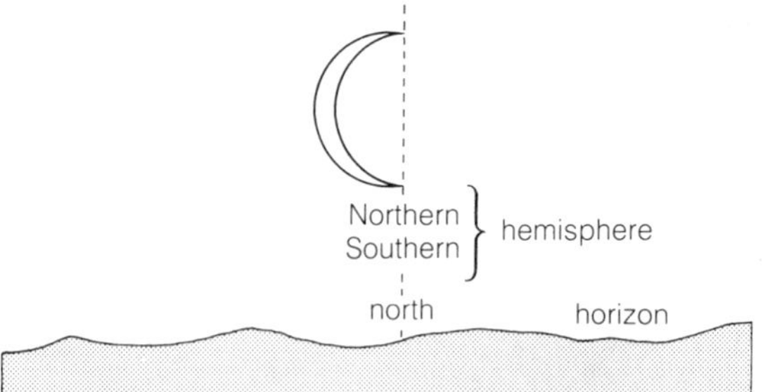

Using a wristwatch

The following method of using your watch to fix your direction is probably one of the simplest and best known.

In the northern hemisphere the watch is held in the flat of your hand or laid on a level surface (stone etc.) with the hour hand pointing directly at the sun. An imaginary line is then drawn between the hour hand and twelve on the watch face. True South is then midway between them.

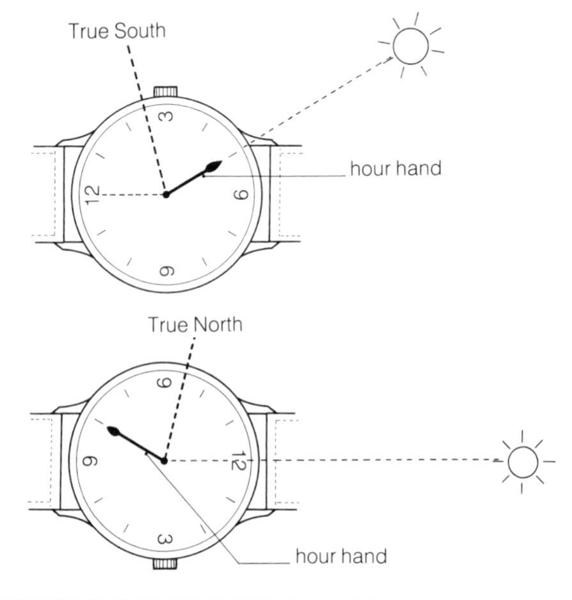

In the southern hemisphere the twelve on your watch face is set in line with the sun and the imaginary line this time between twelve and the hour hand gives True North.

Finding South in the Southern hemisphere

Seek out the Southern Cross. This is easily recognizable as a large group of bright stars in the shape of a cross. If you follow an imaginary line from the longest axis of the cross down to a point just above the horizon (use your finger as a guide) you come to a South landmark.

An alternative method of locating the South landmark is to draw an imaginary line from the two trailing lower stars of the cross. Where these two imaginary lines meet will give you the South landmark.

Navigation, as with everything else, can't be learnt overnight. The more you get out and practise the better you become. Remember, we are in the northern hemisphere, so all your calculations and studies will have to be reversed if surviving in the southern hemisphere.

Mother Nature has provided you not only with a wealth of basic survival skills but also the ability to feel if things aren't right. Try reading natural signs; if they don't feel right use your compass. It's as simple as that. Learn to trust your judgement. If you make a plan, stick to it but do allow for mistakes – that's how you learn.

Navigation need not be complicated. Even the best of the world's travellers make mistakes, but it helps if you use your instincts.

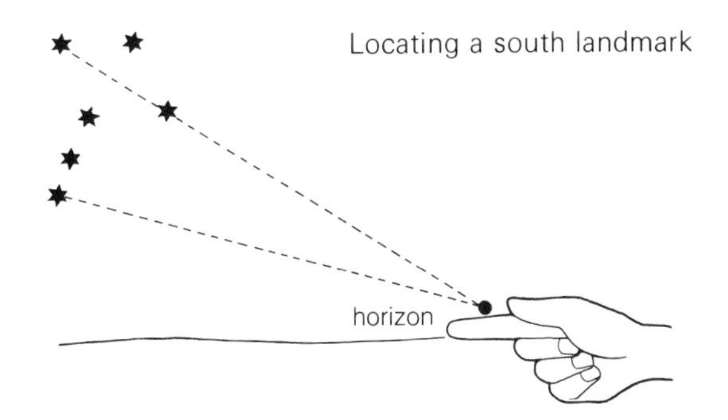

Locating a south landmark

CHAPTER 3

Survival at Sea

The great oceans of the world can be split into three environmental regions: Tropical, Sub-Tropical and Antarctic, each with its own individual climatic characteristics. The further north or south you travel from the equator the colder and stormier the seas become and your chances of survival lessen greatly.

In tropical waters hurricanes, tornadoes and violent storms are quite common and take many lives, yet each year hundreds of people manage to survive and live to tell the tale, often after spending many weeks adrift in small boats or dinghies. The warmer the waters, the greater your chances of surviving. In the cold regions most people adrift die of hypothermia and not of dehydration or starvation. In tropical waters there is an abundance of fish, mammals and rain storms so most people tend to be able to find sufficient food and water to sustain them until help arrives. Those who die, do so because of excessive exposure to the elements, mainly from dehydration.

Adrift in a small dinghy it's almost impossible to protect yourself from the elements unless you have the right equipment, but Mother Nature, as always, is on hand to help you. For instance, a basic knowledge of cloud formation could mean the difference between life and death.

A great deal of unnecessary discomfort can be prevented simply by knowing how to read the elements: for example, what various cloud formations tell you about pressure changes, whether you are north or south of the equator, knowing the sun rises in the east and sets in the west. As we've seen already, being able to recognize and navigate by various star constellations is useful, as is knowing the main shipping lanes and aircraft routes and being familiar with bird migration.

Cloud formations

Different cloud formations indicate changes in the weather. Dark heavy clouds clustering together obviously warn you of heavy rain and storms. These clouds are generally followed by strong blustery winds. Long streaky clouds indicate a warm pleasant day. Small, white fluffy clouds give a similar indication. The old folk lore tale 'red sky at night shepherd's delight, red sky in the morning shepherd's warning' is often true, especially at sea. Fog, mist, hail and sleet are generally signalled by a drop in temperature, a flattening of the water surface and a sky full of grey misty clouds.

Clouds can also point you in the direction of land. They are formed by moisture being drawn up into the atmosphere, where it cools and then falls as rain. This mostly occurs on high ground such as mountains, hills and moors, tropical islands and rain forests.

Clouds over large areas of ice will give off a bluish tint.

Clouds over forest/jungle will be dark and full of rain.

Clouds hovering above still, placid water will have a faint shimmer.

Cloudless skies may be fine during the day, but be prepared for a dramatic drop in temperature as night draws in.

Knowing these simple facts will enhance the odds of your survival.

Cumulonimbus clouds indicate rain, snow or hail (*top*); fairweather clouds in the background (*above*). Look for the bottom edge – it should be parallel to the ground

Equally important is having a basic knowledge of wind strengths. These are numbered 1 to 12 on the Beaufort Scale:

Numbers 1–3: Completely placid water surface with no wind.

Numbers 3–5: Winds beginning to rise up to 40/50 mph.

Number 5 upwards: Considered unsafe for small boats e.g. dinghies to be out sailing.

Numbers 8–10: Gale force.

Numbers 10–12: Hurricane winds.

Navigation at sea

During the night keep your eyes and ears open for large boats or land lights. Knowing that stationary clouds mass over land, head towards them. Storms are generally preceded by raging winds, a drop in temperature and the sea beginning to swell as the wind worsens. White horses (wave tops breaking) normally happen around three to four on your scale. Remember, using the Beaufort Scale, one to four is about as much as you can handle in a small boat. From then upwards it's almost impossible to maintain any control at all if you don't have a sail or any power to drive the boat along.

Drifting foliage, discarded fruit, debris and drifting seaweed are also generally a good indication that land is nearby. Watch for the change in water colour too; the closer you get to land the lighter it becomes. Deep water is often dark with a large swell running. Drifting seaweed indicates currents. Fresh seaweed floats, old seaweed sinks.

Most mammals are found pretty close to shore, though dolphins, whales, porpoises and seals often spend long periods far out at sea. If dolphins and porpoises are splashing around you it is very likely that sharks are in the vicinity. A dolphin will attack a shark if need be. Sea snakes are found mostly close to shore as are sea crocodiles. Both very rarely stray more than a few kilometres or so out.

Drifting palm leaves tend to become limp and discoloured after a few days in the water. When fresh they can be chewed. At this stage they will be yellowy green and give a characteristic 'crack' when bent, not having absorbed a great deal of salt water.

Listen and look for upsurges in the water. These often indicate water oozing from the land in underground currents. Listen and look for the water changes on reefs. Remember, some reefs and atolls can be found hundreds of miles away from the mainland. If you do manage to run aground on one and it's safe, take the opportunity to stretch your legs.

Once whilst sailing in the Pacific Ocean, our boat suddenly became grounded miles from the shore. We were eventually left high and dry for twelve hours, until the tide changed. One minute we were at sea, the next we were sitting on a small island!

On board most modern liners are lifeboats fully equipped with everything that is needed to survive; all you have to do is follow the instructions and stay calm. Technology in survival equipment is changing so fast, it's almost impossible to keep up with it. Thermal suits, radios, flares, water stills, dehydrated food, repellents – the list is endless.

Cold and adrift

In most terrains the human body is extremely adaptable, but not so in the sea. Yes, as I've said, there are cases where people have survived for long periods in almost sub-zero temperatures, and there are cases of people in warm tropical waters having died of exposure within hours. It all depends on the individual. It's safe to say that in 'semi-tropical' waters such as those around the coast of southern France and the Mediterranean the chances of staying alive for any length of time are pretty good, but the further North you go – northern England, Iceland, Russia – the chances of survival after as little as half an hour are virtually nil.

Cold water quickly saps your energy and you need energy to swim or even tread water. During the war men fell into the water after being torpedoed and died within minutes because of the intense cold, some after sitting for hours in rubber lifeboats.

Ask any old sea dog and he will tell you that the sea has two faces. Work with it and you're safe, work against it and it will have you. Its power and enormous expanse frighten most men, but man can increase the chances of survival. Recently, whilst doing some research for this book, I came across the case of an old sailor who had been torpedoed no less than *nineteen* times during the war. Twice he was seriously hurt and at least ten times he found himself splashing around in the North Sea before being rescued. Sadly he's no longer with us, but can you imagine it, nineteen times! If ever there was a survivor who lived to tell the tale it was he.

In rough seas try to avoid letting the boat come broadside on to the waves and don't forget to tie yourself and your equipment down. A capsized boat can still save your life. Lots of sailors have hung on to upturned boats for days before righting them again. Remember that search aircraft are limited as to how far out to sea they can fly, so don't build up your expectations; be prepared for a long wait. Bobbing around for days in a wooden boat and perhaps hour upon hour of rowing will certainly cause you lots of aches and pains, bruises, sores and maybe splinters, so take care. If possible let nature do the work. Run with the currents, hoist a sail, sleep when tired. If it's stormy you'll get very little sleep and remember, storms often last for days, sometimes weeks. On the other hand the sea can be as calm as a mill pond without a breath of wind for days.

Have faith in your own ability to survive. If you feel like praying, pray; the time-honoured 'mariner's prayer' gives spiritual strength in any survival situation. People who have been in such straits speak of the boredom and 'plonk', yes that's right – 'plonk'. This term refers to the mind and body seeming to wander off into limbo, neither of them wanting to work. If this happens it's imperative that you quickly get back into a routine. If you're drifting aimlessly around, the sea is calm and it's daylight, keep fishing. When it is dark take care. If it's very hot take off your shirt or blouse and drape this over the dinghy gunnels to make some shade. Stretch your clothes, socks, dress or trousers across the gunnels. As you bob around and the sun rises and sets, the cooling shadows will move with you.

Signalling

Remember your international distress signal – six flashes every minute or so – and knowing how to send morse code can help. (See pages 94 and 95 for complete alphabet in semaphore and morse code.) Normally air-sea searches are carried out until the authorities are satis-

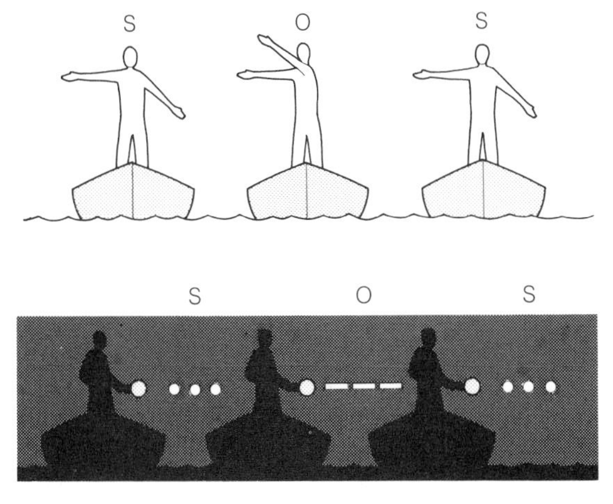

international distress signals
six flashes every minute

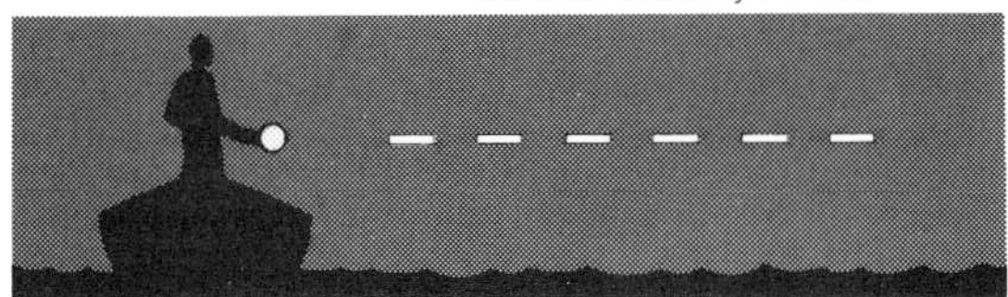

signal flares

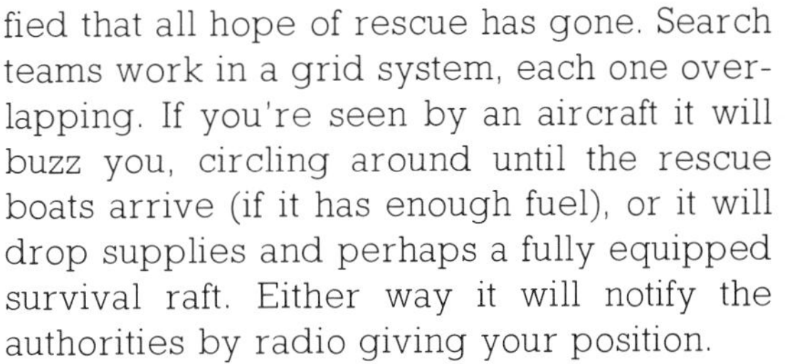

fied that all hope of rescue has gone. Search teams work in a grid system, each one overlapping. If you're seen by an aircraft it will buzz you, circling around until the rescue boats arrive (if it has enough fuel), or it will drop supplies and perhaps a fully equipped survival raft. Either way it will notify the authorities by radio giving your position.

If you're fortunate enough to have any supplies in your dinghy use them sparingly. Flares should only be lit or sent up when you're absolutely sure you can see a boat or plane. Marker dyes are best seen from the air, not from passing ships. Flash or flashes must be continuous. Allow for your silhouette disappearing beneath the swell of the waves. Don't despair if they do not see you first time. Keep trying.

A boat without an engine/keel/sail will drift aimlessly over the water surface, which could mean turning into or away from the sun. A crude sea anchor can be made by using your pants or shirt as balloons. Simply tie the legs into knots, scoop them over your head and cast them astern. Even when the air seeps out they will still act as a drag anchor.

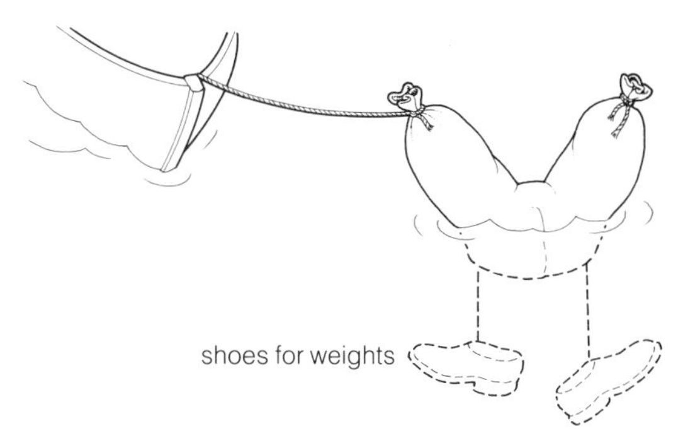

A paddle strapped to one side of the boat will serve as a keel. A running noose made from strips of clothing will support it, and if you are lucky enough to rig up a sail this will give you stability. (See diagram overleaf.)

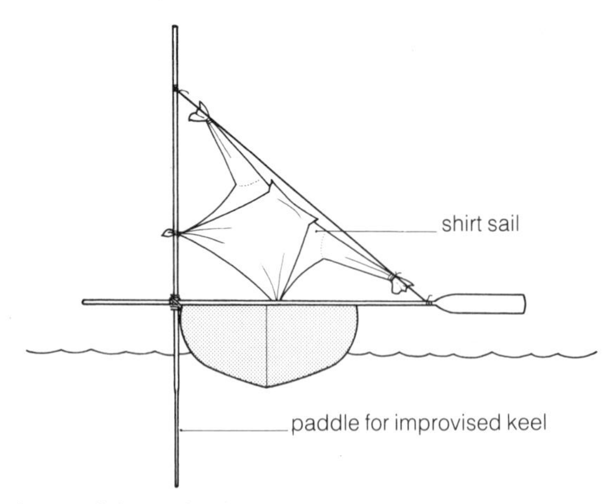

Improvising a keel and sail

Water

We already know how important water is to our survival on land, but at sea we are even more dependent on it. Ironically, adrift in a dinghy you are literally surrounded by millions and millions of gallons – all completely useless for drinking. Therefore precious drinking water must be gained from any source.

Melted fresh ice will provide you with one drinkable supply (see page 159–60). Ice placed on the eyelids will relieve soreness and irritation. Equally ice, fresh or old, melted over a wound or blister helps ease the pain. To get water from the ice make a simple ice pack from your handkerchief. Hold this over your mouth and let it drip.

Fresh drinking water may also be had by freezing sea water in a container. As the water freezes, fresh water rises to the surface and the salt becomes trapped in a soggy layer. This top section can then be removed and the salt waste cleaned off. Re-melt the ice and you have your fresh water.

If there are icebergs around take care. Some of the smaller ones are very unstable and easily topple over. However, because they have drifted away from the main stream, fresh water may be had from the tops of them, the ice having been melted by the sun.

If you have any old sails, tins or buckets, lay them out to collect rain water and drink all you can immediately. Remember, it's better inside you than slopping around in some bucket. Fresh water floats on the surface of salt water, so scoop out any sea water from the floor of your dinghy if rain is imminent. If necessary mop it clean with your clothes (this will prevent any contamination by salt). Collect as much as you can.

Avoid using precious drinking water for washing.

Food at sea – anything goes!

Fish is an excellent source of food, and as you would expect, readily available at sea. It's rich in protein and highly nutritious. The problem is, of course, how do you catch fish if you've no fishing tackle handy? Well, as always there's a way. For instance, even without a regular meal the human body still has natural functions, one of them being the passing of faeces. Repugnant as it may seem faeces makes excellent bait, and remember, in a survival situation anything goes.

More than once I've caught fish and eels simply by using a forked stick and an old sock as a net. Place the faeces in the sock and hang it over the side of the boat. You'll be surprised how fish will push into the sock to get at it. Having caught the fish, rinse out and tie the sock round your chest to dry it. Remember what my army instructor taught me – live like an animal.

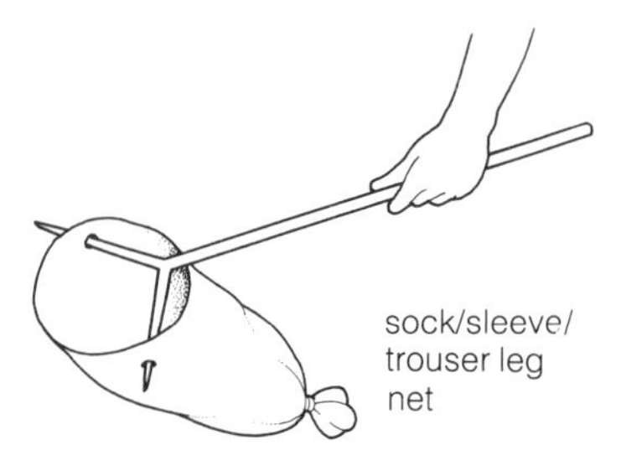

A simple fishing net can also be made from your socks, sweater or scarf. Lay unwound strands across the boat and tie each one up individually across the gunnels. You could use your paddle as a temporary fishing rod.

A scoop net can be made by using your shirt or blouse (see below). Sprinkle bait, faeces etc., on the water surface. Another way is to fasten the paddle to the shirt or blouse and snatch it up when the fish swim across.

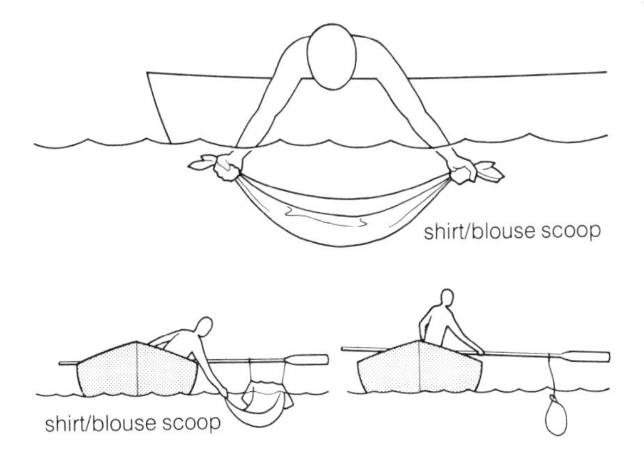

Turtle soup à la survival

Turtle soup is very succulent and rich in protein. Whether or not you can make soup at sea, the shell can be used as a bailer, a scoop, a plate and even a hat if need be, and the flesh is excellent. Turtles are easily caught as they swim slowly on the water surface. If you strike the turtle in the water with your paddle it will probably sink before your eyes. It's better to scoop it up in your shirt or net. If you want to, you can actually lift turtles out of the water simply by grabbing their back legs. As soon as you grab the back legs quickly dunk the turtle under the water and lift it into the boat on the rebound. Some of the larger ones can be quite heavy so you may have difficulty getting them into the boat if you don't dunk them first.

A word of warning! Turtles do bite, and in the confines of your boat could do damage to you. To kill one, you can make a noose from your shoe laces, belt etc. and strangle it. Or you could turn it onto its back and beat it with your paddle or the heel of your shoe. If you are in a wooden boat try cracking the undershell down hard on the bow. More about cooking turtles in the next chapter (page 39).

Safety first

Discarded food will attract sharks, so when fishing in tropical waters be extra cautious. Once sharks know you regularly discard your waste they'll continue to follow your boat. If a shark appears, cease fishing and lie still. *Remember! A fully grown shark can easily bite through a light sailing dinghy or inflatable.* Don't cast your shadow over the water and never enter the water. Soon he'll become bored and swim off.

At night, if you have a torch you could in an emergency use it to attract fish, but again, beware of sharks; they never sleep. Better to keep your torch for signalling.

In tropical waters the puffer fish is quite common but to be eaten it must have very special preparation. Its intestines, liver and kidney are deadly poison, and the meat or flesh needs to be boiled. It's safer to throw the fish back or use it for bait. Shark flesh is tough and often foul smelling, but as a last resort it can be eaten raw or certainly used as bait. Sharks fins are used to make soup and considered a delicacy in the Far East.

Obviously it would be impossible to list all the edible and inedible fish in this chapter and even experts can't agree on what is and what isn't edible anyway, so if you've any doubts at all about a fish, discard it and try again.

Take a tip from the natives: eat only what you *know* to be edible; use the rest for bait. *Never* handle barbed fish or those with tentacles. The bigger the fish the more likely it is to be edible, including the whale. Mud skippers aren't very palatable and without a net are difficult to catch.

Remember, there are *no edible* species of *jelly fish*; in fact most are poisonous and in some cases deadly, particularly the stings of the ones found around the northern shores of Australia. To dilute this poison, alcohol or spirit should be applied immediately to the sting and professional medical help sought.

Apart from those of the stingray most fish eggs are tasteless and not recommended as a source of food. I always put fish eggs on the same par as sheep's or goat's eyes. They are tasteless and of no nutritional value, and that goes for frogs' spawn too. My advice is to leave all of them well alone.

If you have to step into shallow water, wear footwear and carry either a forked or spiked pole. As always, use common sense.

Another word of warning: remember that fish and turtle flesh quickly deteriorate unless cooked or cured. If you're adrift in the tropics you could sun dry it by cutting it into thin strips. In the arctic you have a little more time before it begins to go bad. However, if it does go off, keep it for bait.

More on fishing in the next chapter, and on *cooking* fish in chapter 8.

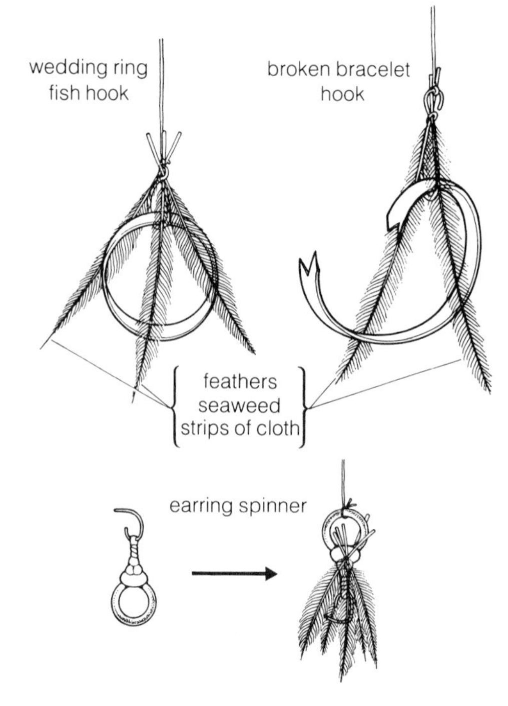

Improvised fish hooks

Sea birds and other meals

Any sea bird that lands on your boat can be considered as food. Retain the feathers and fix them to your improvised fish hook which can be made from fish bone, bones from the bird, even the buckles of your belt, brooch or comb, and as a last resort you could even use your wedding ring. All these and more have been used in the past quite successfully.

With care, a float can also be made from bird feathers. Always be willing to improvise. I have actually caught a small shark on a rope with nothing but frayed ends tied in a knot. The shark's teeth became embedded in the knot.

Plankton, minute living organisms, may be eaten but you'll have to scoop them up with your net. Also, if there's one flying fish around there will be many, many others. Seaweed boiled is excellent for moving the bowels. See chapter 8 for advice on choosing and cooking seaweed. Clams, algae and in fact most molluscs are edible, including sea slugs and lug worms. The latter, often a metre long, need their intestines removing and then drying in the sun. Lug worms may be eaten fresh, but alas you only get them along sandy beaches or small atolls. Sharks and barracuda may also be eaten. Mushed fruit, such as pumpkin, is often used to attract these bigger fish.

Survival rules in a dinghy

The dinghy and its contents, no matter how minimal, are all there is between you and death, so stay with it. Have any flares, marker dyes or flags handy and available. If fresh water supplies allow it (and *only* if there is sufficient to spare) rinse salt from your clothes and body daily. In tropical regions during the heat of the day wear light clothing to protect the head, face and shoulders. Attend to any small cuts and bruises immediately.

Rest at night, fish by day.

As in all survival situations, everything depends on your own individual survival instincts and the will to live. Calmness, confidence, fitness, cunning and improvisation are the key words. Man is tenaciously adaptable even at sea. Keep yourself fit. Have a daily massage and stretch your limbs. Keep as dry as possible, especially during the night. Keep a watch out for ship lights and ships bearing down on you. If there's anything to record keep a daily log.

When storms are imminent stow away or tie down all loose items. A small sail is better than no sail at all during a storm.

Take care when stepping onto coral, it's razor sharp! Normally after crashing through reefs the water is much more placid. Any land must be considered a respite. Take the opportunity to rest on an island no matter how small. It's easier to spot than a small dinghy.

Never be tempted to jump overboard for a swim unless it's absolutely safe.

Daily hygiene is of paramount importance in any survival situation. If it's possible to move the bowels daily do so, especially if you're getting food, but don't be alarmed if you can't go for two or three days. It's quite common. Being close to the water surface as the boat bobs around, it's almost certain that you'll be a little sea sick. Remember that you're in a survival situation. If possible vomit into some old clothing. Repulsive as it seems vomit makes ideal bait; nothing must be wasted.

Swimming and rafting ashore

Remember when swimming in to shore to beware of the sharp coral. Don't underestimate its danger. More than one diver has found to his cost just how sharp it can be. To be on the safe side, as you get closer to the shore adopt the sitting position in the water with your legs stretched out slightly in front of you and do the breaststroke with your arms. As the swell of the waves lifts you, go with them. If the surf is very rough try not to allow yourself to be propelled forwards head first. Retain the sitting position. If you have shoes wear them, feel with your feet.

If you have to swim across a river without any aids try to swim down and across; go with the current. Never swim upwards – it's tiring and time consuming. Use the side stroke. Remember, ice cold water can kill! Swim only if you have to.

If you have the time, make a raft. A simple raft can be made by lashing some bamboo poles together using grass rope or liana fronds. A raft will only travel at the speed of the water surface unless it has a sail or engine.

Use a pole to push yourself through the water rather than paddle.

CHAPTER 4

Fishing

In the last chapter we looked at sea fishing from a drifting craft. Of course, angling is itself a major survival skill. Most of us have been fishing at some time in our lives and those of us who have never fished have certainly seen films or read books about it. What could be more basic? A length of string with a hook and a worm attached to a pole. Millions of people every year fish this way and most are reasonably successful. Fishing is a very important and simple technique for staying alive. It is said by some historians that fish were probably the first alternative food source ancient man turned to after his diet of berries, nuts and roots.

Fish, like all other living animals including man, are continually on the lookout for food, and in their search they become very inquisitive. It's this inquisitiveness and constant quest for food that drives them to your hooks, nets or traps. When you understand this you will be able to use these weaknesses to your advantage and your chances of catching food become that much better.

Fish are usually very territorial and though at the first sign of danger or when suddenly disturbed they rush off into the deepest water and dark shadows, they will nevertheless return soon afterwards to their feeding grounds. So wait and be patient.

My father taught me the first rule about fish poaching. To be a good fish poacher it was not only essential to be able to fish well but also to be able to read the elements. He taught me that, as the sun rises in the east and sinks in the west, the shadows cast by the trees and steep banks along the river edge change. In the early morning the shadows are long and are cast across the waters. As the sun climbs higher in the sky the shadows become shorter and the water surface heats up. This in turn brings the fish closer to the surface to feed and thus they become more accessible and easier to catch.

As the water's surface temperature changes, so do the feeding habits of insects, which we all know fish like to feed on. 'It's all a case of working with nature,' my father would tell me. Having learnt these skills I was amazed how much easier my fishing became. More than once I've sat on a river bank using an old garden cane and pin hook opposite a more conventional fisherman. I was the one who caught lots of fish whilst he sat in frustration catching nothing.

Remember, every living thing must have oxygen to survive. To bring fish to the surface simply stir up the river bed and if possible make a small dam, cutting down the flow of water and decreasing the oxygenating process. Once the oxygen ceases to flow into the water the fish will soon surface to breathe.

A simple guide to whether there is animal life or fish present is to study the feeding habits of the various birds that come to the water. Birds with short stubby beaks are mainly seed eaters so only come to drink. Birds with long pointed beaks, or curved ones such as hawks, are flesh eaters and they obviously come to feed on the fish or animal life within the water. Sometimes molluscs, crabs, cray fish and the like, may have been eaten close by, so look for the tell-tale signs of discarded shells.

Nets

The net is undoubtedly the most effective trap in use today. Think of a spider's web. Making a net isn't all that difficult. You need only a few lengths of string, strips of cloth, vines or whatever is handy – even wire netting. Therefore in a survival situation, if time allows, it's well worth the effort to build a strong net. It can also be used as a trap, a storage container, hammock or in an emergency, as a sling for an injured arm or leg. The beauty of the net is that it not only snares the fish but helps keep them alive for long periods so if need be they can be held for a later meal. If it's made properly and set in the right place (for instance across a stream) it's almost certain your net will work.

Making a survival net

1. String a pole across two supports about chest high or use a nearby tree branch.
2. Hang a series of lengths of string down from the pole either with weights on the end such as dried mud balls, or attached to a heavy pole.
3. Now make yourself a net card or weaver block to pull the cord through.
4. Work from one side, left to right. Weave across the line starting at the bottom.
5. Keep an even weave and, depending on what you want to use the net for, keep the mesh small. A good guide is to make the mesh so that you can push only one finger through. Alternatively use a thin long pole the thickness of your finger.

An unravelled sock, scarf or glove will give you sufficient material to make a fair-sized net.

Double use of your trap is also important. For example, in the Far East they peg out long lines of nets along the coast to catch the fish. These are set out in such a way that only certain sized fish can swim through the net's mesh at the top whilst lower down the mesh is woven much smaller. The net keeps out sharks, barracuda etc., then when the tide recedes, it traps the smaller fish in the fine mesh. Whilst the tide is out the net is left

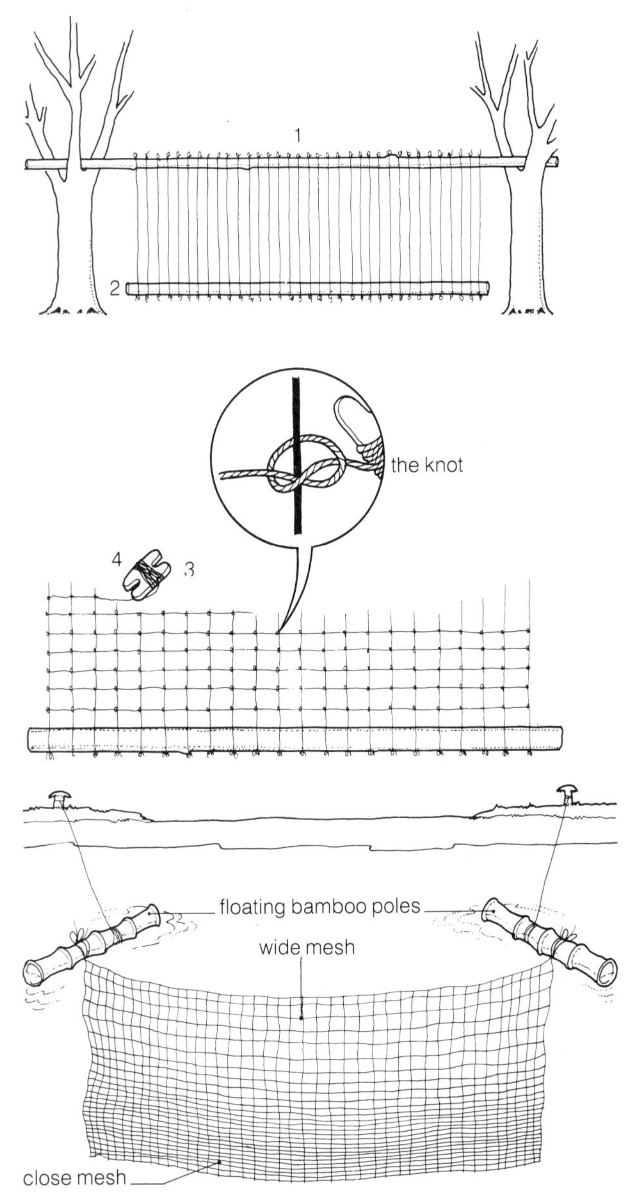

Making and using a survival net

exposed and often traps incoming birds that have been sea feeding. A classic case of making Mother Nature work with you, and multiplying the uses of your traps.

Remember, few fish swim backwards, though some can as a means of defence. Most swim in a forward motion and as a result become entangled in a net as they attempt to swim through it. The more they struggle the more they become entangled and eventually suffocate through lack of oxygen. Of course, their struggle may attract other fish – sometimes the dreaded shark, so take care when wading out to inspect your nets. Nets can be set across streams, along beaches, below weirs, around ponds, along river banks – in fact wherever there are fish.

Before setting your net walk up and down the river bank or beach a couple of times looking for the best anchor points. The siting of your net is just as important as the setting. Like all other traps nets are non-selective and will take anything that becomes entangled in them, for instance rats, fish, crabs, eels, molluscs and even reptiles that browse in the water such as crocodiles or snakes.

Nets set along the shore have to be set in such a way that when the tide is in they are almost altogether submerged. They must not be fully submerged beneath the water because if they are, as the tide recedes, the fish will simply swim back out over the top. Remember to curve the net a little so that the fish are drawn and trapped in the net-like basin; and do not make the net too tight. Let it flap a little, otherwise they will bounce off it.

Nets can be cast over the water surface and if weighed down will sink and trap any passing fish. On many of the great lakes in Africa all fishing is carried out in this manner, and in the Far East you will see great armadas of fishing boats spread along the coastline fishing in exactly the same way.

Other methods of catching fish

Fish can be caught in improvised baskets made from the branches and bark of nearby trees. Coconut fibres make an excellent twine substitute and so too do the fibres from papyrus reeds. Both stems and fibres make excellent building materials for baskets. On the shore, wait until the tide ebbs then take the baskets out and tie them to a stake driven into the sea bed. Along river banks set them just below the water where it is rushing through a gap. Remember to anchor it well.

A simple fish trap (basket) can be made by pushing half a dozen saplings into a scooped out hole in the ground. Place a stone in the middle of them to fan them out, then use your rope to weave the basket.

A simple fish trap

When teaching students the art of survival at my training centre I always emphasize to them that the secret of being a good survivor is to be able to adapt to any situation and that they must be able to improvise with anything to hand. For instance, I tell them buttons from a jacket make excellent fishing weights and improvised hooks can easily be made from old animal bone. A brooch, ring or bracelet will make excellent fishing spinners; hair pins or slides, even a penknife can easily be adapted to make a good strong fishing hook. Laces from your shoes, strips from your handkerchief, cord from your clothing can be adapted to make a crude fishing line.

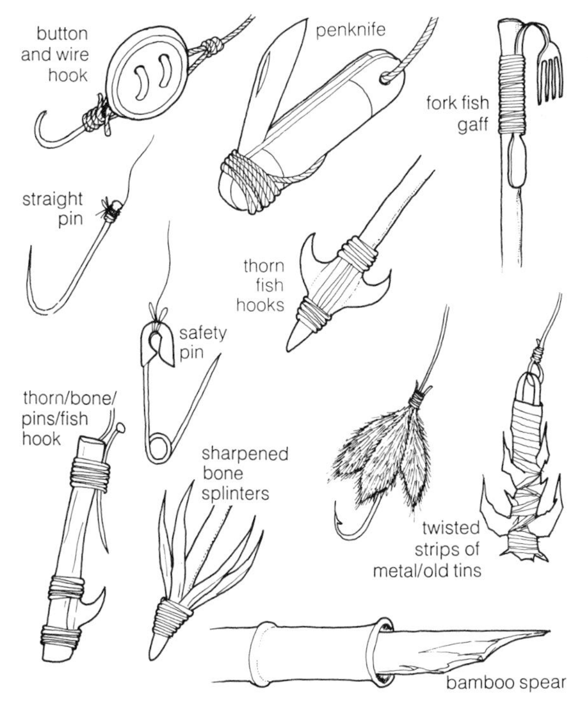

Almost anything that floats can be used to make some sort of fishing net or trap. Old tights, stockings, plastic bottles, balloons and plastic bags have all been used successfully in the past (see illustration on page 38).

I often used to go fishing with an old coke bottle. I'd wedge a small length of stick into the neck of the bottle and then wind my fishing line round the base, bait my hook, and, holding the stick, allow the line to be swung out as I waved the bottle above my head. With the line weighted it would skim out way across the river or pond. When I got a bite I simply wound it in back around the bottle.

Sometimes I'd find an old feather and strip the feathers from the quill. Then I'd take an old oak apple or the liner from inside a pop bottle cap (these were often made of cork), stick the feather through it and I'd have myself a bob float. Oak apples are old wasps' nests left hanging from the oak tree. If you don't use them to make floats, when dry they make excellent tinder.

To make the tip of the float more visible take some sap from a nearby tree, rub the feather top in it and then stick on the petal of a flower. When the water is choppy it makes it much easier to see.

There are many ways of improvising for your needs. The eyelets from your shoes/boots make good snare ferrules and the laces could be used to fasten up a splint, make

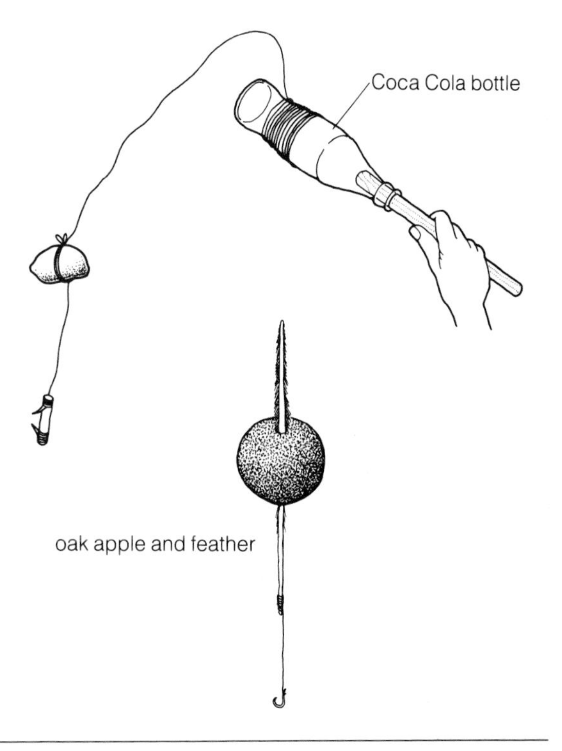

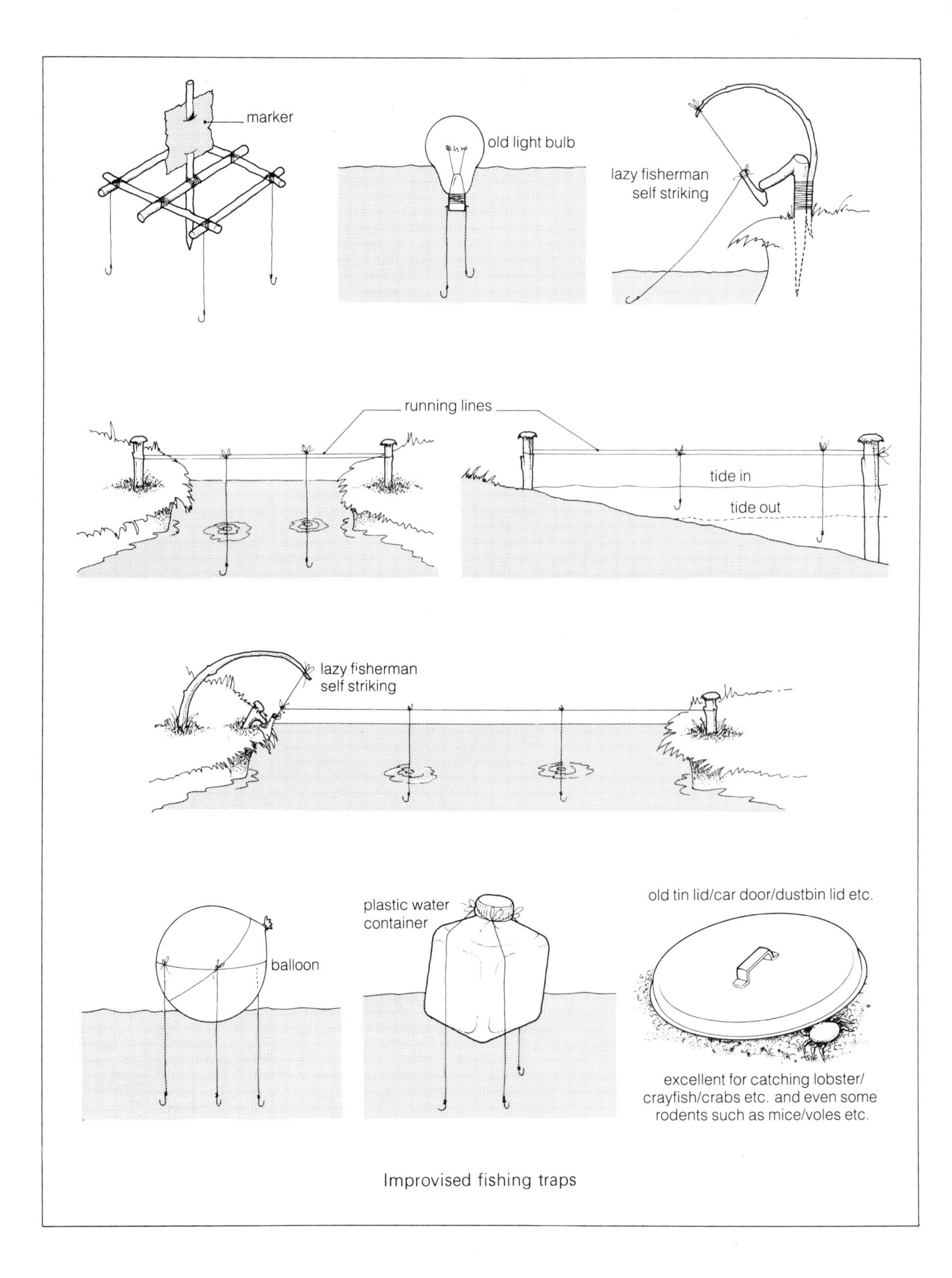

Improvised fishing traps

a snare or use as a fishing line. We know that we can use strips of cloth to make rope or nets and if need be to make bandages. Smouldering cloth helps chase away mosquitoes from your shelter. Human and animal hair will bind together coins from your pocket to make fishing weights. Or if you wish you could stick them together using resin from trees. Even the zip from your clothing can be used to strike a precious match on. The list, as always, is endless and the number of survival aids you can improvise from your personal possessions is unbelievable. Just use your imagination.

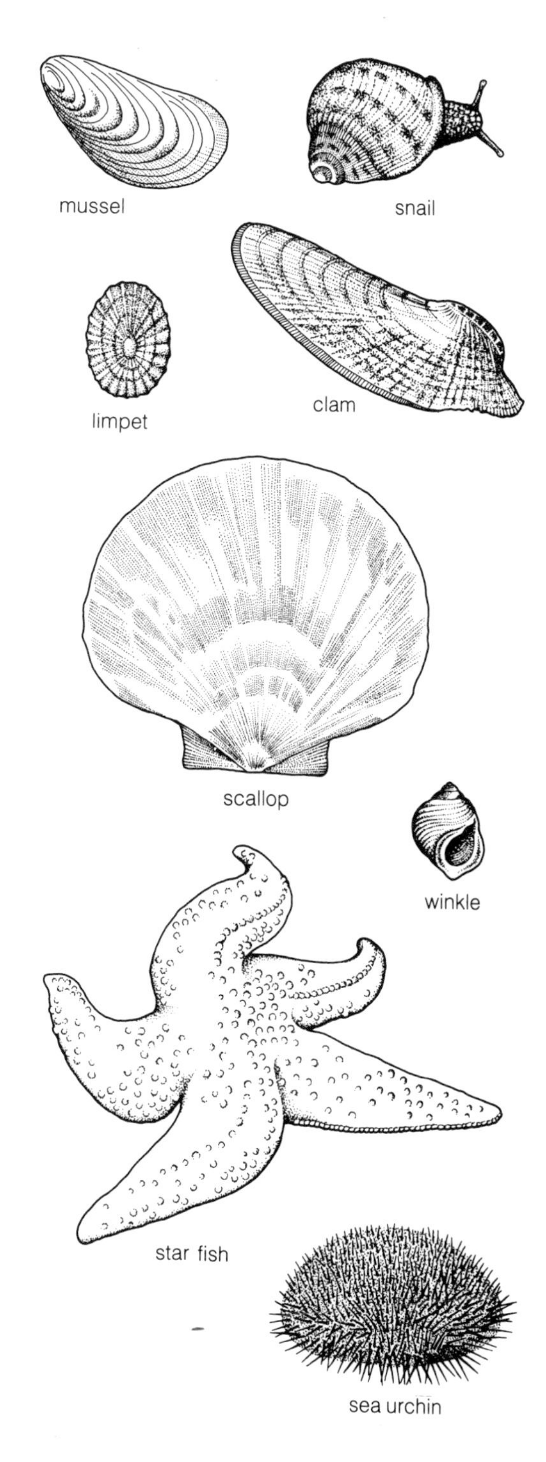

Reptiles and shellfish

You may be unsure how to handle reptiles or shellfish. A net is probably the best trap to use if you want to catch tortoises, turtles, large lizards and even crocodiles and the occasional snake! Many of these creatures tend to move very sluggishly in the early hours of the morning, especially if it's cold, as they need the heat of the sun to warm up their circulation. Common sense tells you that this is the best time to trap them.

A word of advice here: except for the lobster and crab, in the case of most shell-carrying animals such as the tortoise, turtle or large sand snail, remove them from the shell first and if possible gut and clean the flesh before cooking. The smell of turtle flesh can be overpowering when removed from the shell so quickly roll it in the hot embers of your fire. This not only helps preserve the flesh but makes the smell less offensive.

Many of the smaller molluscs will need a good boiling before the flesh can be removed – limpets and winkles for example. Having boiled them for a good thirty minutes, tip them onto a stone (or better still into a sieve), then pick them out. Remember, once out of water all molluscs and fish deteriorate rapidly, so never be tempted to leave them and reheat.

Eels are another excellent source of food and all are edible including the giant Moray eel found in the sea, although special care must be taken when handling the latter as it can give you a vicious bite. In the case of the electric eel, this can still give a slight shock hours after it has been killed. My advice is to leave both these well alone. If there are eels around you may rest assured fish will be there also. Snatching freshwater eels out of the water with your hand is possible but requires a lot of practice. Eels are extremely slippery and without a great deal of experience it's highly unlikely you'll be able to catch one this way. Eels are best caught in a net, and one can soon be improvised from grass or brambles.

The simplest eel trap to make is a net basket. This is nothing more than a few thin willowy twigs tied together with thin grass rope and then suspended just below the surface of the water. (See pages 118–9 for how to make a grass rope.)

Eels tend to congregate at the bottom of weirs and rapids feeding on any food that may be washed down. Once you've set your basket, bait the area with any old scraps of food or any insects you can find. A skill I often used as a youngster, and one that I have used many times since, is the old sock and faeces trick. Remember how we used the same ruse to fish from our dinghy? Take an old sock, push a forked stick through the opening and then drop a little dried animal faeces into the bottom. Lower the sock into the water and very gently weave it backwards and forwards until the faeces begin to break up. If there are any eels around they'll soon come swimming

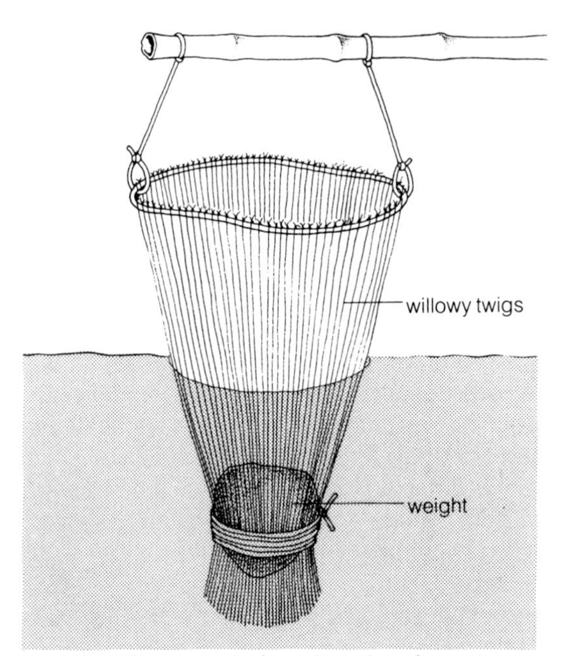

A simple eel trap made from lengths of marsh reed or thin twigs

and providing you hold the sock still they will enter through the forked stick opening and become trapped. Animal intestines make excellent bait, and no eel, or any other fish for that matter, can resist them.

Remember, fish is highly nutritious and in most cases easily available. Make the effort – don't just set one trap, set many. The more lines you have out the better your chances are of catching something. Fish and water go together. If you can't catch your fish one way, try another. Nothing ventured, nothing gained.

CHAPTER 5

Water

In any survival situation, it cannot be too often repeated, water is much more important than food for keeping you alive. As we have seen you can live a lot longer without food than you can without water. Most people can survive without water in moderate climates for four or five days, though even this can be dangerous to health. In semi-tropical climates it's more likely to be three or four days and in extremely hot regions, such as deserts, two to three days will probably be the most you can last, often less than that. If you understand the nature of dehydration, avoid unnecessary panic and thus wasting precious energy, you can help slow down your natural water loss. Knowing how to conserve body water is just as important as being able to find water – which under no circumstances should you consider drinking if it has not first been distilled or purified.

The normal human body temperature is 98.6° and any deviation from this will result in a change in the body's efficiency. To survive, our body converts food and liquid into energy reserves and immediately, when there is a change in body temperature, either up or down, there is a reaction. For instance, when heated the body releases fluids as sweat to bring down the temperature. When our water or food supply runs low our body draws on its energy reserves and this sets up an automatic demand for a further supply – we feel thirsty and hungry.

It isn't surprising that the body's need for water is of paramount importance when you consider that almost 70 per cent of our actual body weight is due to water storage. The average person can loose between 2½ and 3 pints of water per day without any ill effect. In some extreme cases up to 10 pints have been lost, but this would leave you very weak and thirsty. But whatever the amount, without replacement, you would die either sooner or later.

Think Survival! Even without exertion you loose valuable body fluid, and if you exert yourself strenuously you lose even more.

Since approximately two-thirds of the human body weight is fluid – about eleven gallons on average – every drop is critical to our survival. And since water is without any doubt the most important life-sustaining factor, we must clearly understand how the body conserves it and loses it. The body's most unobtrusive method of releasing fluid is through evaporation, or sweating. We also use up body moisture on digesting solid foods and a significant quantity of fluid is lost through urination. Moisture is also needed to help the circulation of the blood. As it's relatively easy to control to a certain extent some of these functions affecting the body's water loss, it is important to try and make this as effective as possible. Too often in survival situations, far more fluid-expending energy goes into the search for food than water when it should be the other way round.

The average adult, in normal conditions, will require up to four pints of liquid a day, much of which will come from food, especially fruit and vegetables which have a high water content. So at the risk of stating the obvious, wherever possible, when you are in a survival situation, try to eat and drink regularly. The old adage of saving water until later doesn't work. It's better to drink as much as you need – the body is an excellent reservoir of liquid.

Concentrate on controlling water evaporation from changes in body heat by wearing the right clothing, eating proper food and conserving your strength. Soldiers are taught to eat little and often as they move across country. They are also taught to drink small amounts regularly. Excessive sweating will result in the loss of body salts and it may be necessary to remember to take a little salt from time to time to keep up the balance of salts in the body. But be careful, as too much salt in too short a time will only have the reverse effect and result in making you more thirsty or sick.

Before we look into more specific aspects of the importance of water to a survivor, I want to give a general warning: we know how vital water is, but remember that it is also one of nature's most effective silent killers. It is sometimes impossible to know whether water is contaminated. If you drink contaminated water and it begins to poison your system you may not realize until it's too late. Therefore the importance of water mustn't over-ride the necessary precautions we need to take to ensure that drinking water is clean.

Dehydration

Providing you can restore any water loss from dehydration within a few hours, the body will not suffer any serious damage. But it must be stressed that time is of the essence and even a few hours may be too long, especially in extreme heat. It's therefore always advisable to try and make up water loss as quickly as possible. No-one is immune from dehydration. Immediately the body starts reacting a wide range of symptoms may occur. Their speed and severity will depend upon how bad the dehydration is, but even a mild case will produce some common symptoms that are relatively easy to recognize.

The first symptoms of dehydration are thirst, discomfort, lethargy and sleepiness. There will be loss of appetite, the body's temperature will begin to rise and the sufferer may feel nauseous. The colour of urine may change from pale yellow to orange. If no water replacement is possible and the dehydration worsens, additional symptoms will include dizziness, headaches, breathing difficulties, an extremely dry mouth and throat, as well as increased fatigue in all limbs. As the water deficiency increases the symptoms will include deafness, swelling of the tongue, cyanosis (skin becoming blue), a growing inability to walk, loss of vision, general spasticity and eventually death. When victims of dehydration become delirious they often do dangerous and stupid things, such as walking out into the sun or the sea and drinking sea water. Watch carefully for early signs of dehydration and try to deal with the conservation of body fluids and the replacement of fresh supplies as a matter of priority.

If possible increase the amount of liquids taken as soon as the first symptoms are noticed. A reduction in drinking will lead to a reduction in sweating and increase the risk of heatstroke, though drinking more than the body can sweat out will result in fluid loss by urination. Any loss is to be avoided so drink small amounts regularly. Keep cool and quiet. Place wet clothes, grasses or leaves over the body to help reduce body temperature; even salt water can be used very sparingly.

Dehydration can kill in several ways. These include causing kidney or heart failure. As the water loss increases the amount of blood decreases and the decrease in blood circulation lessens the amount of oxygen to the body and increases the work of the heart. The kidneys need a certain amount of blood flow to function and when the pressure and volume drop too far, the kidneys fail. Later in the chapter we'll look at ways of collecting and purifying water but first we'll see how you can control sweat loss and preserve the bodily fluids you have. Never forget that dehydration is a killer. Hikers have been found not far from safety and carrying water in containers, dead from dehydration.

Sweat loss

There are a number of simple and effective ways of minimising sweat loss and of preserving bodily fluids, the most obvious being –

Keep in the shade

Conserve energy; avoid walking or working during the hottest part of the day; move slowly; work at night and if possible rest often. Keep calm; stress can increase the rate at which you sweat. Keep covered in intense heat – remember how desert nomads always appear dressed from head to foot: it keeps down evaporation and avoids sunburn (which increases the rate of dehydration). Keep clothing loose to increase ventilation and always keep your head and neck covered.

If in or near the sea, use sea water to keep the skin cool but try to prevent a build up of salt on the skin or clothes as the body dries out. Too much salt on the skin may cause sores.

Other forms of fluid loss

Diarrhoea and vomiting are both very serious causes of fluid loss and it's not easy to avoid them.

Avoid drinking sea water. Salt water can be used as a means of *inducing* vomiting but it also increases the thirst. Excessive salt water kills.

Avoid alcohol – it usually results in greater thirst and can cause dehydration (even in the safety of your home).

Avoid cigarettes as they are also known to dry the mouth and throat and increase the desire for further liquid.

Useful hints

Sucking buttons or stones or chewing a piece of cloth or gum, as I mentioned earlier, won't stop your thirst – only a fresh liquid supply will do this. It simply makes you feel better and may prevent you from panting and taking in hot air which will dry up the moisture in your mouth.

When you've obtained some water (see below for collection methods) you must drink it carefully. Sip it – don't gulp. If you're very hot and the water is cold, the rapid drop in the temperature of your stomach as you drink may cause you to be sick and lose the life-giving water anyway.

If you expect to be rescued don't bother to ration your water supply too strictly, otherwise you may lapse into unconsciousness without using all the water. Keep yourself going as best you can while trying to find adequate fresh supplies.

Don't drink urine, stagnant water or sea water. Test for contamination (see page 51), check there are no dead animals or insects in the water; choose a fast-flowing source if possible. If you're in arctic conditions melt ice rather than snow (it produces water in less time and with less heat). Sea ice more than one year old is usually salt free. You can identify it by its colour and texture: it is blueish, has rounded corners and has a more crystalline structure than older ice contaminated by salt water which is milky grey and opaque. Snow contains less water than ice, melt some in your hand then suck it slowly.

Collecting water

All rain water can be drunk at source without purification provided it has been collected in clean containers. Obviously any tin cans, plastic bags and other man-made containers which you have will be of help. Leaves of large plants can be used as well, as can sections of bamboo.

It's extraordinary how far apart sources of water can be and you may have to travel some way to find one. You should make sure that you have adequate containers with you, and other tools such as string or rope, pieces of cloth and so on, in order to maximise any discovery of water you make.

The easiest pure water to find is usually rain water but when that isn't available you'll have to make do with other sources. In a tropical jungle you may not find fresh drinking water easily, but you will find plenty of muddy pools. You need to know how to deal with water under these conditions. There are some general geographical points to remember; wherever there are hills there will probably be a supply of fresh water and the higher the hills, the greater the amount. Hills hold moisture (hot air rising to meet cold air), this moisture builds up into clouds which give rain, the rain creates streams and rivers and wherever there's water there will be life – animal, vegetable and insect. Where these exist your chances of survival are increased.

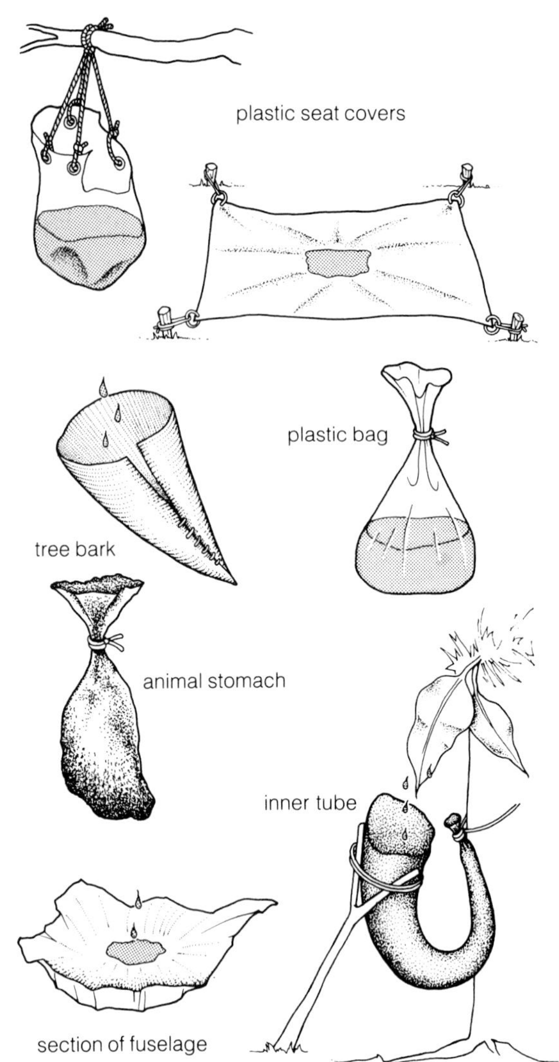

Containers

What containers can you make from your environment if there are no man-made ones around? One of the simplest and best is made from the bark of a tree. Silver birch bark is ideal. Cut a section about 10 in. square, place it in hot water for a while (this makes it more supple and easier to bend) and scoop out a hole in the ground. Put the bark over the hole and fill it with boiling water, place a heavy stone into the water and allow it to cool. Afterwards remove the stone and you have the perfect basin.

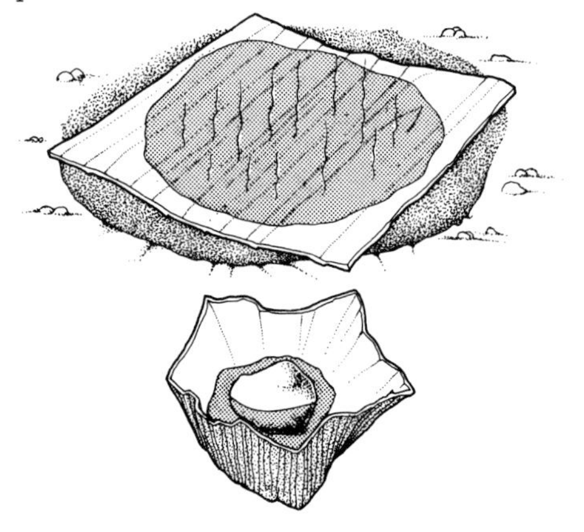

You should bear in mind that stored water isn't always safe unless it's first boiled or purified. In most survival situations man-made containers such as hubcaps, pieces of canvas, water bottles or empty petrol cans (dangerous unless *very* thoroughly cleaned out) will prove to be of great value.

Rain

Even if there's an abundance of water, rain traps using pieces of metal, cloth or very large leaves should be set up so that any water supply you're using is as fresh as possible. A rowing boat or inflated dinghy can also be used as an excellent method of catching rain water.

Containers left outside around the bottom of a tent can also fill up quite quickly during rain. Large leaves placed over a framework may also be used. If you tie a shirt around the trunk of a small tree with a bowl underneath you'll find the shirt absorbs water which drips into the bowl.

More water will of course collect if you just let rain splash into the bowl and if you line a small hole with a plastic bag you will find that this method produces a mouthful of clean water quite quickly.

Rivers

Rivers are an obvious source of water whether they're full or empty. In a desert area the most likely source of water will be an oasis – but these are very few and far between. You can usually see them from some distance away because of the palm trees. You can be sure that if there is any water the locals, both human and animal, will know about it, so follow the trails in the desert.

Only once have I come across a water hole in the middle of a barren area of desert with no signs of vegetation or animal life near the pool. Just a large clear pool of fresh water sitting there! Most pools tend to have lots of vegetation around them and in major deserts are almost always used by local nomads. These oases are natural springs providing a constant supply of water. A word of warning here! Remember both humans and animals take water from them. Some may be dirty or contaminated.

It can sometimes pay to travel along a dry river bed as you are likely to come across indications where animals or birds have been digging in the sand to get at the moisture. I would usually find that if I dug a little further, water would begin to seep up to the surface. This usually happens when the diggings are on the inside of the river bed, particularly under a rock overhang. A tried and tested method of obtaining water from the desert is one used by nomads: search out a possible site along a dried river bed and probe the area with a long, thin stick. If the stick glistens when removed from the sand you know there is water present. You may find, on digging, that you end up with handfuls of wet mud. This alone can produce life-saving amounts of water.

Having dug deep enough to allow the water to flow to the surface you then cover the water with grass or reeds. Push a long thin reed tube, or improvised version of one, down into the water and grass and draw the water out by sucking on the reed. If you've any doubts about the purity of the water, spit it from your mouth into a container and then boil it. This method is one of the most basic desert survival techniques used throughout the world.

Mist and dew

On the edge of one of the world's driest deserts, the infamous Kalahari on the south west coast of Africa, many animals and plants get their water by collecting the heavy dew from the thick sea mists that drift inland. One species of insect stands in the mist and waits until its body is covered with dew, which it then drinks. Desert nomads lay thick heavy woollen blankets out in the mist and then squeeze the dew from them, collecting seven or eight pints a day. This method is used by many desert dwellers the world over. It's one of the easiest ways of obtaining moisture.

You can collect dew from the underside of sheets, parachute fabric, canvas, hubcaps or whatever you have at hand. If you're lucky enough to find the grass covered with dew, collect water by dragging a piece of cloth or your shirt through the grass so that the fabric absorbs the water. Squeeze this out into a bowl or even directly into your mouth, and you'll get a refreshing mouthful of reasonably clean water.

We know that we can collect water like this from condensation, but for it to happen, the dew or mist has to be heavy. If the nights are too dry we may be able to make our own 'dew still'. For example, I used to collect the dung from my camel and carry it with me in a small plastic bag. Similarly, I used to collect my own urine. Using a couple of tins to make the still, and the camel dung to light the fire, I would boil the urine to produce my own water vapour. In my survival kit I always carry a small length of thin plastic or rubber tubing. This has many uses, such as a tourniquet or a tube for siphoning water or petrol. In this instance it's used as a water still condenser pipe. I never obtained a great deal of water using this method but quite often it provided me with enough to be able to cook. Once boiled, the acrylic salts from my urine would settle in the bottom of the tin and the steam would condense out in the plastic tube. As you can see from the diagram a substitute pipe can be made using radiator hoses.

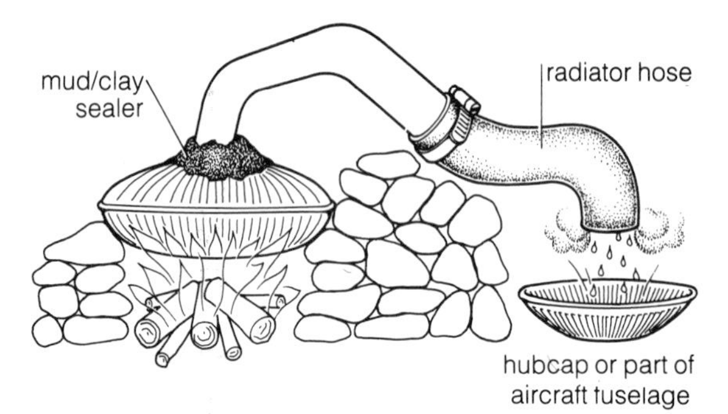

The biggest problem I had was keeping the tube cool, so I had to build a small protective shelter over it and sit there gently making a breeze by waving my sandal.

The desert still

If you have to make your own improvized desert still it will help if you understand that a water still works on the following principle: when air is heated the water vapour present in the air begins to form into droplets. If you heat air in a container, droplets will form on the cooler outer surface of the container. As long as there is a difference in temperature between the outside and the inside, as you have no doubt seen when drops of moisture condense on the outside of a cold glass of beer in a warm room, you can create water to drink.

The desert 'survival still' (see opposite) requires a small bucket or container, a sheet of clear plastic (five or six feet square), and a length of plastic pipe to suck up the water.

As the sun's rays strike the outer surface of the plastic, the air underneath, between the plastic and the ground, heats up and droplets of water will form on the underside. These droplets trickle down to the lowest point of the plastic where they will fall into the container you've placed there. The reason for having a plastic tube is to save you having to lift up one edge of the plastic sheeting every time you want some water.

It's worth trying to set up more than one still at a time. The water vapour that will be extracted from the soil beneath the plastic sheeting will eventually be exhausted and therefore you may need to keep moving your still. It you find you're not getting any moisture out at all and there isn't anywhere else you can move it to, place any fresh green leaves or grasses in the hole, as a kind of lining. The plant material will give up some water, or you can even urinate onto the soil around the container you are using to collect water. The still will gradually extract the new moisture from the soil. The vapour will condense on the underside of the plastic and drop into the container. This will be perfectly drinkable.

During the night the still will continue to work in so much as the air inside cools and moisture falls back into the ground. When the sun rises the next day, the process carries on where it left off, condensing fresh moisture from the soil.

It's also possible to collect condensation (dew) at night simply by laying your plastic sheet on the ground. As the air cools, so the underside collects condensation. This method

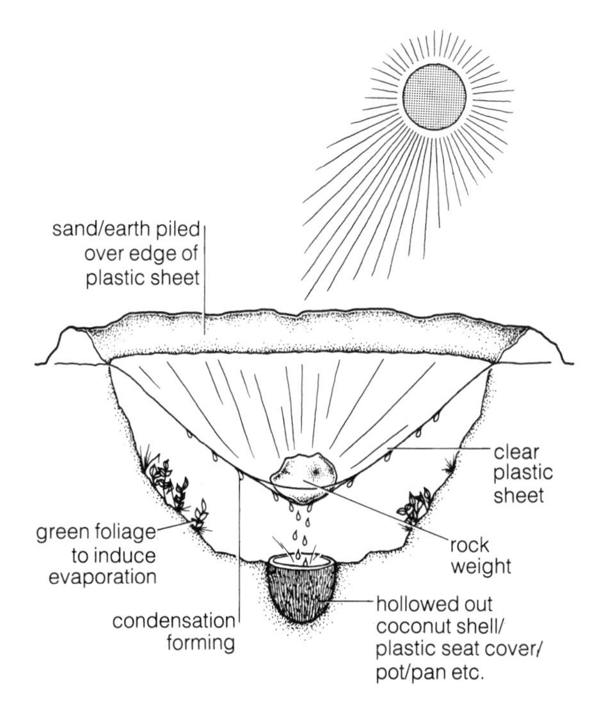

will not give you a steady supply of water, but it will provide you with a couple of mouthfuls until your still begins working again.

Remember, every little helps, so think ahead.

Divining with Sally

In my younger days I did a considerable amount of desert travelling. On one occasion I was crossing a vast expanse of open desert with very few water holes. Those that were there belonged to desert tribes and were very aggressively protected. If you attempted to take water from their wells without permission they would retaliate in the severest possible way. So in general I thought I'd be self-sufficient wherever I could. My trip was to take me from the east coast to the west, a distance of 3000 miles. Making the journey with me was my favourite camel, Sally. Sally and I had been together for many years, and though at times she could be a stubborn and cantankerous animal, we were firm friends. More than once when I fell asleep as she plodded on, she took me to water holes. Just like humans, camels require a regular supply of water; contrary to popular belief they don't carry spare water in their humps. As every schoolchild knows, the camel's humps are simply used for storing fat.

On one occasion Sally found me a water hole deep inside the crevice of a very large rock. However, the hole leading into the well wasn't much bigger than my fist and it was also a long way down to the water, but I used a trick taught me by the Aborigines in Australia. I took my towel from my rucksack and some fishing line from my survival kit and lowered the towel down the well (the Aborigines used tree bark instead of a towel). Once soaked it took only a couple of seconds for me to squeeze out as much water as I needed to refresh both Sally and myself. After we had finished drinking I used the wet towel to wash most of the sand from my body, then used it to cover my head from the hot sun as we progressed across the desert. Sally's water divining worked on many occasions.

She contributed to my welfare in other ways. Each day I'd take milk from her and sometimes I'd turn it into cheese, as this was easier to store and carry. First I made a small lattice plate from strips of pine fronds or bamboo. I'd pour the camel milk onto the plate, letting it seep through into my container. I would then repeatedly dip the lattice into the milk until gradually the creamy curd began to thicken. In minutes the milk would provide me with a thick creamy cheese. Goat's or cow's milk of course can also provide you with cheese using the same method.

Camels, like my survival equipment, have multiple uses. Dung for fuel, milk for cheese, hair for rope-making, skin for shelters, meat for food, intestines for string, bladders for water containers – the list goes on and on. Mind you, I would have had to be desperate before I'd even have thought of killing Sally off. We were a team and once we had crossed the desert I let her go her own sweet way. The least I could do was to save her life. She certainly saved mine.

Other natural guides

Knowing a little about nature is a tremendous morale booster to the survivor. For instance, all birds and animals that feed off corn, wheat, grass, seeds etc. need to have a regular daily intake of drinking water to allow them to digest their food. In the desert, pigeons, grouse, partridge and even parrots can be seen winging their way each evening to the nearest water hole. So keep a look out for them.

Game trails are both potential trap-setting areas and guides to finding water. A good indication of a game trail in use is well-trodden ground, chewed foliage and shrubs, lots of animal droppings and birds feeding off droppings. If the game trail is unused, fresh shoots will be sprouting from the shrubs and foliage, and the droppings will probably have turned to dust. Very often you can smell a well-used game trail long before you come across it. The closer you get to the water, the muddier the ground becomes, especially if used by herds of animals. Around the water hole itself there will be a strong smell of urine.

In East Africa the Masai tribesmen drink the blood from their cattle to ease their thirst. I've tried it and it's not as offensive as you may think. The drink was fresh, warm and thicker than I'd anticipated but once I'd taken my first sip the rest wasn't too bad. Yet it didn't ease my thirst. I still had to have a fresh water drink. Perhaps I wasn't as used to it as they were.

Plants as a source of water

It's in the desert that most people fear the lack of water and yet as always, nature provides nearly everything you need to survive.

Barrel cacti

For instance, every species of cacti is edible and will provide you with some liquid refreshment. One in particular, the famous barrel cactus, a native of South America but now found in most deserts around the world, is a great desert survivor. Protected by its many large sharp spikes, it stands proud and upright in the burning sun. Most animals are prevented from getting to it by the length of its thorns and its outer skin becomes so tough that it seals off any loss of evaporation from the soft, white, water-logged flesh inside. But with a little effort on your part it's possible to get through these barriers.

To remove moisture from the cactus you first have to break through the tough outer skin. If you've a knife or machete this is no problem; if not you'll have to use a rock, stick or the heel of your shoe. Once you've removed some of the outer skin, tear out the soft spongy flesh. You can then squeeze out the moisture into your mouth or a container. The flesh itself is edible but will taste a little bitter. Not all cacti, though, will produce the same amount of water or succulent flesh.

The prickly pear

Many cactus plants are extremely tough and more often than not the effort involved just to wet your lips may not be worth it. It's important, too, to remember that any plant which secretes a milky liquid should be avoided. (The barrel cactus is the *only* exception: here the liquid tends to be milky anyway.)

Should you be fortunate enough to come across prickly pear cacti, then you're in for a bonus. As well as the inner flesh, you can also eat the delicious fruit that grows from it.

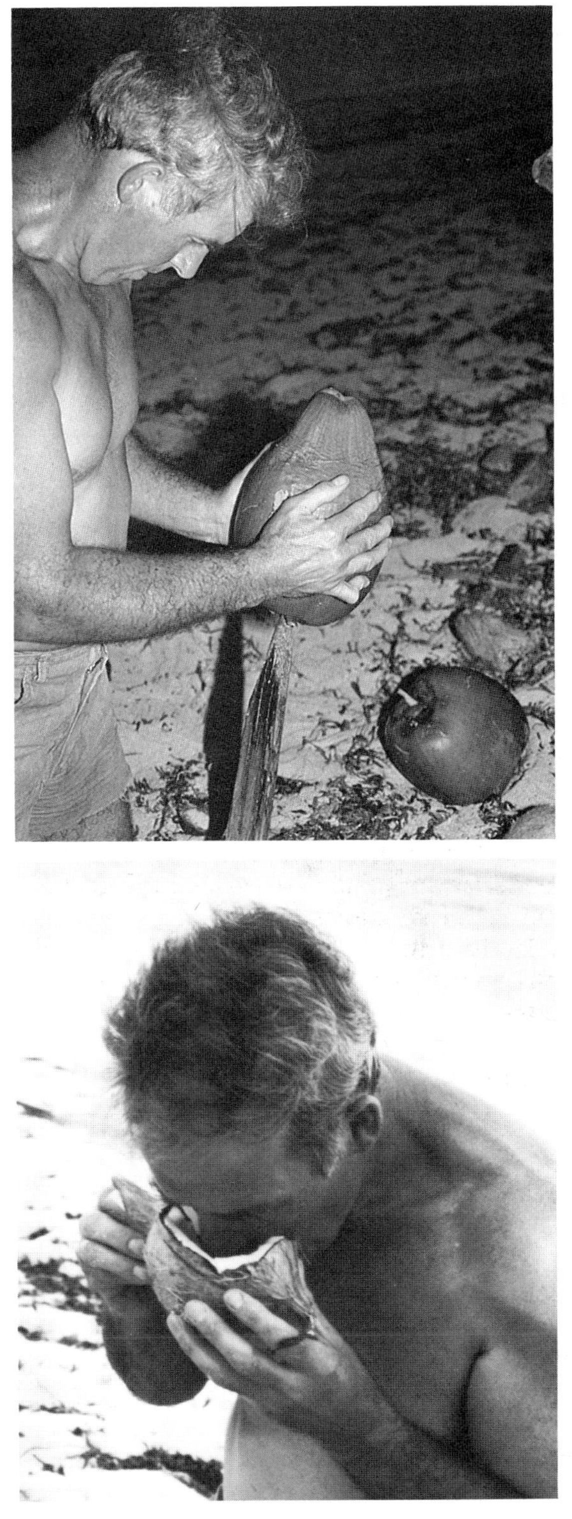

Prickly pears also originated in South America, but can now be found worldwide in most hot climates, especially on the fringes of deserts and particularly where humans have lived. They smell fresh, taste delicious and with a deep rich red succulent flesh are easily recognizable.

Jungle taps

In a jungle you'll find water held by large leaves or you can obtain it from jungle vines. If you cut a length of several feet from the lower section of the vine you'll find it contains cool, drinkable water. Soldiers call them the 'jungle tap' as they drip for hours. Remember to watch out for vines which give off a milky sap, as this is not drinkable. Some roots also contain moisture, usually in desert areas. And fruit such as the coconut can supply you with drinkable milk. Avoid drinking too much at once though as it can have a laxative effect and you can't afford to waste precious body moisture and energy by having the runs!

Purification

So far we have only been concentrating on finding and collecting water, but it is equally important to ensure any water we do drink is safe and free from contamination. It's a fallacy to assume that water already used for cooking will be free from bacteria, so don't use suspect water even for cooking.

Boiling

Boiling is a straightforward way of getting reasonably pure water. You should always boil it for at least thirty minutes if you can, and shake the water afterwards to try and oxygenate it. This will also help eliminate the flat taste associated with boiled water. If the water you've collected has come from a muddy pool or stream, try leaving it standing overnight so that any sediment goes to the bottom, then boil the water taken off the top. It's important to remember that oxygenated water not only tastes better but is usually purer, which is why water that's running over stones in a river is better for drinking than water taken from a stagnant pool or by the side of the bank where there is little or no current to oxygenate it.

Remember too that at sea level you should boil water for longer than you need to at higher altitudes, where it tends to be much purer and free from contamination.

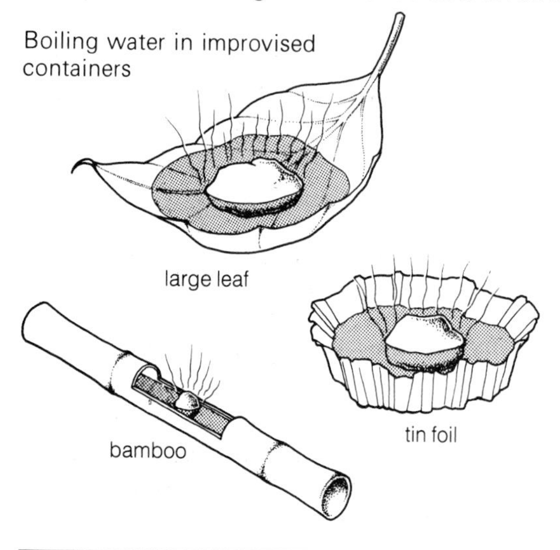

Boiling water in improvised containers

Hot stones

If you have water in a container you can kill some of the bacteria by putting heated stones into the water. Water collected in a plastic bag can be treated like this. Place a loose covering of fine sand or stones at the bottom of the bag to prevent the hot stones from melting the plastic. To ensure you get the best results you will have to keep adding hot stones at intervals. Why the sand? Well, sand or charcoal act as a filter, so heat up the sand first on a flat rock. This will kill off most of the nasties. Charcoal, of course, will already have been heated. Once you have heated the water sufficiently to your satisfaction, simply pour it into a clean container. The charcoal or sand will settle on the bottom, leaving you with fresh drinking water. A similar technique can be used with a tin or carved out wooden container.

Remember that water can be a silent killer and the only way to *ensure* that it's fit for human consumption is to thoroughly boil it (the longer the better) or treat it chemically. Any water that has a greasy feel to it, an oily surface or foul smell should be discarded. This doesn't include water extracted from vines, cacti and so on. There you may expect some discoloration and a slight bitterness.

Filtering

Generally speaking, water filtered through a canvas bag, a pocket liner or handkerchief will remove most of the grease, scum and debris, even if the water has been taken from the rut of a tyre on a road. But no matter how much you filter it, if the water is visibly contaminated don't take chances. Any water with a definite smell of petroleum should also be discarded. Boiling doesn't remove the taste and this water shouldn't be drunk under any circumstances.

Water used for cooking meat or vegetables should always be included in the meal as a soup or broth. In a survival situation, drinkable water is too valuable to discard. In some parts of the world such as Mongolia or Tibet the hot greasy water left from cooking is used to wash in. This leaves a thin layer of protective grease on the skin that helps keep off the cold and prevents chafing. Even in the high mountains where there is an abundance of rain and snow, water supplies are still protected and preserved. Heated water is as precious as fuel is scarce, and none should be wasted.

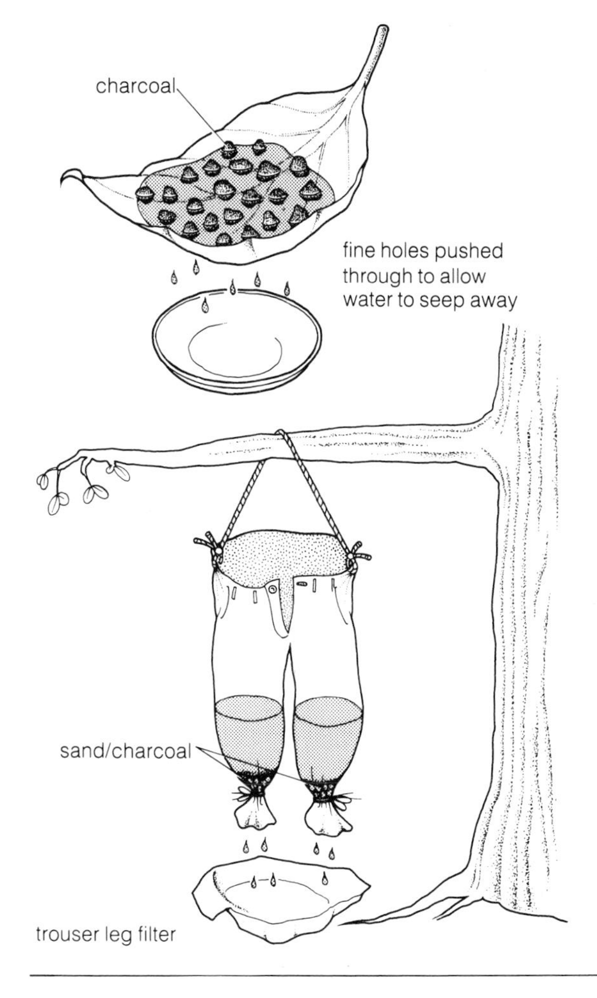

trouser leg filter

Chemical purification

It's relatively easy now to buy water purifying tablets or iodine but these tend not to work if the water already contains sediment. If you've a canvas bag it's always best to strain any water first before using up your perhaps scarce supply of purifying tablets. Some people prefer iodine to chlorine, which used to be the most common form of chemical purification. Iodine has a longer shelf life. If you're setting out on a journey and it's possible you may have to use some form of chemical purification, be sure you know in advance what to do. The instructions, the quantities to be used and the length of time the process takes, all need to be dealt with as if in a scientific experiment.

In jungle circumstances water may be readily available but will seldom be clean enough to drink and therefore one or more of the techniques described should be used for purifying it.

Testing for purity

It cannot too often be stressed – water can be silently lethal. Inexperienced people frequently cause themselves greater problems by drinking the water they eventually find than by going thirsty. Water tends to carry bacteria and diseases including such notorious ones as dysentery, cholera and typhoid. Sea water may look very inviting as the sun beats down on you but it won't increase your chances of survival. If you drink it you'll feel even thirstier as the fluids in your body will be used to dilute the increased salt.

As already mentioned, there are other liquid hazards. Alcohol if drunk in the absence of other fluids can cause terrible thirst. However, alcohol can be used for other things including bartering and fuel for fires, even as an antiseptic or throat gargle. Alcohol is ideal for washing out wounds, and if circumstances demand, it can be used for cooking in.

But to return to the hazards of water itself – how can you test if water is pure? Without the proper chemicals it's practically impossible for anyone to be able to tell. So what chance has the survivor of finding out if the water is safe to drink if he doesn't have either the chemicals to purify it or the materials to light a fire to boil it? Well, there are some tips that have been tried and tested. For instance, all running water will be cold and nearly all water trapped in mountains and small lakes is drinkable at source without purification. Water that's filtered through bracken, sand and peat can also be drunk at source, providing of course it hasn't been contaminated with any chemicals or dead animals. A simple method of telling if water has any chemicals in it is the ear wax test, which I must emphasize is only a rough guide and in no way foolproof.

Most chemicals have a petroleum based product in them which fails to mix with water. Classic examples are oil, petrol and paraffin. As soon as any of these meet water the latter immediately takes a colour spectrum, that is the surface will have a rainbow.

To test for this contamination collect a handful of fresh stream water in your hand or in a clean container. Using one of your fingers, not a stick or anything equally dangerous to eardrums, remove some of the wax from inside your ear. Now place your finger end into the water and let the wax float there. If the water has any chemical contamination, the wax will immediately break down and the colour spectrum will appear. If the water is pure, the bits of wax will float down to the bottom of the water and settle. This will at least give you a rough idea of what *not* to drink.

Whatever the effort and trouble of purification, filtering, boiling and testing – remember: without clean water, we die. It's as simple as that.

CHAPTER 6

Fire Lighting

Ask any professional explorer or outdoor adventurer what they consider to be one of the most essential of basic skills necessary to stay alive and they will tell you that it is the ability to light a fire, and keep it going, even in the most adverse conditions. After shelter and water it is the next most important aid to survival.

Not just to a survivor, but to anyone who spends time living outdoors and travelling across the world, a fire is a terrific morale booster. The moment it is lit, no matter how small, the area around it immediately becomes 'home'. Even the effort involved in just getting your fire going, i.e. collecting wood, tinder etc., can be a life-saver. When cold, wet and miserable we quickly become depressed and unless we motivate ourselves to work and get the fire going, we could easily become a hypothermia victim and yet have the means for our survival close at hand. In other words, we must have the ability to light a fire, with or without matches.

Throughout the world, wherever there is a fire used for domestic purposes such as cooking, it also becomes a focal point for meetings and discussions. Just as we in the so-called civilized regions gather around our kitchen fire for comfort, so too do the many thousands of nomads who still roam the world. Since man first discovered fire and learnt how to control it, it has become a major life-saver, because once he was aware of the potential of fire, both domestic and industrial, he became totally dependent on it. The diagrams below show various methods of laying and building your fire.

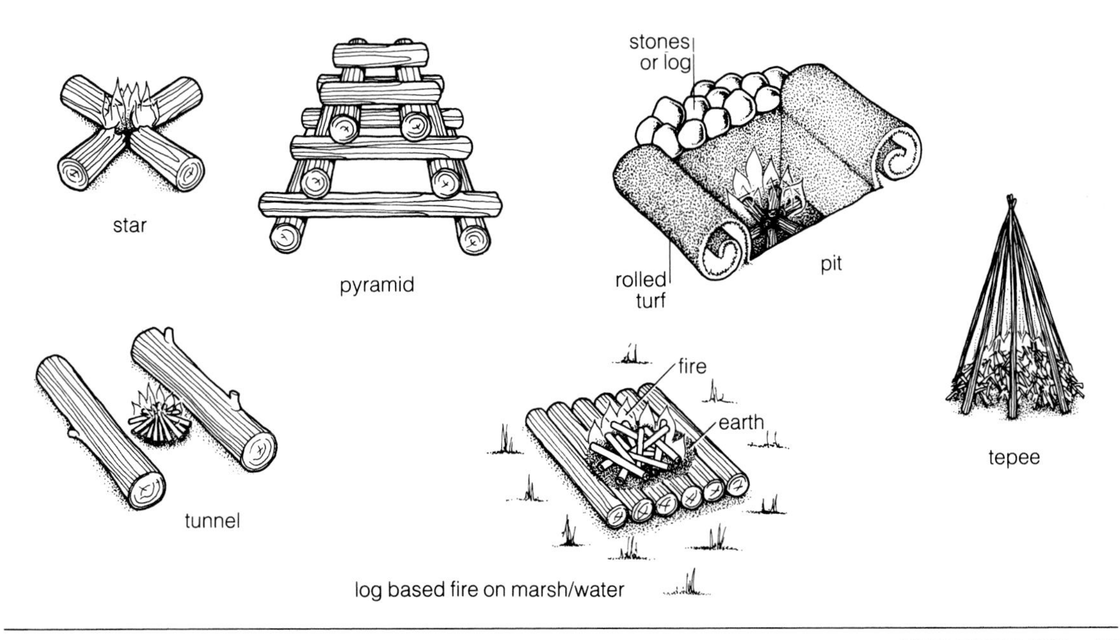

log based fire on marsh/water

Having discovered the value and benefits of fire our primitive ancestors quickly developed the skills involved in making it themselves and probably did so by knocking hard rocks together to create a spark, or by rubbing dry wood together to create friction. Both these methods we know work and have been used for centuries since. There is a great deal of mythology about lighting a fire by rubbing sticks together, but in fact it's not nearly as difficult as some writers would have us think. Basically all you require is a couple of strong pieces of wood thoroughly dried, and a little elbow grease. With these anyone can light a fire, providing you use the right method and have the determination to see it through. Be careful, though, *not* to start a fire where it may get out of control – especially in forest areas.

Many times during my courses I've stood back and smiled as groups of students slipped away into the nearby woods to practise their fire-making skills using the bow and spindle method. Hours later you can still hear the squeak, squeak, squeak of the firebow grinding away.

Recently, at my survival training centre, I ran a course for adult outdoor leaders and it came as no surprise to me to discover that not one of them had the ability to light a fire with primitive tools, yet most of them were responsible for leading groups of youngsters on expeditions high on the moors and mountains. A couple of the students actually came from overseas, from an area where nomadic tribes still survive and use primitive methods, yet they hadn't the slightest idea of how to go about it.

The firebow

The bow

Choose a length of green springy sapling about half a metre long and roughly the thickness of your little finger, preferably with a natural curve in it. If the bow is any longer it becomes uncontrollable when you try to spin the wood; any shorter and on the thick side, it becomes too strong to allow the friction stick to spin. It also tends to break the rope or twine needed to make the bow.

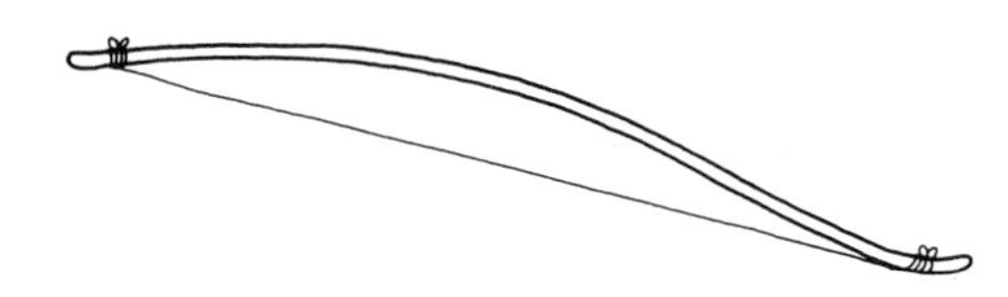

Spinning stick

The spinning stick needs to be about the same thickness as the bow but much shorter, preferably about nine inches long, as straight as possible with the ends slightly rounded and, of course, bone dry.

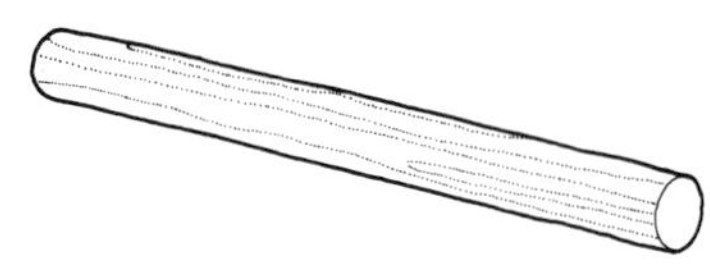

Base log

The log or branch that the spinning stick has to rotate in must also be dry and preferably of a softer or harder wood.

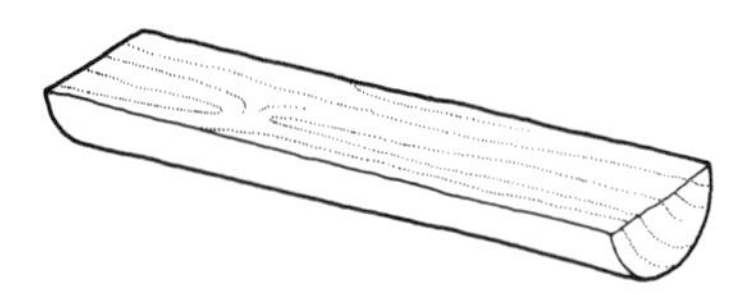

The next phase is probably the most important part of all. For the spinning stick to work there must be a small hole dug into the base log to prevent the stick from spinning loose. The hole must be positioned in such a way that the edge of it breaks through a very crucial notch or groove to allow the hot ash created by the friction of the spinning wood to fall onto the waiting tinder.

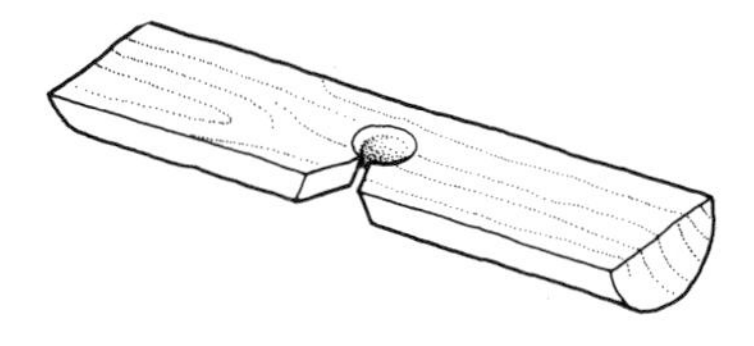

The groove needed for the firebow to work, it must be emphasized, is critically important. Without it you will never get your fire going.

You will also need something to hold in the palm of your hand to stabilize the spinning stick as you rotate it with the friction bow. A small grooved stone or a log with a hole in it will do, and on some occasions I have actually used the bottom half of a broken bottle, but if you do this take great care.

The hole in the base log (for the spinning stick to work in) can be made by simply taking a sharp stone or the point of your knife and twisting it around until the indentation is about a quarter of an inch deep.

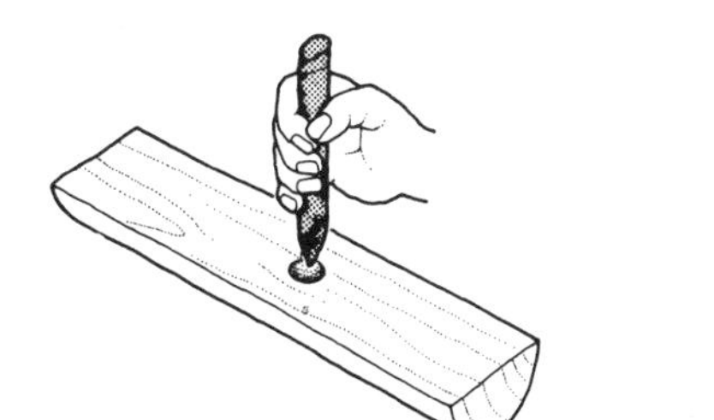

Once you've done this you must work on the groove. Using the edge of your knife make a small cut from the log edge to the edge of the spinning hole.

Then turn the base log over and proceed to cut out a 'V'-shaped groove as shown. Take care not to break *too deeply* into the hole for the spinning stick.

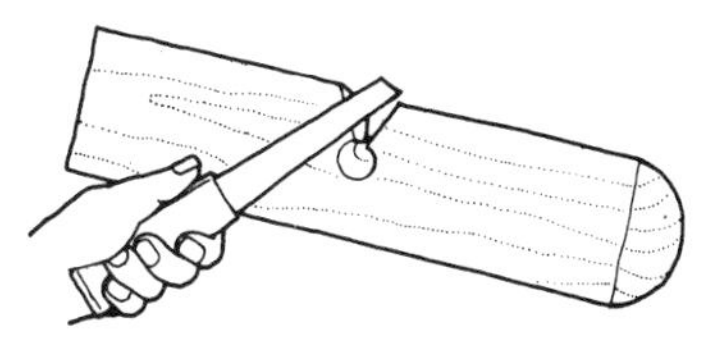

The firebow is now complete and is operated as shown opposite and below. Until you get used to working it you may have to adjust the tightness/tension of the string on the bow. As you get more skilled, this can be done by simple upward pressure of the fingers against the underside of the cord. Hot ash falls through the groove and onto the tinder below. Remember, you'll need good dry tinder for the hot ash to fall onto. As soon as it begins to smoulder you will have to stop spinning and gently blow it into life.

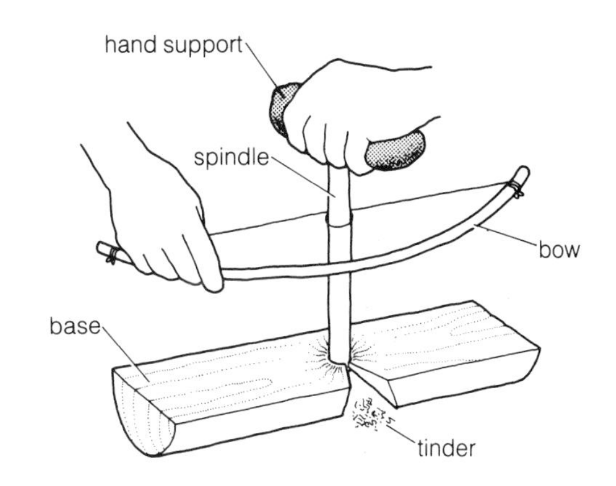

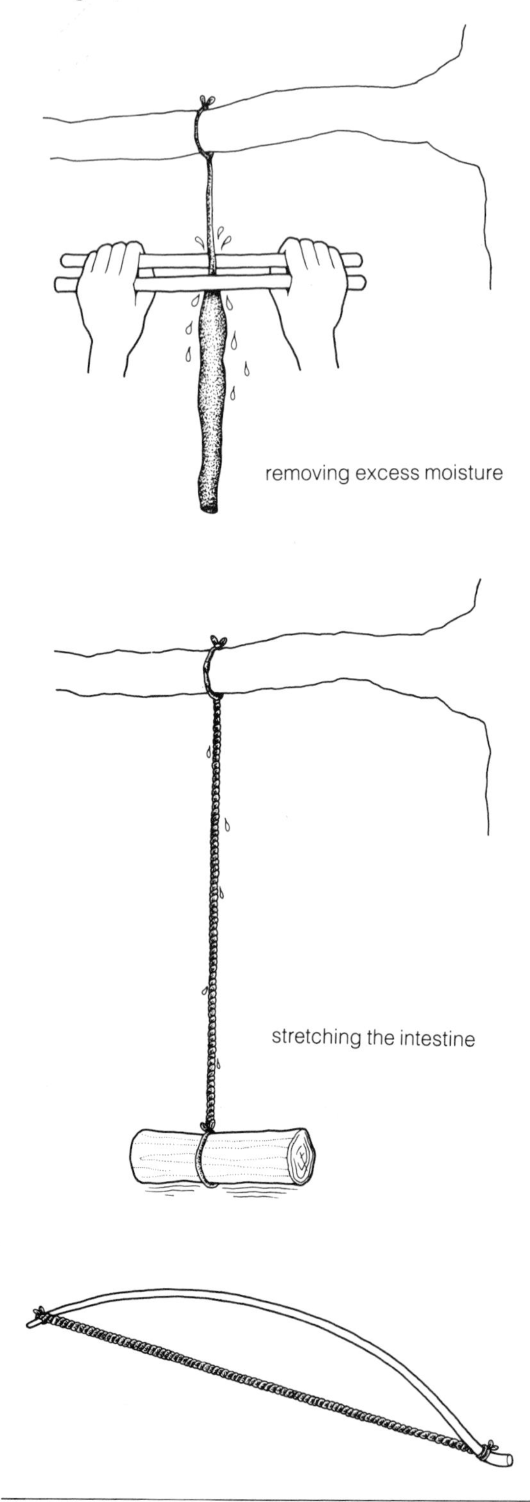

Making rope from animal intestines

When you first attempt the firebow technique you'll find that the spinning stick will fly out of the groove every time you try it. Don't despair, soon you'll get the feel of it and in just a few moments will be able to keep it under control.

Steady the base log with your foot and if possible try not to use nylon or other synthetic fibres for the bow string. They tend to spin and slide giving very little drive to the spinning stick. An old leather bootlace will create much better friction, especially if slightly damp. Ancient man used animal intestines twisted into thin gut ropes. This he did by cleaning out the intestines, then soaking them in hot water. He would then tie a heavy weight to one end of the gut and tie the other to a tree branch. Next he would spin the gut and weight until all the water had been squeezed out and as the gut spun so it stretched. Once this was done he would fasten it to his bow.

In a survival situation you will of course use anything that is available. Strips of animal hide make excellent bow strings; so too do many of the vines and creepers you find in the jungles and marshes. As a last resort, try twisting together a couple of lengths of wet cloth. Long lengths of cloth strips plaited are even stronger. (See pages 118–9 on rope-making.)

The rubbing block

The next simple method of starting a fire by friction is with the hand-held rubbing block, and effective as this method is, a great deal of physical effort is needed even to get the stick warm. With practice this difficulty can be overcome, but I would only use this method as a last resort. Often I have spent many frustrating hours pushing with nothing to show for my efforts.

For the rubbing block method, once again it's necessary to have the right kind of wood. Instead of rotating the spinning stick in a hole to create friction, this time we have to rub the stick along the base log in a groove. The rubbing stick, or pushing stick (whichever you prefer to call it) will have to be much stronger as it now becomes necessary to apply a great deal of pressure on it to create sufficient friction. You'll also find that it works much easier if the stick is a little longer, this time about twelve inches long and as thick as your thumb. The base log will have to be a little stronger too, and will need a small groove about three inches long cut into it for the rubbing stick to slide along.

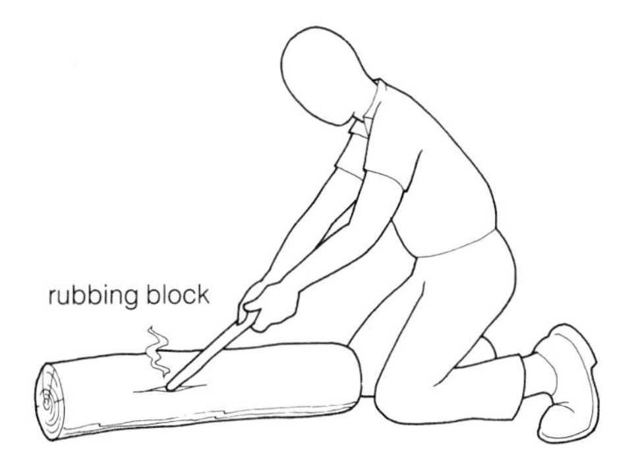

The hand-held spinning stick

This is similar to the bow method except the stick is rotated in your hands as shown. The base log, made of very dry wood and preferably opposite in texture to the spinning stick, will still need that critical groove and spinning hole. The two main problems with this method are keeping the spinning stick rotating in the same spot, and keeping enough pressure on the spinning stick to create sufficient friction.

As an alternative to holding the base log with your feet you can try wedging it between two rocks or in the base of a tree. Ensure that you have lots of dry tinder to hand and that you keep downward pressure on the spinning stick all the time. Above all, be ready to crouch down and blow the fire into life the moment it begins to smoke.

At first you'll find that your hands quickly become very tired and as you apply pressure on the stick they tend to slide down to the

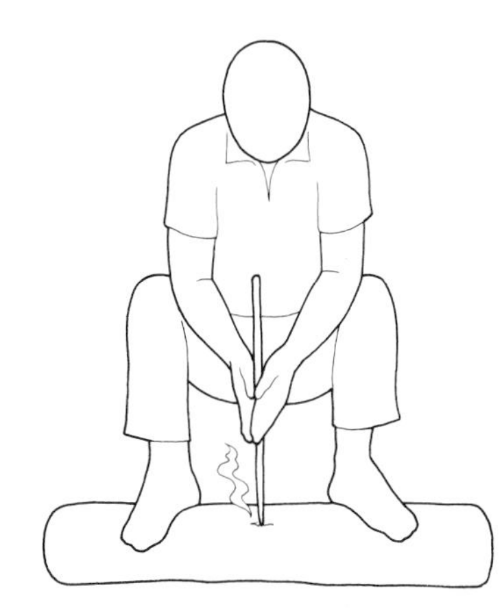

bottom. To counteract this it's not necessary to have the spinning stick as smooth down the shaft as you would the one used with the bow method. In fact, the whole stick need not even be the same thickness. If anything, it works best if it's slightly tapered, the thicker end held in your hand. In any European country this method is practically impossible to use as the wood will never be sufficiently dry unless it has been dried in an oven or kiln. Also, there is too much moisture in the atmosphere and if you leave your tinder on the ground for any length of time it quickly becomes damp.

The Archimedes drill

An alternative method is the Aborigines' Black & Decker, as I call it, or to give it its proper name, the Archimedes drill. This one is much easier to work than any I have shown you so far, but takes a little more time to make. It works on the same principle as both the bow method and the hand-spinner.

Again, it's necessary to ensure that you have the right kind of wood to make it with, but this method is nowhere near as tiring as the others once you have mastered it. As with other methods you'll require a good dry base log with the hole and groove. This is not a rubbing fire aid but a spinning one. You also need a small heavy log about two to three inches thick and about twelve inches long. In the centre make a hole right the way through to allow the spinning stick to rotate easily. Some kind of weight will be needed – either sun-baked clay, another log or a stone with a hole in it. You also require a good strong, dry spinning stick about eighteen inches long, slightly tapered at one end, which must pass freely through the small hole in the heavy log. Cut a groove in the thin end of the stick. Then having got these items together you finally need a length of twine or cord to complete the drill.

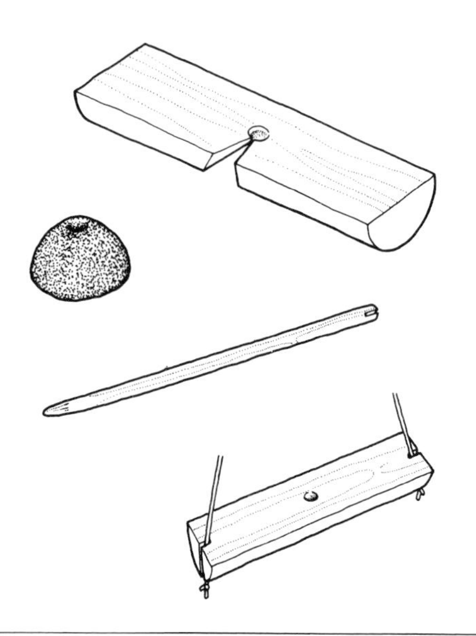

Now you're ready to assemble the Archimedes drill. Take the spinning stick and place the selected weight down its stem, stopping about two inches from the bottom. Next take the log with the hole in it and slide this down the stem so that it rests on the fixed weight. Now tie a length of string to either end of the log and into the groove cut in the top of the spinning stick. The drill is now ready for use.

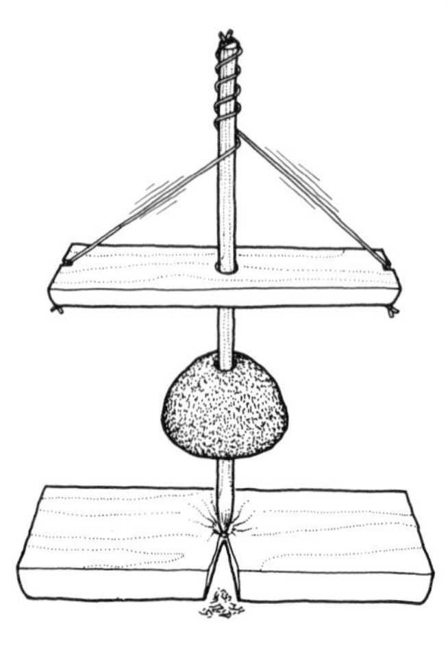

Fix your base log firmly by either supporting it with your feet or wedging it with stones etc. Twist the log above the anchor weight and wind it round. It will gently rise until it's fully wound round the spinning stick. Now, push the support log down until you see the spindle start to rotate. When you reach the bottom of the string ease the pressure off the support log and it will then rewind back to the top. Repeat this, speeding up the action until you have sufficient friction to make your fire work.

The draw string

This is nothing more than a very dry base log or stick, supported on two stones or another log and a very strong rasping cord or vine drawn backwards and forwards across it until it creates the necessary hot dust. This method is popular among the bushmen in the Kalahari desert and the Aborigines of Australia.

An alternative to drawing the cord by hand

is to make a small bow, but, if using the bow, it's necessary to have that critical groove again. If using the hand-drawn method a groove isn't necessary.

For either of these two to work it's necessary to have the right kind of friction string. Dry rotang, or a jungle creeper will make an excellent draw string; so too will some thin semi-dried bamboo saplings. Hemp rope or nylon can also be used, but they must be very strong and not damp. Strips of dry cloth won't work, but leather thongs will; however, they take an awfully long time to generate enough friction.

The lazy firelighter

How about this for an ingenious device! I first saw this method being used in the Middle East when I was a young soldier. It's a mixture of the Archimedes drill, the bow method and a modern bench drill. The model I saw working was in a remote Arab village and was there for anyone to use: it was a communal firelighter. Every morning I would see young Arab girls sitting around the machine working away to get a fire going.

As you can see, the weight from the log holds the spinning stick upright and as the cord is drawn backwards and forwards, friction is created inside the hole in the base block,

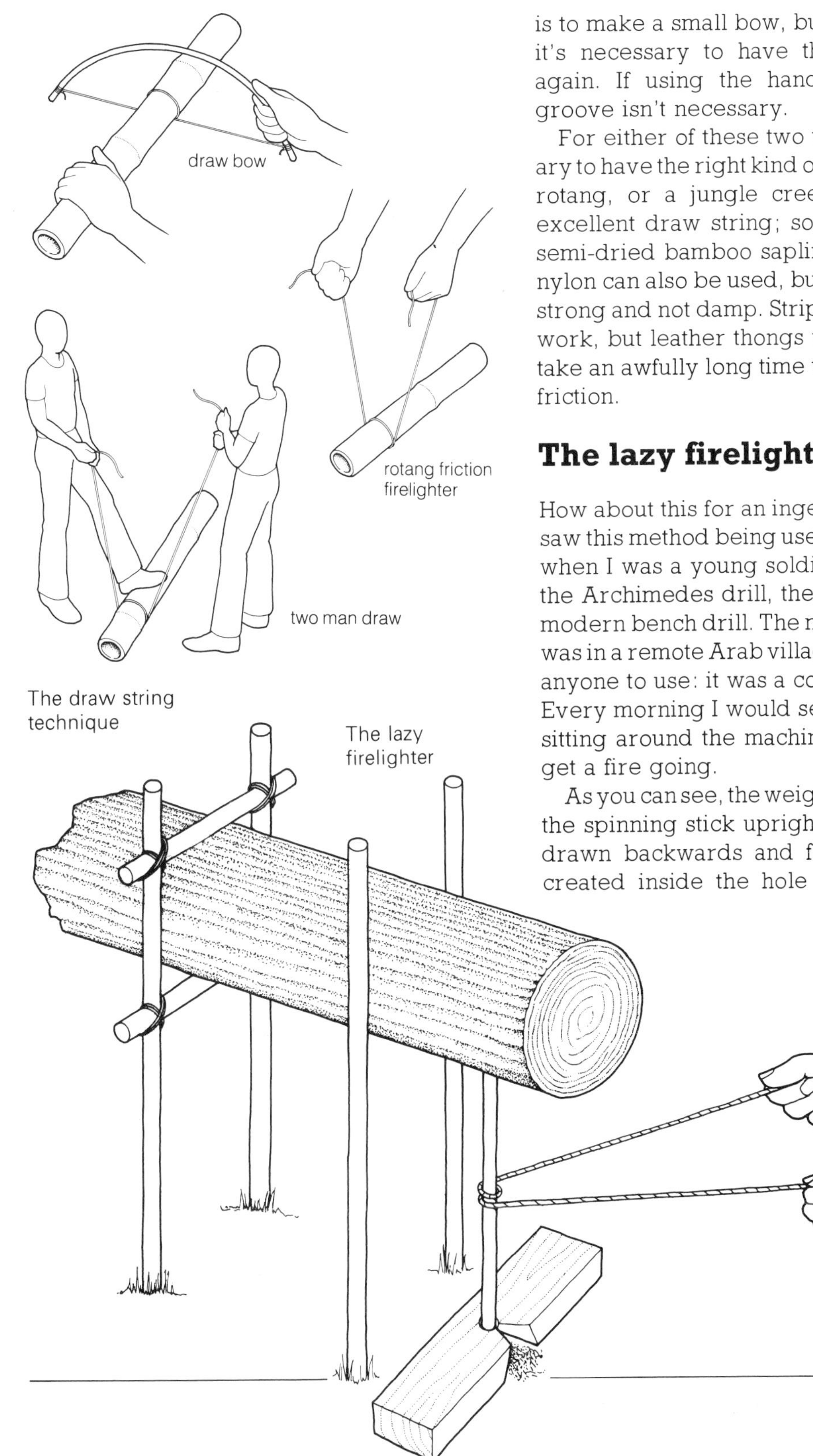

The draw string technique

The lazy firelighter

making the crucial hot dust ready to be placed onto some dry tinder and sparked into life.

To prevent the top of the spinning stick biting into the log it's smeared with camel grease. This makes it turn smoothly without causing its own friction.

Flint and steel

This method has also been around for a long time. Basically it consists of nothing more than striking a piece of very hard rock, preferably flint or quartz, with a lump of steel in order to create a hot spark that can fall onto your prepared tinder. Sounds easy doesn't it? But just you wait until you try it! This is a skill that requires a great deal of practice.

Flint is by far the best of stones to use. It's extremely hard yet pretty easy to break into manageable pieces. Alas, it can only be found in chalky regions. Granite sometimes will produce a spark when struck hard but no matter which rock is used, without the right sort of steel it will never work. Try striking a lump of flint with the rounded edge of your eating fork and you'll see that no amount of strikes will induce a spark. However, turn the fork round and use the pointed prongs and you'll see the difference immediately. The best thing to use is the sharp edge of your knife (unfortunately this doesn't do the knife much good).

Hold the flint firmly in your hand just above the prepared tinder and strike hard down on it. (Be careful not to injure yourself with the knife.) The secret is to get the hot spark to drop into the waiting tinder and smoulder. As soon as the spark falls you must immediately begin blowing gently until the tinder bursts into flames. The difficulty then is to keep the fire going, so make sure you have enough spare tinder available.

No doubt there are other equally effective methods in use around the world, but the ones I've shown you can be made fairly easily and, given sufficient dry wood and tinder, applied almost anywhere.

Tinder

By far the easiest method of setting out your tinder to catch that vital spark is to form it into the shape of a crude bird's nest and place it on a dry stone or rock – somewhere where it won't absorb the damp from the gound, preferably on a small platform of dry twigs. As soon as the tinder takes fire, the small wood platform serves as a base and eventually as firewood itself.

There are all sorts of tinder you could use, the best one being cotton wool. The moment a spark touches it, it immediately bursts into flame. So too does the fluffy down of the willow herb, thistle, cotton plant, dry coconut husk, the end of a hemp rope or the teased out corner of your handkerchief or shirt – anything that's dry and easily combustible when ripped into fibres. I've used lots of different tree barks and even dried nettle stems. So combustible are the flower seeds of the dandelion and willow herb that the slightest spark will cause a fire. During the steam train era, fires were started every day because of this. If you're attempting to light a fire by using a magnifying glass, broken bottle or the lens from your camera etc., you couldn't find a better tinder for the job.

Setting out the tinder, in this case tree bark

You can also use dry grass if there's any about. To collect it run your fingers along the tops of the dry grass and gather it. Don't reach down and pull up handfuls. Gather grass that's been fully exposed to the drying wind. Once you've sufficient, very gently and not too tightly form it into the shape of a bird's nest. Now place a few dandelion seeds inside it but don't compress them, and then place just a couple of very fine dry twigs across the nest. It's now set to receive the crucial spark that will start your fire.

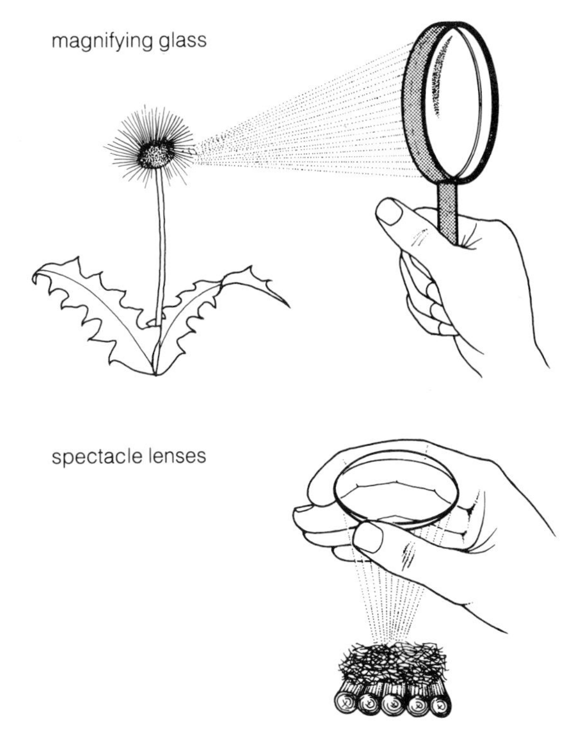

Using a magnifying glass

Lighting a fire with a magnifying glass is probably one of the most tried methods used by boy scouts, girl guides and school children. All you need is something like a magnifying glass that will focus the sun's rays onto a small spot and allow the heat to pass through it. When held to catch the rays (angled onto a spot and held steady) whatever it is focused on will eventually begin to smoulder. The finer the spot the more intense the heat. On a normal sunny day it may take a couple of attempts to get the tinder alight, but on a hot summer's day, especially in the desert, it works in just a few seconds.

It's possible to start a fire with the bottom half of some broken bottles, especially the ones that have a concave base and are made of clear glass. You can also use the lens of a camera, which of course you'll have to remove. The same applies if using the lens from your binoculars, and it's even possible to use the lenses from your glasses. Of course for those who are completely dependent on their glasses this may not be the answer. Make sure you can reassemble them again! Gently remove them from their frames and hold them together to form a domed disc. Depending on the type of glasses of course, some work much better than others. The clearer the glass the better the reflection.

To use your camera lens line it up, with the sun and tinder. Slowly bring the lens close to the tinder until the sun spot practically disappears. At this stage the tinder should start smouldering.

If you're lighting paper or cloth, gently tear the edges and fray them out. This way they'll immediately burst into flame when you blow on the smouldering tinder. All the time you're holding the glass the sun will either be setting or climbing, so it's essential that you hold the glass steady in your hand and concentrate the heat source on one spot. If it's hot enough and you were to prop the glass up with a piece of stone or twig, providing the tinder is kept still it will work.

Using the same glass and technique it's possible to make a fire using wire wool, silver birch bark, pine needles, toffee papers etc. Sheep wool off the moors, and indeed most animal hair, tends to have too much moisture, so unless it's completely dry, it's of no use. Once, out in the Yemen, I managed to get a fire going in seconds by simply focusing the heat onto a rubber band, and I've also used dry camel dung.

Using a car battery or hand torch

Lighting a fire using a car battery or your hand torch is quite simple providing the batteries have power in them. In the case of the former, first remove the battery from the car (or boat) to a position well clear of the vehicle's petrol tank. Tie one end of a piece of wire to one terminal and lightly stroke the other terminal with the other end. This will give you a series of instant sparks. To ensure that you only have to do it once, you must have something combustible to hand. A small piece of cloth soaked in petrol is ideal or some wire wool. The cloth needs *only the slightest drop of petrol*. Too much and it'll blaze up in your face.

Using your torch requires a little more skill. If you've a spare bulb you can try to break the glass very gently so as to leave the filament intact; then when you switch on the torch, the fine wire glows red. Again, using the right tinder it's possible get your fire going. Wire wool or cotton wool soaked in something inflammable is ideal.

You can get the same result if you unscrew the top of the torch (the part that holds the bulb), put some wire wool inside and place the top gently back into place. When you switch the torch on the wire wool makes a full contact.

Remember in both cases when using anything inflammable beware of an instant flare-up. If necessary lay the material down on the ground before attempting to light it.

Fire-lighting survival kits

Whenever I set off on any of my expeditions I always ensure that I have at least three different methods with me for starting a fire: waterproof and windproof matches, a magnifying glass and a flint striker. Each of these items is duplicated throughout my equipment. For example, sewn onto the shoulder strap of my rucksack I have one fire-lighting survival kit. Another is strapped to my waist belt, and a further one sewn into my clothing. So that at any time, no matter where I am (unless I'm completely naked), I have several fire-lighting survival kits with me. I even have one tucked into the handle of my knife!

Carbide pellets

I also carry in my survival packs a small amount of carbide pellets which make ignitable gas. These I got from a friend of mine who teaches pot-holing. The pellets are small and easy to pack. I have them rolled in a slip of silver paper to protect them. When I need to light a fire I simply take out a couple of the pellets, place them onto my tinder and gently drop spittal onto the pellets with my finger. As soon as they begin to smoulder and give off gas, I light my fire either using a match or flint striker. Even the battery method will work here.

Some explorers and travellers I know carry with them small plastic petrol-filled containers, such as the kind used for filling cigarette lighters. In the bottom of my rucksack in a small sealed tin I have two such containers as well as a good, working cigarette lighter. Having been caught out many times in my early days without a fire, I've learnt the hard way just how important is a merry blaze to one's survival.

The modern flint striker

If you can, always try to include in your survival pack at least one modern firelighter, preferably a fire stick or striker, as they are called. Basically this is a short length of flint impregnated with iron filings or magnesium deposits. When struck sharply with a piece of steel (a knife blade is ideal, or old hacksaw blade) it gives off a shower of hot sparks. As a substitute I have used the buckle of my belt as a striker and even an old tin lid or razor blade will do.

The beauty of the fire sticks is that no matter

what the conditions – snow, hail, rain etc. – they'll be guaranteed to work every time with the right tinder. So to anyone who spends hours in the great outdoors they are a must. Hold the striker firmly in your hand, just above your tinder. Strike the steel firmly against the flint, ensuring that the sparks fall directly onto the waiting tinder (shaped like a bird's nest as explained earlier). As soon as the tinder begins to smoulder blow gently until it bursts into flames.

If you aren't using inflammable tinder such as dandelion heads, cotton wool etc., you may have to coax the fire before it actually begins to smoulder. Sometimes it may be just a thin wisp of smoke that needs nursing. Take your time, and blow very gently at first using the top lip forward of the bottom one. As soon as the smoke begins to thicken, blow in a series of short, gentle puffs. Once the fire is going make sure that you've sufficient tinder and wood to keep it alight.

Fire by explosives

A method often used by the old pioneering backwoodsmen was to remove some of the black powder, or to give it its proper name, cordite, from their shotgun cartridges. This was then sprinkled onto their tinder. This is so combustible that if one spark struck it, they had an instant fire. Even though this is a sure way of getting your fire going, for obvious reasons it can be very dangerous. If you have to resort to using this method you need only the smallest amount of tinder. Remember, cordite is explosive! It may be obtained from, for example, the shell case in an aircraft pistol flare gun.

Backwoodsmen would spend months, sometimes years, wandering around in the harsh mountains and during the winters often had to cope with sub-zero temperatures. It became essential for them to get a fire going as quickly as possible and to make absolutely sure that the flames from the cordite managed to light the tinder, they mixed it with some sugar or sap from the maple tree. Both, when hot, cling and burn to whatever they come in contact with, thus ensuring a continuous flame.

In the deserts of South America and Mexico there is a small bush that thrives in harsh, barren sands called the creosote plant. This is highly inflammable and, as with the black powder, when a spark comes in contact with it, it bursts into flame. Here in Europe, the common pine needle, when dry, also becomes very inflammable. Even the sap from the pine, when dried and crushed, is combustible. As always, it's a case of looking around and experimenting.

CHAPTER 7

Finding Food

Generally speaking, man can eat almost anything that walks, flies or swims. Add to that anything that grows. There are some exceptions we know, but unfortunately in a survival situation you have to take some chances. Luckily for us there are far more edible foods and plants than there are poisonous ones.

To replenish our energy supply the body must have the necessary intake of fats, proteins, vitamins and carbohydrates all obtainable from plants, birds, fish, animals and insects. The body cannot live on water alone. Vegetarians would argue that eating animals is not necessary, but it's worth emphasizing that there are situations where there is no vegetation edible to humans, only sparse animal life.

Plant food won't actually supply a balanced diet (unless you have a very wide choice), but it can save your life. Green stems and leaves can provide roughage and vitamins; fruits or tree-sap can provide glucose and vitamins and roots are a good source of starch and protein. Mushrooms can be extremely nutritious, but as fungi may also be highly poisonous they should be treated with caution. Animals, birds, insects (see Chapter 8), fish and seafoods can provide proteins and fats. To stay alive a survivor must be able to seek out the most beneficial foods quickly. For example, very often time and effort spent searching and hunting for animals as a source of food will be less profitable than digging and scraping around for roots and tubers. In any survival situation, day-to-day living is far more important than worrying about the future. When you become stronger, fitter and more confident your chances of survival will greatly increase. Then you can plan your larder. Obviously, if the opportunity is there to stock up on your food supply, you should do so. As always take care, especially if a fruit or tuber is unfamiliar to you. There are literally hundreds of edible foods to choose from. Most may be eaten raw whilst others can actually be improved with cooking or used to enhance flavour. Peppers are a classic example. Eaten raw they are very potent if you're not used to them, but used with other plants or fruits they can help enhance the taste.

The obvious advice when trying out unfamiliar food is of course to be sensible. First break off a little and taste it – *don't chew*. Wait half an hour, then break off another chunk and this time chew it. If there's no obvious bitter taste or burning inside your mouth swallow a small amount. Now wait a good hour. If there's still no reaction, go ahead and eat. To stay alive a great deal of self-control will be needed to avoid the temptation of gulping it down without taking precautions. The desire to do this can be overpowering depending on how hungry and thirsty you are at the time.

Once you have eaten something and it *does* turn out to be poisonous, the damage may already have been done. Eat in moderation; don't assume that you can gorge on a food just because it tastes or smells OK. If you're not sure, remember the old soldiers' adage: IF IN DOUBT – LEAVE IT OUT – AND GO WITHOUT.

As always, Mother Nature is actually on your side: if you have eaten something that disagrees with you, it will probably make you

Common Death Adder

King Cobra

Green Mamba

Spitting Cobra in a defensive position

Adder or Viper

Western Diamond-Back Rattlesnake striking

POISONOUS

Death Cap

Fly Agaric

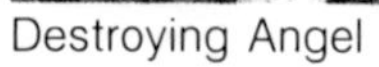

Destroying Angel

Privet in bloom

Deadly Nightshade

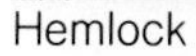
Hemlock

Henbane

Black Nightshade

Monkshood

Yew berries

Castor Oil plant

Fruits of the Cuckoo Pint

Mistletoe

Poison Ivy

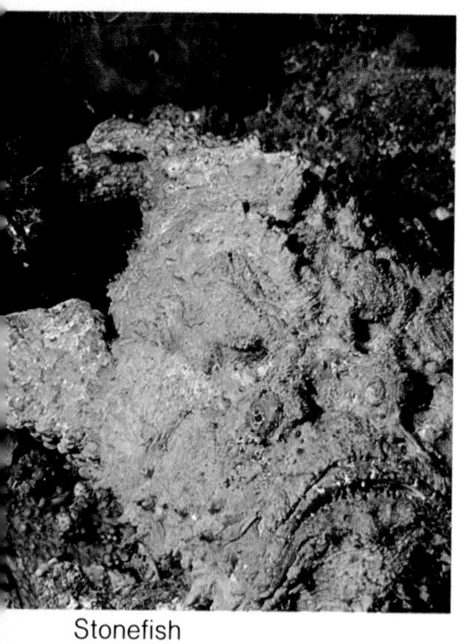
Stonefish

Zebra Fish

Porcupine Fish

Oyster Toadfish

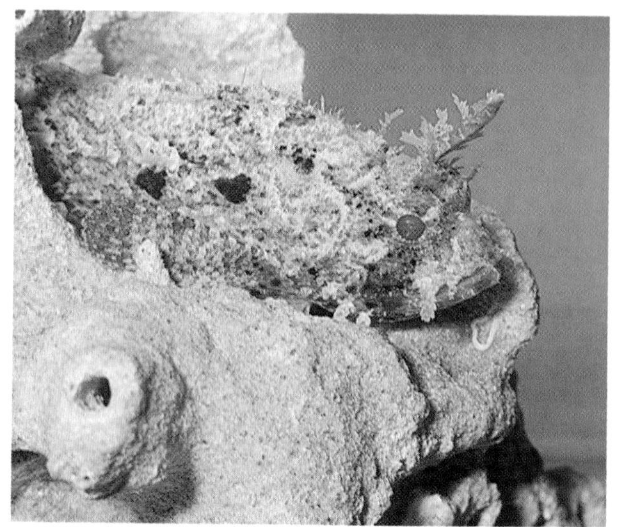
Scorpion Fish

Sting Ray

Slender Filefish

sick, and if not, try to regurgitate it. You could use your finger to tickle the back of your throat or use a clean, sterilized feather as the nomads do. This will make you vomit. Once you have regurgitated, drink as much water as possible to help dilute any poison left in the stomach. It may perhaps sound primitive and a hard way of learning but believe me I've done it hundreds of times and it certainly saved my life.

No amount of literature or photographs can compensate for actual experience. In a survival situation you must expect some dangers and discomforts as you experiment with food. The only way to gain confidence in your judgement is to go out and try the different plants, roots, fruits etc. yourself. It's possible to do this in most Western countries now by simply paying a visit to your local supermarket, as nearly all stock a great variety to choose from. This way you will familiarise yourself with the taste, smell and feel of them. Obviously many foods are peculiar to certain regions, but on the whole the rules for taste, preparation and indeed collection remain the same. Your ingenuity, common sense and the need to survive will generally see you through and determine what you should and should not eat. Use your natural instinct to search for food; watch animals and birds, see where they find theirs, and if necessary follow them.

Even if your situation looks grim don't ignore the possibilities of finding food that may have been planted or harvested. Areas where crops have previously grown could still provide you with sufficient sustenance to help you survive another day and any sign of cultivation will indicate that people may not be too far away.

Nature's supermarket

Being the most adaptable animal in the world, man has the ability to convert even the most offensive-smelling or vile-looking plants and animals into food. For example, the Australian Aborigines eat fat, white, juicy grubs found beneath the bark of certain trees. The Masai tribe of East Africa eat roasted termites. I've tried them and they taste like roasted nuts. Eskimos chew (for hours) the liver and heart of fish they catch. Kalahari desert nomads dig deep into the harsh desert sands for roots and insects and even today many people living in Third World regions often have to eat things that to us seem completely inedible.

The trouble with us in the better-off countries is that we prefer to wrap our food up in coloured paper and packaging before we attempt to eat it. Why? Because we are fortunate enough no longer to have to go out searching for food; we have all we can eat, and more, right on our doorsteps, and we know that everything displayed is edible. This is where our survival skills fall down. Because of the easy accessibility of food, because we've never gone for more than a few days at the most without any, we have never been driven to extremes of hunger (unlike many people in the Third World). Few of us have ever had to go out and scrape around for roots or grubs. But when placed in a survival situation that's exactly what we would have to do to live.

Remember, out there is the biggest supermarket in the world, and you don't need a trolley to put your shopping in.

Food sources that we wouldn't normally touch, let alone eat, can become life-savers. A greasy-looking slug, or a grasshopper near your feet, are both full of succulence and protein. Even the common every day garden worm is perfectly edible. What you, the survivor, must do is to seek out these resources and face up to having to eat them. It isn't just a question of picking up possible meals that you happen upon. You will probably have to hunt, track, trap, kill and skin your meal before you can cook it, and that is where your true survival skills will be tested to the full. Having been forced to live like an animal, you might have to hunt and kill like one. Man is the most adaptable animal in the world. Use your brain, skill and cunning to the full.

You can usually assume that wherever

there's fresh water, there is also food in the form of meat, fish, insects and vegetation. At most waterholes animals come to drink and bathe. They deposit droppings which bring birds, insects and smaller animals who in their turn help cultivate the surrounding area and thus induce plant growth. In the desert, seed-eating birds can be seen making their way to the nearest waterhole to replenish their supply before settling down for the night. As a result of their droppings new plants will grow. Animals that graze during the day, such as the elephant, rhino, buffalo, wild deer and many others, will make the same daily trek to the waterhole, often using the same trails, thus making it easier for you to follow them. You need to identify the pattern of animal or bird behaviour and then you can exploit it for your own survival. Having been forced to live like a nomad because of the situation you are in, it's important to your very life that you also think like a nomad.

Plants and roots

When desperate, the Aborigines pull up large handfuls of marsh and swamp grasses and chew the succulent white stems to quench their thirst, even when they know that the surrounding waters are being used by many animals and could be infested with water-borne disease. By chewing the stems they are obtaining fresh clean water, some starch and a small quantity of solids from the chewed stems themselves. They realize that if they didn't do this they would probably die from starvation. Nomads and Aborigines aren't infallible: some of them die too.

Sometimes Nature likes playing games with us. For instance, very often the only visible sign telling us that there are edible roots or tubers present is a small string-like vine root sticking out from the ground, perhaps only a couple of centimetres long. To the trained desert dweller this is all he needs to see. Digging carefully with his hands he follows the tell-tale stem down until he comes to a large root or tuber bloated with water and succulent flesh. Some of these tubers can be as large as footballs and one of them will provide you with enough water to get you through the day. As we saw in Chapter 5, water doesn't come easy in the desert, so you must be prepared to dig down deep in the sand to find it.

It's possible to gain enough liquid to help you stay alive from various species of vegetation. Many hold an abundance of water and edible food. Melons (all species), coconuts, wild plums, pears, apples, mangoes, tomatoes, strawberries and lots of tropical fruits are all excellent life-savers.

Many roots and tubers, on the other hand, tend to have very little moisture content and even though they may satisfy your hunger they don't always stop your thirst. Indeed, some require a good boiling in water before they can be made palatable. Manioc or cassava are classic examples. Incidentally, both are very rich in starch.

Cassava tree and roots

The Common Dock Leaf (*Rumex obtusifolius*)

The Dock Leaf is best known for its use as a relief from nettle stings. It belongs to the cabbage family and is highly nutritious. Eaten raw it is quite bitter, but when cooked tastes like spinach. Its food value is very good and sustaining. All parts are edible but the roots may need a couple of boilings after you have given them a good scraping first.

Collection time: May/June through to September/October for fresh dock leaves, but they may still be found throughout the year. The millet-like flowers may be scraped from the stems and boiled in water.

Medicinal use: a compress of dock leaves is very good for rashes, bruises etc. Dock leaves pulped and mixed with a little soap can be used as a suppository for piles. Pulped dock leaves and butter make a very good healing salve.

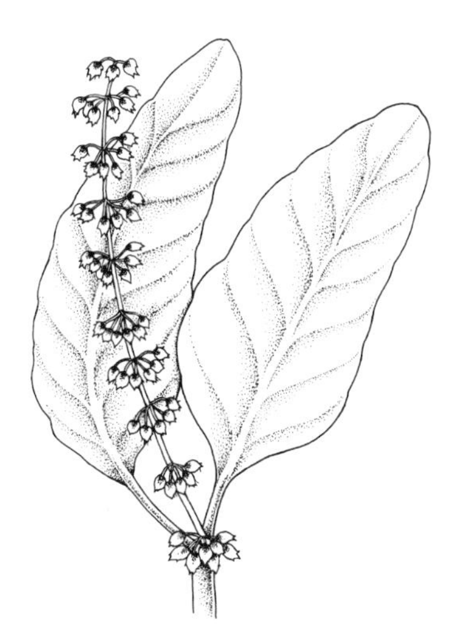

Great Burdock (*Arctium lappa*)

Also a member of the cabbage family, this plant grows two to three feet high. The leaves are large and taste bitter when eaten raw. The flowers (not unlike thistles) eventually turn into the famous 'sticky bud'. When dry the buds make superb firelighters. The leaves

need at least two boilings to remove the bitter taste and the roots need at least three boilings, again after first scraping.

Location: widespread throughout Europe and parts of the sub-tropic.

Collection time: similar to that of the Common Dock Leaf, i.e. May through to October.

Fungi

A mycologist is someone who studies fungi scientifically – in other words, a fungi expert. But so controversial is the study of fungi, especially the poisonous varieties, that even some experts can't agree on what is and what isn't edible. So, what chance has the layman? To be fair, so much folklore and superstition has been peddled about fungi that the experts themselves often doubt their scientific beliefs. One scientist's meaty mushroom is another scientist's poison. But the three poisonous ones I shall describe and which are pictured in the colour section, are accepted by *all* as killers and so they are perhaps the first of the many poisonous species you must learn to recognize and avoid. To learn the others I strongly recommend that you get yourself a good illustrated book on the subject, preferably in colour, and get out into the wilds to see them for yourself. Remember, many fungi only appear for a few days each year before dying off, hence the problem of logging them and classifying their edibility or lack of it.

There is no set method of telling if a fungus is edible or not simply by looking at it. Some need to be boiled first whilst others need to be fried. I don't recommend anyone to work on the old adages, 'if animals eat them so can we'; or 'if you touch them with a silver spoon and they don't turn black they are edible'; or 'if it grows in a garden it's edible' etc., etc., etc. The only way to learn and gain confidence is to read and study under an expert. If in doubt about a particular fungus – *leave it alone.*

In the mountain regions in particular, especially pine forests, you will find lots of edible species and the lower down you come into the deciduous forests, the greater still the variety. Fungi were first gathered by early man, and in later years the Romans in particular placed great store by them, both as a food and as a medicine. In all, there are thousands of different species throughout the world.

Fungi poisoning

If poisonous varieties are eaten by mistake the first symptoms are violent stomach pains, diarrhoea, a strong feeling of nausea, sickness, dizziness, severe shivering, pallor or other change in skin colour, eventual lack of vision, spasmodic and irregular breathing followed by death. To date there is no known antidote for deadly poisonous fungi and the only remedy is pumping out the stomach. However, if caught in time the patient can be admitted to hospital and certain drugs given to ease the pain and perhaps save his life.

The Death Cap (*Amanita phalloides*)

This is probably the most poisonous fungus of them all. It would take only a minute piece to kill you, and this may lie dormant in the stomach for up to 24 hours before being absorbed into the bloodstream. It has been known to grow in almost any habitat but its favourite haunt is deciduous forests, especially where there are lots of oak and beech trees.

The Destroying Angel (*Amanita virosa*)

Equally poisonous, similar in shape but different in colour from the Death Cap is the Destroying Angel (*Amanita virosa*). This fungus has all the same characteristics as the phalloides and is deadly poisonous. It is often picked by mistake for the common field mushroom because in its early state it, too, is white and until the skirt forms on the stem and the bulb from which it grows matures, it is very difficult to tell them apart.

When fully grown it is easily distinguished from the field mushroom because of its skirt and bulb, and because the cap, when touched, is a slimy, sickly white. Like the phalloides it, too, grows mostly in deciduous forests, but it can also be found in pine forests, hedgerows and very often on the edge of bracken-covered moors.

The Fly Agaric (*Amanita muscaria*)

This is another member of the *Amanita* family that is highly poisonous and is indeed responsible for a great number of casualties each year. This fungus is very popular amongst children because it is often shown in children's books with fairies and pixies sitting on it! Because of these associations, children tend to pick the fungus, not realizing that the cap is covered in a sticky substance which when taken into the stomach by licking the fingers can cause severe tummy pains. If the flesh is eaten it can kill. It grows in the same regions as other *Amanita* fungi, and has the same tell-tale skirt, bulb and scales.

The cap may be as large as 20/30 cm and is a very striking red, later turning to a reddish orange. From the moment that it shows itself above the ground, the red cap will have lots of soft flaky white warts sticking to it. These are to attract flies, hence the name Fly Agaric.

Common Edible Fungi

Botanical names	*Common names*
Agaricus arvensis	Royal Horse mushroom
Agaricus campestris	Common field mushroom
Lycoperdon giganteum	Giant puffball
Lepiota procera	Parasol mushroom
Coprinus comatus	Shaggy ink cap
Morchella conica	Morel
Tuber aestivum	Truffle
Tricholoma nudum	Wood blewit
Fistulina hepatica	Beefsteak fungus*
Pleurotus ostreatus	Oyster fungus*

*Tree Fungi

All the following are from the *Boletus* family:

Edulis	Cep
Cyanescenes	known by local names
Elegans	,,
Luteus	,,
Pulverulentus	,,

Morchella conica – morel

Tricholoma nudum – wood blewit

Coprinus comatus – shaggy ink cap or lawyer's wig

Agaricus campestris – common field mushroom

Tuber aestivum – summer truffle

Boletus edulis – cep or penny bun

Pleurotus ostreatus – oyster fungus

Boletus elegans

Fistulina hepatica – beefsteak fungus

Boletus luteus

Lycoperdon giganteum – giant puffballs

Lepiota procera – parasol mushroom

Common Edible Fruits

To explain in detail all the world's edible fruits, berries and nuts would take a book on its own. However I feel I must mention at least a few of the more common ones. Today, because of the speed of modern transport and methods of storage, it is possible for anyone worldwide to be able to sample even the most exotic fruits by visiting the nearest supermarket. Easily available are fruits like these:

Melon	Banana
Bread Fruit	Mango
Monkey Bread	Grapes
Locust Bean	Paw Paw
Avocado	Wild Fig

Figs

Papaya or paw paw tree

Mangoes

Bread fruit

More edible fruit

Wild bananas

Papaya or paw paw, also known as jack fruit

Poisonous plants

As a boy I was always taught never to eat anything that had a shiny leaf, such as ivy, privet, holly etc. or anything that had single berries that were shiny black, bright red or orange and grew on plants and shrubs. I was taught that these should be left alone as they are poisonous and though strictly speaking this was not always the case, for me it provided a good yardstick as I grew up. In later years when I began travelling the world I applied these same rules and I'm positive that is why I am alive today.

It is estimated that world wide an average of two per cent of the people who actually die through eating poisonous plants and berries tend to be in the very young age group and, more important, live in the so-called civilized regions of the world. My own theory on this is that because we no longer have to forage for our food as many people from underprivileged countries do, we have forgotten all our basic survival instincts about what is and isn't good food for us.

It would be wrong to assume that you could never eat poisonous berries, leaves, roots and fruits etc. by mistake; of course you could, but that danger can easily be avoided by applying the same rules as I did. Remember how I suggested eating little and often? This in itself stops you from taking a large overdose of poison, but *be warned*! Some plants and berries are so toxic that only a small amount would kill you. Here is a list of common plants (pictured in the colour section) that *are* highly poisonous, easily recognizable and found in most regions of the world:

Hemlock (*Conium maculatum*)
Monkshood (*Aconitum napellus*)
Deadly Nightshade (*Atropa belladonna*)
Cuckoo Plant (*Arum maculatum*)
Yew Berry (*Taxus baccata*)
Mistletoe (*Viscum album*)
Castor Oil Plant (*Ricinus communis*)
Privet (*Ligustrum vulgare*)

Black Nightshade (*Solanum nigrum*)
Henbane (*Hyoscyamus niger*)
Poison Ivy (*Rhus toxicodendron*)

Lastly, on the subject of plants for food: bear in mind that Mother Nature provided you with a superb set of instinctive survival aids: TOUCH, SIGHT, HEARING and SMELL, as well as a superb brain to co-ordinate them. So use them.

Trapping

Catching food or game is more difficult than most people imagine. It requires forethought, lots of planning and skill as well as luck. It's not always easy locating prey. Unlike fruit, berries and wild plants, animal life doesn't stand still. Often the only evidence that you'll come across of any game or wildlife around is their droppings. I've been in jungles where I've not seen a single animal for weeks on end. So to catch your food you first have to find it and this could mean hours, sometimes even days, of patiently stalking it. Always remember the words that my instructor drilled into me when I was a young paratrooper. 'Think like an animal, sleep like an animal and live like an animal.'

Because waterholes are areas where animals collect, it may seem an obvious place to trap them. Not so; trails yes, drinking holes no. When drinking most animals are much more alert because they are vulnerable, and the slightest disturbance sends them scurrying away. For the survivalist it's better to trap them when they're away from the waterhole, preferably somewhere along the trail leading to it. An animal panicking near the waterhole will drive away all others and it could be hours before they return. Early morning is generally a good time to stalk game, perhaps just before or after they have taken their morning drink. At midday they'll be resting and not moving around, so they'll be more alert to danger. Many animals, large and small, have regular habits and feeding routines which you can use to plan your trap.

First you must have a trap prepared, but before we discuss specific types of traps I'd like to deal with trapping in general.

We know through the study of paintings and sketches left on cave walls by our ancestors, that many of the hunting skills they used to trap and snare food actually came from the study of plants and animals around them. The fishing net, for example, was probably based on the spider's web, and one of the most primitive but effective traps of all – the 'pit fall' – may have been based on the structure of insect-eating plants. Traps were one way of capturing or killing animals without having to get too close to them. Trapping was prehistoric man's way of dealing with animals that were too big and too dangerous to approach and kill by hand.

Possibly the first trap ever used systematically by Stone-Age man was the 'pit fall'.

This was nothing more than a pit dug into the ground, lined with sharpened spikes and covered with a few branches as camouflage. Interestingly enough the same trapping principles are still used today, in some cases with a few refinements such as a tilting platform or drop gate. Modern poachers sometimes line the pit with barbed wire or netting. Trapping today (for those who are legally permitted to trap for a living), is a highly skilled, professional trade and is carried out under strict control.

WARNING

Trapping is illegal in most countries. It is non-selective and terrible pain and suffering can be caused unnecessarily to animals caught in traps and snares. Indiscriminate killing or maiming of animals is to be abhorred.

In a survival situation it may be necessary for you to hunt and trap in order to stay alive and therefore the skill and use of trapping becomes very much an integral part of survival. But the techniques described here are *only* to be used in a survival situation and even then with the utmost care and caution.

Basically traps fall into two categories; those that kill and those that snare or impound. In a survival situation you can use either. What you should take into account is the type of animal you're trying to trap, study the surrounding terrain and vegetation, and then try to construct the most suitable trap to use.

Because of modern technology and the ease with which we can now kill or trap simply by firing a gun or setting off a charge, many animals now instinctively avoid contact with man. This can obviously make it very difficult for the survivor to obtain food, so to trap successfully you should know something about the behaviour patterns of the animals you intend to snare. If you're able to construct a trap and can site and set it correctly then there will be a reasonable chance of it working, but there are ways in which you can increase your chances. You can 'guide' the animal towards the trap, for instance, by placing a wall of branches on either side of the trail leading into the pit. You can try and hide your scent by using animal blood or entrails, even smoke. Inventiveness and patience are a great asset for a trapper.

I couldn't even begin to count the number of times when I was a lad, our poor old cockerel and hens fell victim to my deadfall trap. It never hurt them; it was just an empty orange box balanced on a thin stick. Along they would come pecking at the corn or bread I'd set in a trail. Seconds later – wham – they were caught. I'd turn them loose, of course, and re-site the trap, but back they came. It never failed.

Traps don't have to be elaborate. Generally speaking, the simplest is the best. A running wire is proof of this and is the most commonly used trap in the world.

Two things to remember about traps. First, having made them correctly, a snare, drop-gate or platform trap is of no use if it isn't strong enough to hold the animal securely, and to have any success at all a trap must be set and sited correctly, otherwise you will have spent a lot of time and effort for nothing.

Don't even try to catch large animals. Apart from a great deal of effort involved in making a trap strong enough to hold them, very often when trapped they are only injured and this makes them extremely dangerous to go near. In all my years of travelling the world's jungles and deserts, I can honestly say I've never had to resort to killing anything indiscriminately. I've managed to survive quite adequately on small game, fish, plants, eggs and even insects. So my advice is to leave the larger animals alone, otherwise you could end up on the menu.

With a little effort and ingenuity almost anything can be turned into some form of trap. Many is the time I've used an old rubber band and two bits of wood to catch fish and eels (below left). And for a mole trap you couldn't ask for anything better.

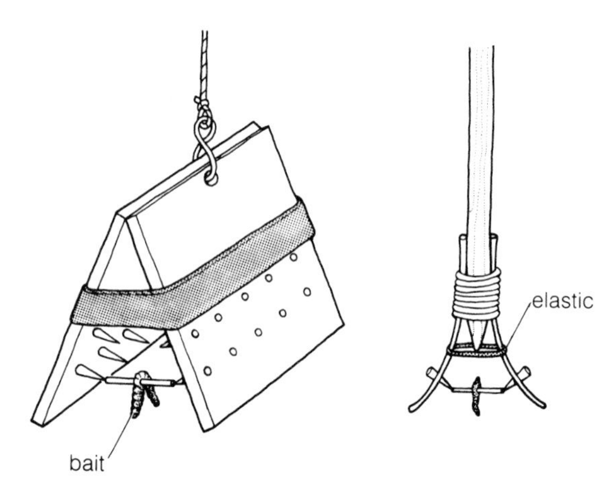

The trap shown in the diagram on the right is simplicity itself. Choose a long stout pole and shape the prongs as shown. Fasten them securely to the pole and prop open the prongs using a small support trigger. Now use the elastic from your underpants or bra, or strips of old inner tubes and fasten them around the prongs. The spear trap is now ready for use. This particular trap is ideal for catching fish, crabs, eels, snakes, mice and almost any small

A trap should blend in with its surroundings as much as possible

A crocodile trap, shown to me by the Aborigines

rodent. Unfortunately it's only as good as the person using it, but with patience and determination you will find it very effective, especially if you don't like putting your hands in water and searching around. I was shown this method by the Aborigines: they use it to catch turtles and lizards etc.

I mentioned earlier that there were two kinds of traps, those that kill and those that snare. It's generally best if you use the trap that will kill the animal as quickly as possible. Deadfalls or spiked pits may be the answer. Cages and snares often cause very painful deaths to their victims. You should only try to trap as a last resort even in a survival situation, because as I've already mentioned, all traps are non-selective. Ideally you want to try and make a clean kill. I was fortunate enough to be able to practise my trapping skills to gain confidence and knowledge without hurting anything. You may not have had that opportunity.

Anyone can set the simplest snare, perhaps a noose attached to a stone or post. My dad used to sit and watch me make a rabbit snare from some old wire and then together we would go off and set it. 'It should be free-running, set at the right height, the right size and in the right place,' he would say. 'What you need to do is look for the rabbit's trail or burrow. Set the snare in such a way that it can't be disturbed by anything else and that it will kill instantly.' My father used to say a running snare should be set four fingers high from the ground, and about the size of your fist. It should be well secured and strong enough to hold the rabbit.

If you set it too close to the ground the snare will probably be knocked over. If you set it too high the game will simply pass under it. Look for a well-used trail. In the case of rabbits you will see that the ground along the trail looks bumpy. To a professional poacher it has 'high

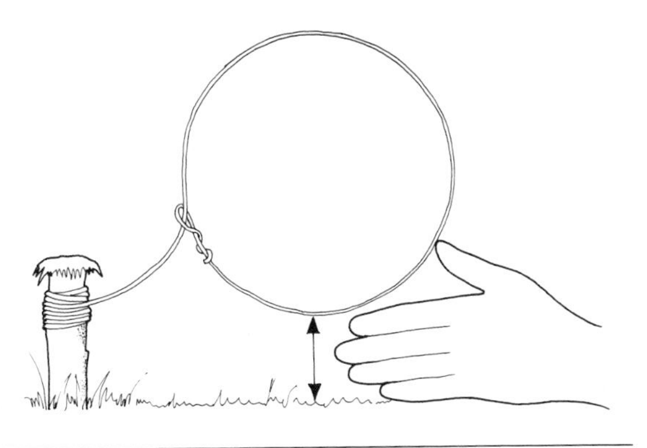

and low spots'. Seek out a high spot and set your snare as instructed.

Snares can be made from an assortment of materials: vines, grass, wire, cloth strips, wool, fishing line or bark. You name it, it can be used, providing of course it's flexible and strong enough. I've caught hundreds of eels in snares using lengths of grass. To make the loops, early man probably used grass and vines with animal hair.

Snares need not only be on the ground. A series of running snares on a tree will help you catch squirrels, monkeys, snakes or even birds – anything that moves in the branches.

Simple twitch-up snares

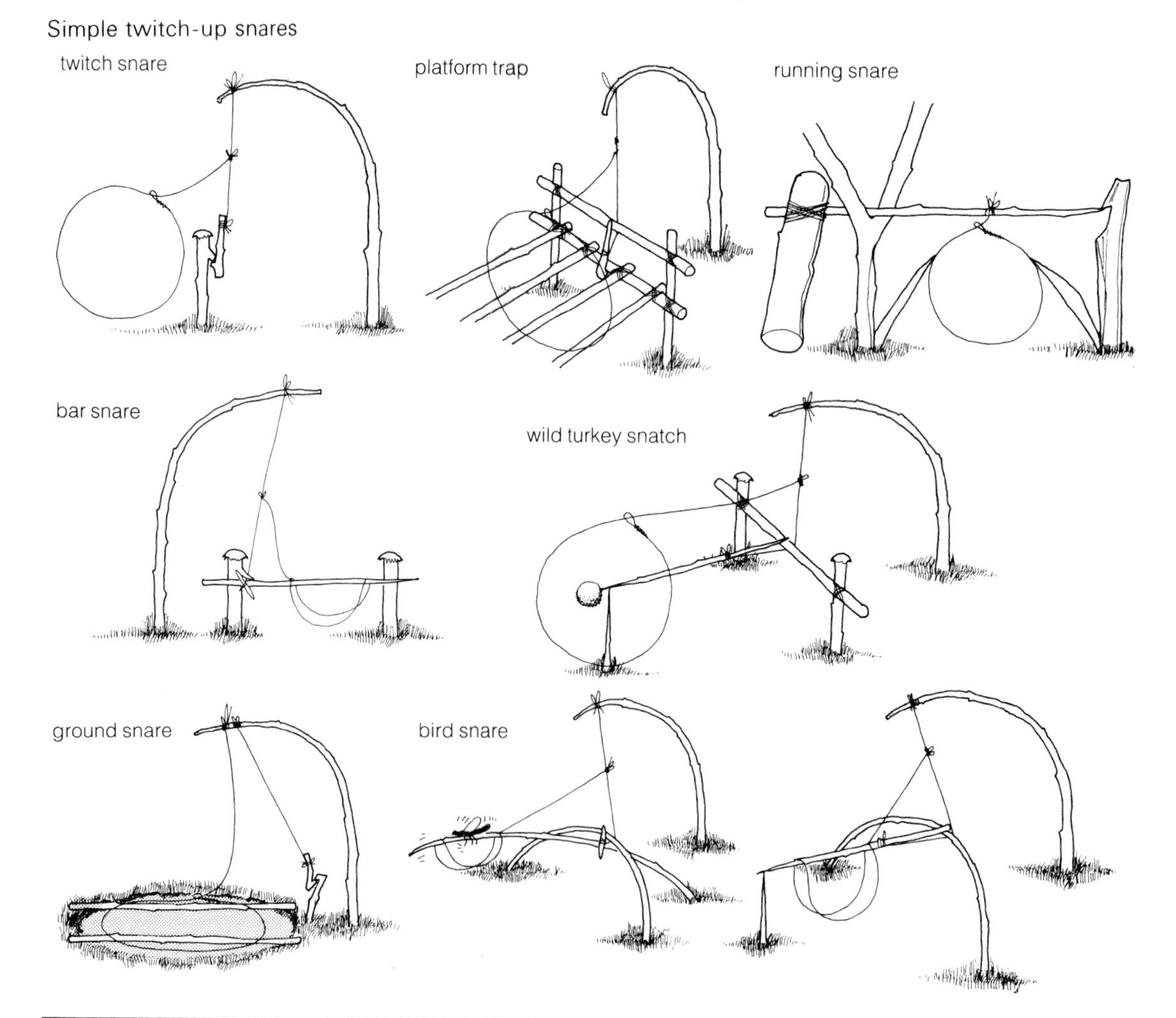

Setting and siting of traps

There are a number of basic points to remember when setting and siting your trap.

- The terrain and environment will determine the type of animal you're trying to catch.
- Look for obvious animal trails and spoor.
- Be prepared to adapt your trap to catch anything.
- Animals partially trapped or injured will become extremely dangerous.
- Animals are naturally suspicious and cautious. Be prepared to re-site your traps if necessary. But in general, once set, leave the traps well alone.
- If possible try to *make* the trap well away from the site where you intend to set it.
- Test the trap to ensure that it works before leaving it in position.
- Try to eliminate any human smell on or around the trap. This could deter animals. Rub hands in soil, rotten leaves or on an old carcass. Leave some animal blood nearby – the smell it gives off may overpower the scents you have left.
- Keep the trap simple, strong and if possible re-useable.

Remember! Traps are non-selective and must only be set under survival conditions when you have no other choice.

- Many animals, birds and insects are protected species.
- Even in a survival situation NEVER leave traps set if you don't intend using them.
- Trapping should only come after you have organized water and environmental protection for yourself. These are always your first priority.
- Don't waste time making and laying traps to catch a meal, particularly if there's lots of vegetation around.

It's better to nibble anything edible throughout the day, than to try and have a very large meal now and again. Eat little and often to establish a good work rate.

Camouflage

A simple technique used by hunters worldwide is to camouflage yourself to suit the surroundings and creep upon your prey. For instance, the Aborigines tie old ostrich feathers to their waists and using their arms imitate the ostrich itself. This enables them to get close enough to shoot the bird with their bows and arrows or spears.

Similarly, North American Indians used to cover themselves with a buffalo skin and stalk the beast.

The Eskimos still use the skin of a polar bear to stalk their prey and sometimes they use this to lie down on the snow and ice to imitate the seal.

As always, *improvisation* is the key word.

Game birds and wildfowl

The same rules apply when catching birds as for locating animals. Find their feeding haunts and sit and observe them. At night when they settle down to roost see how close you can get to them before they fly off. For example, if you try to approach a pheasant or grouse during the day it'll be up and away at the slightest disturbance, yet at night if you know where they are lying up you can mesmerise them with a torch, walk right up and pluck them from their perch. Some poachers don't even use a torch.

All birds need to push downwards before they can lift off and they will always take off in a forward motion. Many of the larger birds need lots of room before they can actually get airborne, so a well-placed net or bunch of knotted twigs will soon slow them down. Very few birds fly at night. If disturbed they will take to the wing, but few fly further than a couple of metres, so don't give up after the first attempt. Wait for them to return from feeding and drinking. As soon as they settle down they'll become drowsy, heavy from the day's pickings and, as a result, much slower in trying to escape. Familiarise yourself with the area before trying to catch them whilst asleep.

The problem with snaring birds is that if they are not killed immediately they do make a lot of noise and tend to warn off others in the area. A classic example of this is a jungle turkey or grouse.

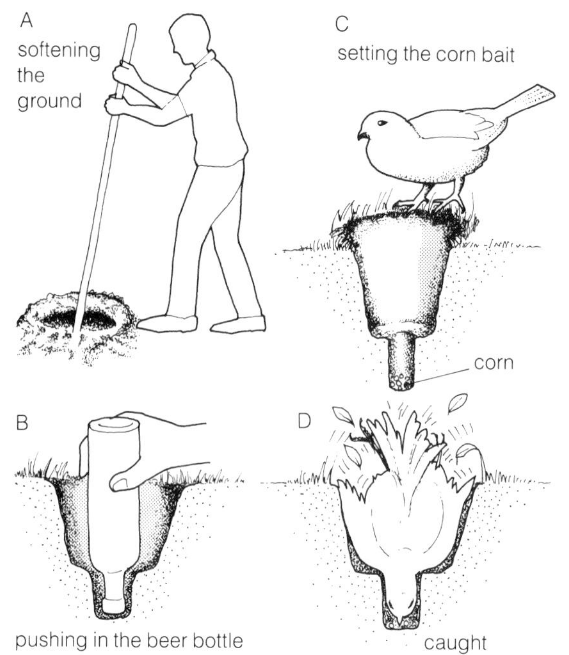

Jungle turkey trap

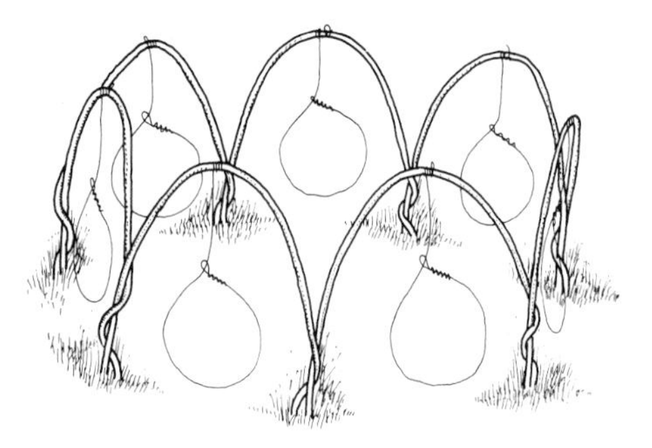

When caught in a snare they make the most unholy row and very often this compounds their downfall, for as soon as they begin squawking they attract larger predators such as pythons, leopards etc. But trapping birds can be done quietly and efficiently. My father and I often used to go out onto the moors and take the odd grouse with nothing more than an old beer bottle and some corn.

Once having found where the grouse were feeding Dad would twist and push the bottle deep into the ground, neck first. Then after withdrawing it gently and not damaging the sides of the hole, he would sprinkle fresh corn around the top and finally drop a small amount down into the bottom of the hole. When the game birds came along they would feed off the seed round the edge and then proceed to peck out the corn in the bottom of the hole. As they gorged themselves they became greedier and greedier until eventually they fell in the hole, wedging themselves tightly and leaving only their tails and legs sticking out in the air.

The trick was to get the hole deep enough to enable the birds to reach right down to peck the corn, and large enough to hold them when they fell in. On a good night I have collected a dozen or so grouse in this manner. Dad used to wear an old ex-army overcoat with a large pouch sewn into the back lining. He would pop the birds, still alive, into the pouch, and if the farmer ever came along he simply pulled a cord and the pouch opened, leaving the birds to flutter off.

Waterfowl

I think nearly all of us have seen films or read books in which the Indians swim quietly just beneath the water surface, breathing through a hollow reed, creeping up on some unsuspecting duck and suddenly dragging it under the water. Believe me, it works! I've used the method more than once. The thing to remember is that the water needs to be reasonably clear and, if possible, warm. A pond or lake is ideal to practise this skill. A river or stream could prove too dangerous as

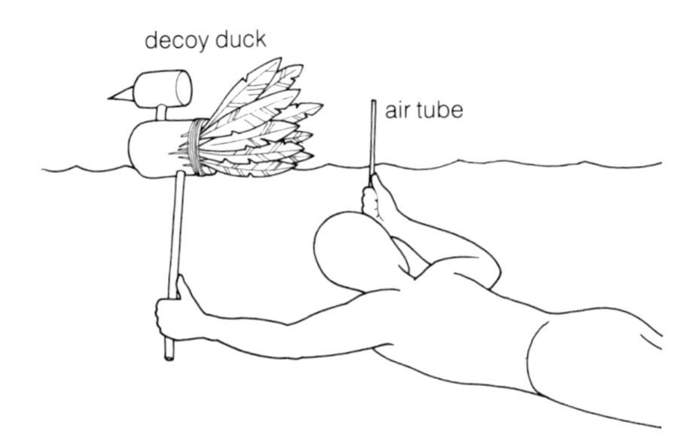

running water is always cold and the current may be too strong. But the trick really is as simple as it sounds.

A similar ruse is to make yourself a decoy bird (see diagram above) and strap this to your head. The problem here is staying below the surface of the water and at the same time breathing through the reed. You'll achieve your best results if you swim in shallow waters and move along the bottom either in the crouch position or pulling yourself forward on your hands, and instead of strapping the decoy to your head, fasten it to a stick. This way you can move in any direction as you swim beneath the water surface.

This decoy method can also be used to drive game into a waiting trap. Build your trap close to the bank and preferably in the reeds. Attach two lengths of twine, one to the gate and the other to the rear of the trap. To the rear twine attach a small decoy and gently pull on the twine to attract the game. As they enter the trap pull the other twine and release the gate to trap them.

Knowing how important water is to our survival and indeed to any other form of life, it's inevitable that where water exists some species of wildlife will be around. If there is a lake, stream, dam etc. you can rest assured waterfowl will be frequent visitors to it. Waterfowl, as with all other animals, have their predators both from above and below the water. Thousands are taken each day by large fish, crocodiles and snakes. Hawks, foxes, even hyena and dogs will take a passing duck, goose or anything else that takes their fancy. Like most living creatures waterfowl are extremely inquisitive, even to the point where they can actually be hoodwinked into almost walking into your traps.

Every schoolchild knows about duck hunters who use imitation whistles to attract the

A duck trap

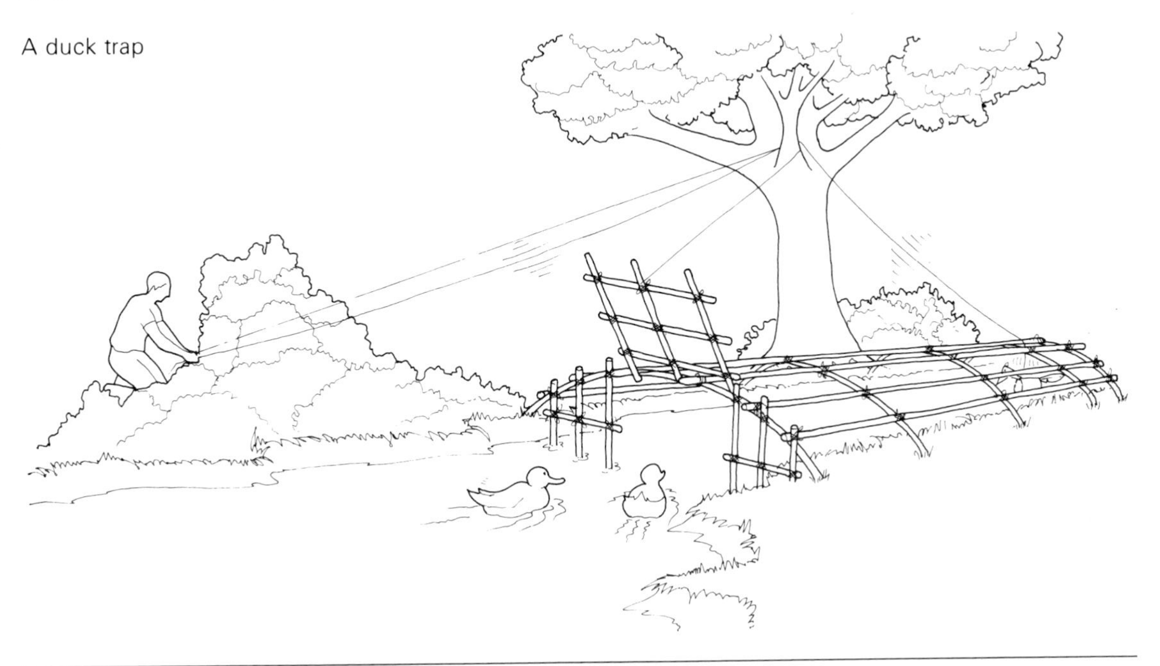

ducks, and many is the time I've used a floating decoy duck made of wood with a bit of clay and feathers stuck onto its back to lure real ducks into my net. Once when I was working with a group of scientists, we set up a large funnel net by the side of a pond to snare waterfowl in order to check their migration movements. To attract the birds I tied a small piece of silver paper shaped as a butterfly to some fishing line and hung this down from the inside of the net. From the front of the net I hung another piece of fishing line, attached to a small flat piece of wood.

Hidden in the undergrowth I gently tugged on the butterfly line to attract the birds as they began to swim nearer to the net's entrance. When just inside the trap I quickly dropped the flat piece of wood onto the water surface behind them, making a big slap and splash. The birds then rushed forward into the net. The more I slapped the wood, the further up the tunnel they swam. A painless but extremely effective method of trapping. This trick is not new; it has been used for hundreds of years. So too has the technique of setting out lines of woven hurdles spaced along the banks. To attract the ducks' curiosity a dog is made to run between the hurdles darting in and out. The inquisitive ducks swim across to investigate and in so doing, as the dog moves down the hurdles, the ducks in the water will follow blindly into the waiting trap.

Often I've used the hard hollow shell of a coconut as a duck trap. Having removed all the edible flesh, cleaned out the shell and tied a large handful of grass or reeds around it (as shown below), you affix a couple of snares – fishing line being the most suitable – three-quarters fill the shell with water and leave it floating nearby. In the Far East I saw this method being regularly used and to ensure the birds were attracted they had tied a large beetle or dragonfly to the rim of the shell as it splashed around. The duck, being as inquisitive as ever, would swim forward and snatch at the bait. In so doing it would catch itself on the snares, the splashing would cause water to pour into the shell and down would go the duck. This must be done in shallow water, generally waist high.

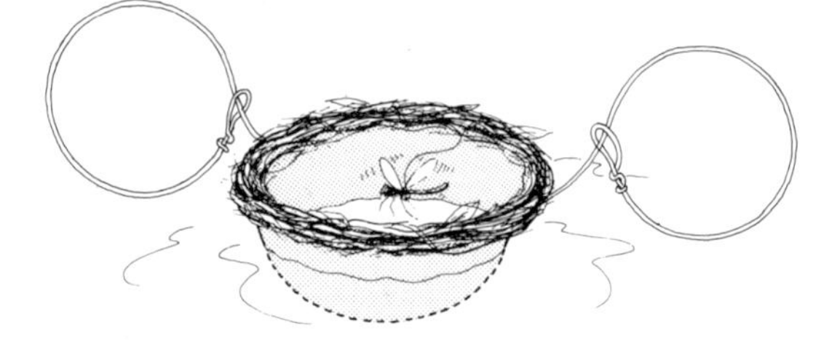

The slipway

A less complicated method of the dog-and-hurdles trap would be to find a section of the river bank that drops gently into the water, one where ducks etc. can waddle out easily. Drive a series of pegs into the bank, fasten some lengths of fishing line on string between them and at intervals hang snare loops from it. Bait the area leading from the water to the rear of your trap and just sit back and wait.

Equally effective is a technique used by the North American Indians. To guide waterfowl up a slipway they run a length of fishing line from a post set in the water close by the entrance to the slipway, to a nearby bush where they hide themselves. When any waterfowl are close by the hunters gently tug on the fishing line and cause a piece of wood attached to it to slap on the water. Being inquisitive the birds move closer to investigate and see the bait set out on the slipway. A quick pull on the fishing line startles the fowl and they rush forward into the hanging snares.

Another method I often use is a water hoop platform. This is nothing more than a couple of dry logs tied together by two supple bows and with a simple loop trap to catch the birds. A live beetle or grasshopper, even a piece of silver paper hung down between the bows, would attract the birds into the snare.

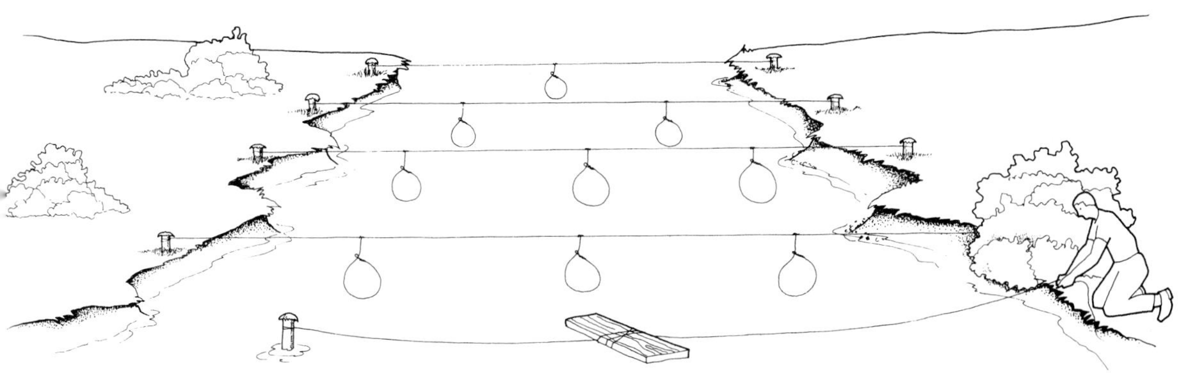

Estuary duck trap

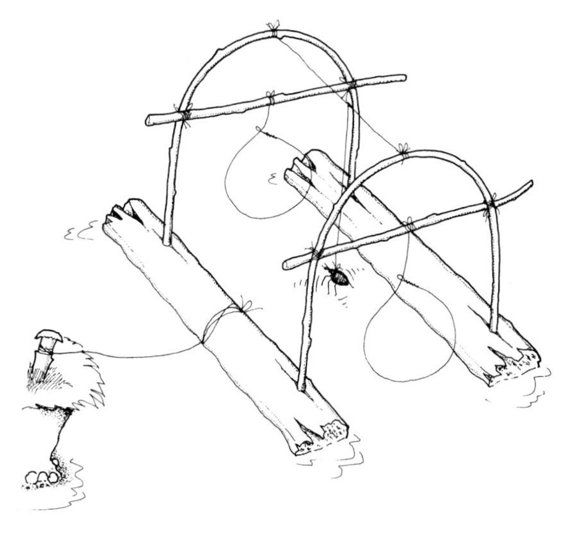

Water hoop platform

Bird liming

This is a means of trapping birds simply by making the perch they land on sticky. Unable to grip the perch as they land, the birds topple off the branch and hang upside down or drop into a funnelled net. Bird liming is highly illegal in most Western countries, including the United Kingdom. However, in certain parts of the world it is legal and every year many thousands of birds are trapped in this way.

Finally on the subject of trapping, like all serious survivalists, I'm also a keen naturalist and believe very much in the conservation of all wildlife. No doubt some people will think that I'm being hypocritical, but as always I emphasize that this book is written for the survivalist, someone who could easily die without this basic knowledge. It's acceptable to kill for food in order to survive.

Eggs

If you are lucky enough to come across any fresh eggs during your search for food, keep them. All eggs are edible, some may taste a little stronger than others, but they are a good source of food and should not be discarded. Eggs can be eaten raw or cooked: fried, boiled, grilled or poached. They can be added to flour to make cakes and bread. Boiled eggs are excellent for absorbing stomach poison and in many parts of the world eggs are mixed with flour into a gooey paste and then used as a cover for open wounds and grazes. More than one desert traveller has used a couple of eggs (cracked) in his radiator to help seal off a leak.

The egg of an ostrich is a meal in itself and even fresh crocodile eggs taste good when you're hungry. Turtle eggs taste very fishy but are a good source of food, especially to the desert island survivor. They can be found in large quantities, sometimes as many as 150 to 200 per nest. Raw eggs act as a binder and even today in the Western world many people who suffer with stomach problems will eat half-a-dozen raw eggs a day.

Eggs may be cooked by using hot water from a car radiator, fried on the hot metal of a plane/car wing, dropped onto a hot flat stone, popped into a tin of hot water or, if you wish, you can cook eggs simply by wrapping them in mud and setting them in hot charcoal. A simple egg poacher can be made either by shaping a piece of tin foil in the last embers of the fire, bending a piece of tin from a crashed aircraft or hollowing out a piece of good, clean, hard wood.

Turtle eggs may be cooked in mass simply by placing them in a ground oven and covering them with hot sand or embers.

You can also cook them by wrapping them in a plastic bag containing clean water, covering the bag in hot mud and placing it on the fire.

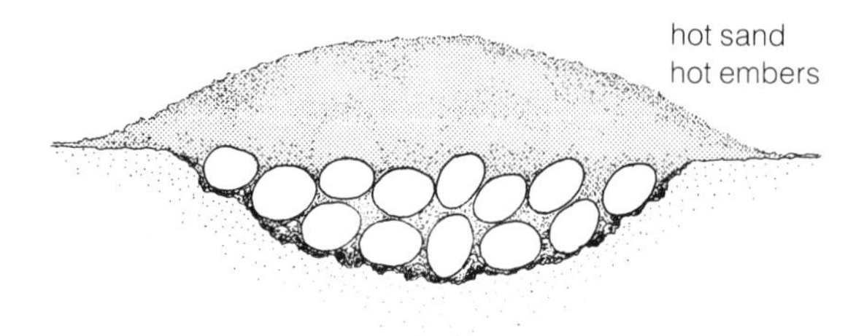

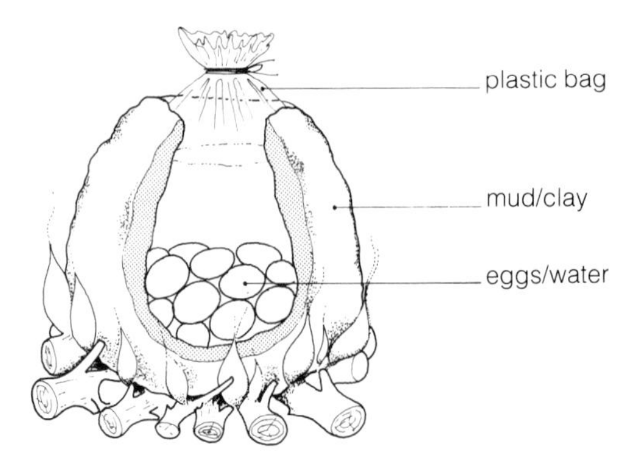

CHAPTER 8

Preparation and Cooking

Having successfully caught your game the next thing is to be able to kill it, then skin it, gut it and finally cook it. Even in a survival situation it is unwise to eat any meat or fish unless it has first been cleaned and cooked. Fish deteriorates rapidly so you may have to cure it before eating, by sun drying or smoking it. Meat also deteriorates quickly, but not as quickly as fish. However, meat exposed to the air and not protected or cured will soon attract flies, insects and perhaps flesh-eating animals. In the Arctic, for instance, it's said that a polar bear can smell a dead seal from over a mile away, and as any African bush traveller will tell you, as soon as you've made a kill any hyena in the vicinity will seek you out. Both of these animals are ferocious carnivores and wouldn't hesitate to attack when driven by hunger. So, once you have your food move away to a safe area.

Firstly, let's deal with the killing of your game. Having set your trap or snare and caught something, the next obvious thing is to remove it. Never, if possible, approach the trap from the rear, always from the front. Look directly at your game and approach slowly. It may be that the animal is not dead, only injured (or sleeping) and if this is the case it could be dangerous to get too close.

Most animals caught in a trap are flesh-eaters and as such will have very sharp teeth, powerful jaws and extremely sharp claws. Depending on what kind of trap you have used always take with you your knife, bow and arrow, or if you have one, your gun. If you have none of these, at the very least you should take a strong, long, sharpened pole to fend off any surprise attacks. Remember this is a survival situation and cruel though it may seem, the catch in your trap may be the only food you'll have to live on, so being squeamish or feeling sorry at this stage won't help.

After approaching the trap from the front give the game a couple of prods with your pole to see if it's sleeping or dead. If it's dead there's no problem. Remove the body from the trap and if necessary re-set the trap. If it's not dead then you'll have to kill it yourself and this isn't as easy as it sounds.

There are two basic methods with all living animals and the first of these is asphyxia – death through suffocation, in this case through strangulation. So if the trap you've set includes a snare it's important to try and ensure that when the game is caught the snare takes it around the neck and kills it quickly. Believe me, this is very difficult, even for the most experienced of trappers. The second method of death is equally agonizing to the animal – death by wounding and pain. Kill the animal quickly and as humanely as possible. Even in survival situations unnecessary suffering can be avoided. If possible strike the animal hard at the back of the neck with a heavy object such as a log, stone or any blunt instrument, possibly the starting handle from your car or a piece of heavy metal from the wreck of your aircraft or boat. Put the animal out of its misery as quickly as possible. If you have a gun shoot it in the head just above the eyes. If you have only a primitive bow and arrow shoot it in the heart (if you know where it is), behind the ear, in the throat or anywhere that will kill it quickly and humanely. Wait for a few minutes to ensure that the animal is dead before removing it. Smaller game such as rabbits, birds and even fish can be held in the hand; a powerful blow to the back of the neck will soon kill them.

Skinning

Skinning a snake/lizard

Having killed a snake you can either hang it, tail downwards, from a tree or drape it over a rock. The skinning procedure for both is the same. Either remove the head completely, or cut around it. Using a sharp knife slit open the stomach and remove the entrails. Where you've cut just below the head take hold of the skin and gently peel it downwards. If you are skinning the snake on the ground it might be easier if the body is cut up into sections first. Larger game can be skinned using the same methods, though for convenience and hygiene it's better to have it hanging. Remember if you skin your game properly you can use the skins for clothes, shoes, shelters etc. Skin as soon as possible after killing.

Skinning small game, e.g. rabbit or hare

1. Lie the rabbit on a flat surface and remove the feet at the first joint.

2. Turn the rabbit onto its back, head away from you, and using a sharp knife make a small incision in the skin, just above the back legs. Slit the belly open and remove the entrails. If fresh keep the liver, heart and kidneys for eating. When washed and dried, entrails make excellent bow strings.

3. Using thumb and forefinger gently ease the skin off the flesh and over the leg stump. Do this to all four legs. Ease the skin away from the flesh under the animal's tail.

4. Holding the two skin-free rear legs, gently ease the skin down over the rest of the carcass until it stops at the head. Using your knife remove the head and skin in one go.

5. Wash the rabbit thoroughly and it is ready for cooking.

Cooking

Fire pit

Probably the first method of cooking used by man was simply to throw pieces of meat or fish onto an open fire. The advantages being (providing the fire was both hot and large enough to accommodate the meat) that it can be cooked literally in a few minutes. The disadvantages are, firstly, that the food will almost certainly shrink; secondly, that it may not be cooked through sufficiently and third, that it requires constant watching, otherwise it will burn away.

Boiling

To boil your food simply place it in a suitable container and immerse it in water. This is a quick and very effective method of cooking providing there is sufficient water and heat from your fire to boil the food thoroughly. The disadvantages are finding clean water, finding a suitable container to boil in and undercooking because of insufficient heat. Any food, especially meat, when not boiled for an adequate length of time could become infected with bacteria.

Stewing

The food is placed in a container with a little water and cooked slowly until tender. Disadvantages: as above, and length of time involved waiting for the food to be ready. Advantages: if stewed correctly, all the goodness in the food is retained and tough meat will become more tender. Also, it isn't necessary to stand over it.

Simmering

Similar to stewing but on a much smaller flame or less intensive heat. The food is allowed to simmer gently for a long period. The disadvantage is that it takes a long time before it's ready and the fire or cooker will need constant attention. There's also a tendency to overcook. The advantages are the same as in stewing.

Roasting

Here the food is placed in a container and hot fat is poured over it as the meat cooks gently on the fire. Disadvantages: often, if not supervised, the meat will shrink and not cook properly. Heat is needed all round to ensure even cooking unless the meat is suspended on a spit. There is also a tendency to burn the outer flesh too quickly and thus prevent the heat from cooking the inside. For the hungry survivor, though, the advantage is that whilst the carcass is still cooking, pieces of meat that are already done can be cut off and eaten.

Grilling or braising

Similar to roasting but in a very hot clay or stone oven or grill. Disadvantage: it has to be watched continuously and the heat supply maintained. Also there's a very good chance of undercooking, especially if hunger pangs are gnawing at your stomach.

Pressure cooking or steaming

Food is placed in a sealed container and submerged in water. Pressure is built up in the container and the meat cooked by steam and hot water. Disadvantages: undercooking and finding a suitable container. In a survival situation without the right equipment, you may have to use a mud pack. The principle is the same except that the food is encased in soft mud clay then placed on an open fire.

Poaching

Food is gently simmered in water until cooked. Fish, mushrooms and eggs are the most common food prepared by this method. To attempt to cook meat by poaching can be dangerous. It will almost certainly be undercooked if not done for a very long time.

Baking

Food placed dry on a hot plate, grill or dry oven. Food wrapped in mud or tin foil can also be cooked in this fashion. Disadvantages: needs constant regular heat and continuous supervision. Food tends to shrink and may be undercooked.

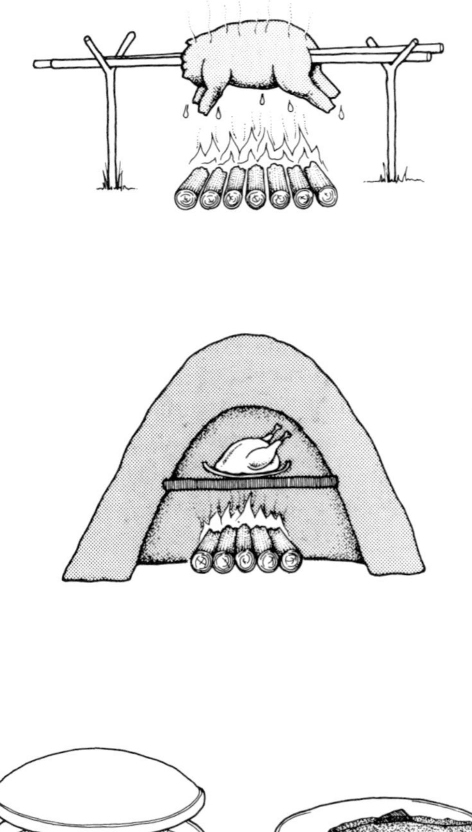

Frying

Food placed on an open frying pan, flat plate, hot stone etc. An excellent speedy method of cooking though needs constant attention and possibly some cooking fats or oils (preferably the food's own juices).

Making an oven from an old tin/oil drum

A very simple, but extremely effective, cooker/oven can be made from an old tin or oil drum. Nothing should be wasted in a survival situation.

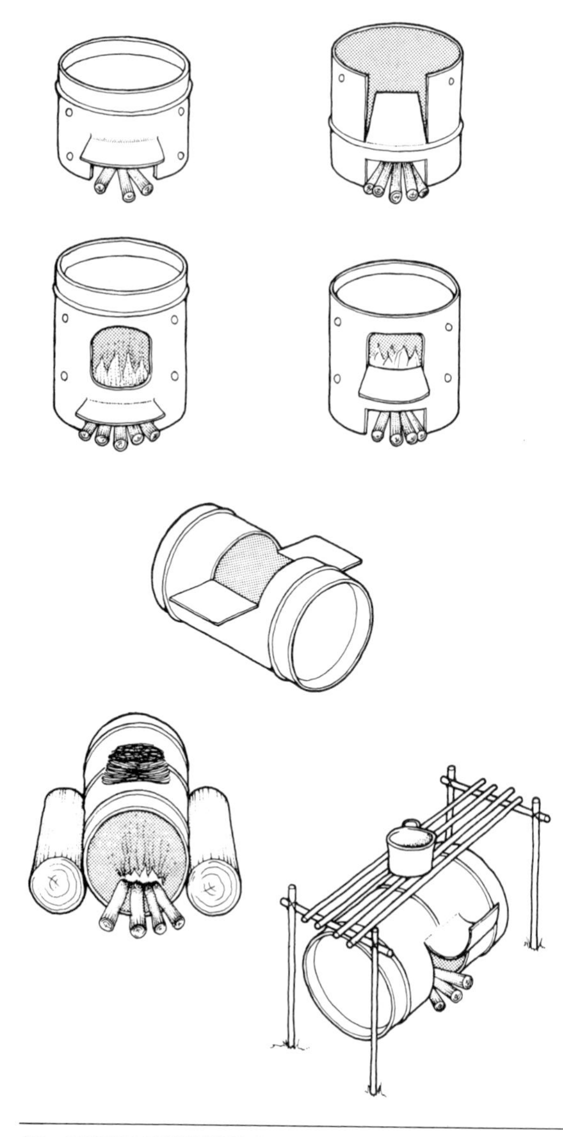

Caution! The golden rule to remember when cooking meat, be it red or white (especially white) is to ensure that it is properly cooked. Contaminated raw meat is a very likely source of food poisoning, which can be fatal. White meat in particular is very prone to carry bacteria.

Before cooking: SKIN, WASH, GUT and CLEAN, INSPECT and COOK THOROUGHLY. Use your common sense. If it doesn't smell right don't eat it!

Preserving and curing

To summarise, basically in a survival situation there are three ways of preserving and curing your food quickly.

1. Simple sun drying or planking.
2. Curing in an improvised oven using smoke.
3. Preserving by cooking and then soaking in salt or vinegar.

All of these methods can be easily carried out by the would-be survivor and without too much effort or skill. One word of warning here, though. In the early stages when you're experimenting there is a tendency to either over- or undercook the food. It's only by trial and error that you'll learn to cook or preserve food in such a way as to suit your needs. Remember, it's always better to overcook than to undercook meat. Burnt, charcoaled meat or fish is much safer to eat than partially cooked flesh.

The good thing about using any of the three methods described is that, providing there are no animals or birds around to steal your catch, you can't lose or spoil any of your food by leaving it for a long time. Indeed, in the case of smoking, or soaking in brine, the longer the food is left, the better it will be.

Just as their ancestors did thousands of years ago, people who live alongside the sea in the tropics today still cure and dry their meat and fish using the same methods. After cleaning and gutting it is cut into strips and

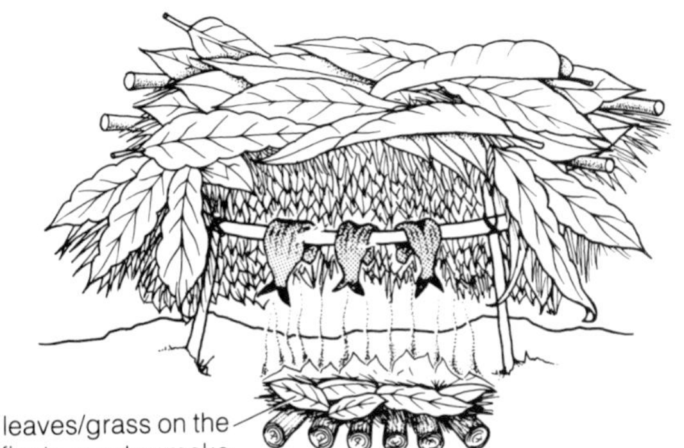

A curing kiln (this would be completely covered with foliage); and fish drying in the sun

One way of smoking fish

hung on racks either to dry by the heat of the sun or to cook in a smoke filled kiln. Often it is simply left out to dry on rocks upon the sand. Meat and fish can also be cured by planking. Here the food is staked out on a log and placed close to a fire. This is a fairly quick method of curing depending on the heat of the fire. To

Smoking fish

get the best results use wood shavings if you have any. In Polynesia, after the people have chipped out the centre of a log to make a canoe, they use the shavings for a communal kiln.

Building a curing kiln

Dig a small hole in the ground about one foot square and one foot deep. Then build a simple box enclosure around the fire and cover this with green leaves, moss, seaweed or grass. Before covering ensure that you have built a small trellis support to hang the fish on. Light your fire and remember to place some green foliage on it to help the smoking process.

The beauty of this method is that you can leave the curing pan, as it's called, working whilst you attend to something else. The disadvantage is that if you don't have a good fire and lots of smoke it could, if left unattended, go out and the food wouldn't be properly cured. However, if you've covered the pan correctly you shouldn't have too much trouble.

Curing by brine or salt is also a simple process. The food is washed and then allowed to soak in salted water. In the case of large chunks of meat it may be necessary to regularly keep dipping the meat until the salt has soaked right into it. Salt may be obtained by taking buckets of sea water and continually boiling it until only the salt remains. Or if you're lucky, you may stumble across a salt flat and use the natural dried crystal salt.

A salt water still

Once, whilst living alone on a desert island, I used an old oil drum that had been washed up on the shore to make myself a salt water still. Painstakingly I scored a groove around the tin until I could separate the two halves with a few deft knife cuts. One half I made into a ground oven and fire, the other half I used for boiling sea water. A large plastic sheet was draped over the area and the steam from the hot water condensed and dripped into my collection pans.

The whole purpose of curing is to preserve your food for a later date. In a survival situation it may not be possible for you to do this; circumstances may dictate that you could be on the move all the time and of course you must eat your food as and when you find it to keep up your energy. The good thing about curing food is that if you have to travel you can always take your food with you.

Curing fruit or vegetables is possible but not in the way described. Apples and onions can be preserved by slicing them and holding them over a hot fire. They seal themselves and will retain their sweetness and smell for many months. With the apples this is an excellent way of preserving your sugar supply.

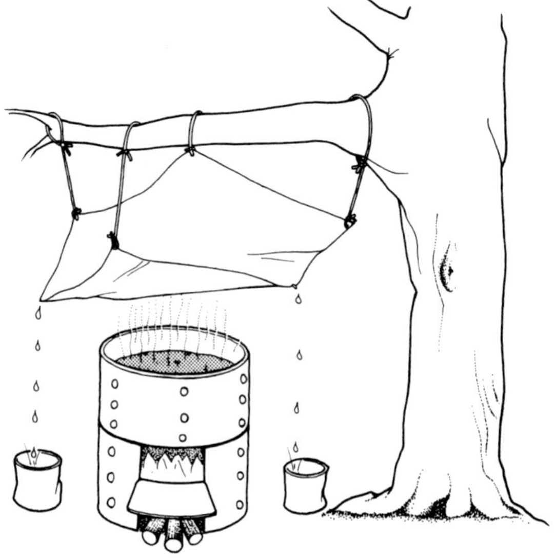

A salt water still

slices of apple drying over fire

onion rings drying

Corn, wheat, maize and many herbs can be stored for a long time in containers made of clay or earth and if a little charcoal is added to the base of the bowl it helps to absorb the moisture and keep the food fresh. Many of the common nuts such as acorns, chestnuts, almonds and hazel nuts may also be preserved by mixing a little salt and sand in a container and then roasting them over a hot charcoal fire. Peanuts are generally cooked in this way.

Soft fruits (unlike apples etc.) require specialist curing so there's little point in trying to explain this in detail to you as it's very unlikely you would want to build yourself a kiln drier or hot air dispenser and moisture evaporation unit. Some fruits such as blackberries, loganberries, cherries and elderberries may be left to soak for a week or so without too much problem though once exposed to the air they quickly mildew and deteriorate if not eaten.

Insect cuisine

In a survival situation food from any source must be considered if you wish to stay alive. I've mentioned some of the more commonly known foods available to you – foods that you'd have no hesitation in eating. There are, however, many, many others equally nutritious but not perhaps as well known so it's up to you to do a little extra reading to familiarise yourself with them.

Probably the food most readily available to the survivor is going to come from the insect world. Insects of various sizes, shapes and colours can be found in all regions. They provide a good source of protein and fat and in many cases are very nutritious. Anyone who has travelled widely abroad will probably have seen the way in which many nomadic peoples still depend on insects to boost their diet. Termites, grasshoppers, crickets, locusts and even stick insects are all edible.

To get the best from your insects remove wings, stings (if any), legs, antennae and any other bits and pieces sticking out. Even if you're really desperate all insects must be cooked and most taste better when roasted. An excellent method of roasting (without letting them shrivel) is to drop them into a container of hot sand. Keep shaking the sand covering the insects until they turn a deep brown and become brittle. Cooking this way helps to keep all the nutrients inside the shells and allows no wastage.

Termites are easily caught. First find your termites' nest, then seal off all but one of the entries into the mound and poke around the open one with a stick. As the termites become agitated they begin to pour out, many clinging to the stick. I was taught this method when living with the Pygmies, although it is a skill learnt originally by man watching animals. (Chimpanzees in particular use this method.) Sometimes the Pygmies knock the top off the nest, carry it across to a stream and gently lower it into the water. Within seconds the water surface is covered in termites. These

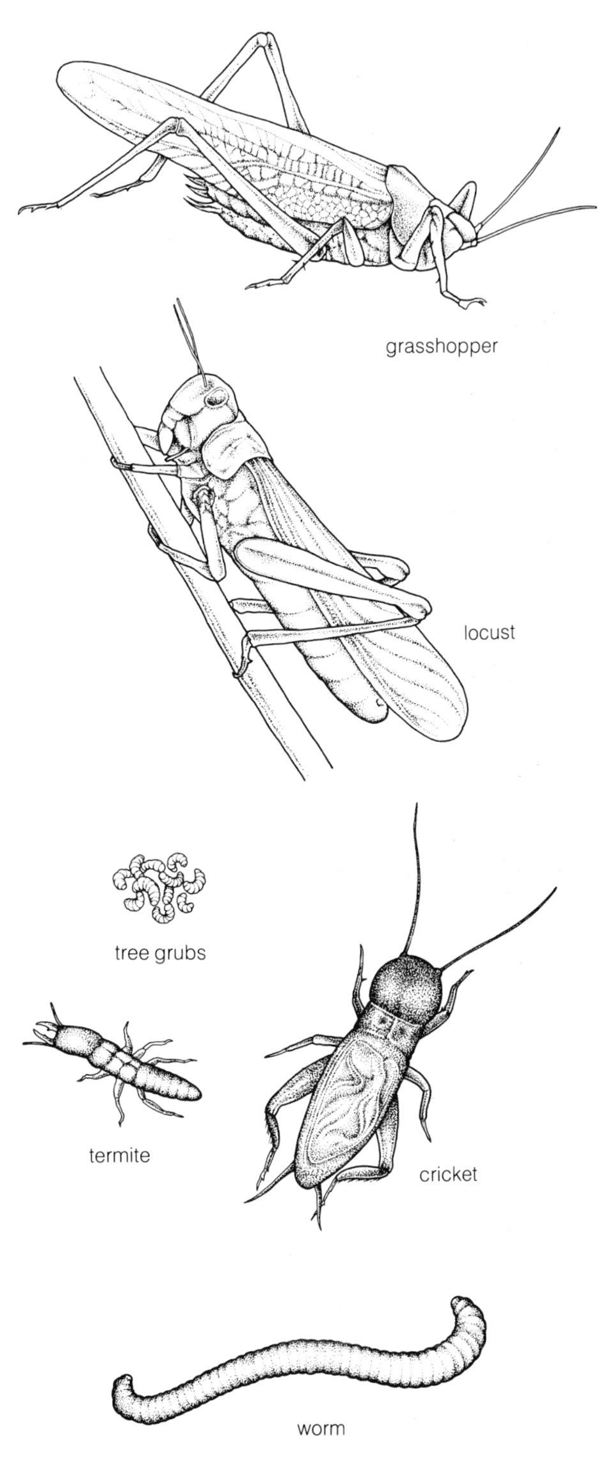

Edible insects

Chimpanzee catching termites. You can use the same method

are then scooped up and either eaten raw (not advisable) or taken for roasting. The Australian Aborigine gathers termites and ants, squashes them into a pulp, then rubs them onto his body. They claim this helps ward off colds and other illnesses.

If your camp is continually plagued by ants, open up a termites' nest and drag it away from the camp leaving a trail on the ground. Any marauding ants will quickly pick up the trail and zoom in for the kill. Both termites and the inner nest make excellent fishing bait, and the hard-baked mud surrounding the nest makes perfect fire bricks. As always, 'everything you need Mother Nature will provide'. A word of warning though: lots of snakes and scorpions use old termite nests to rest in during the heat of the day. So take care; poke around with a stick first.

Worms, as I've already mentioned, are edible and very rich in protein and contrary to what some experts claim may be eaten raw, though it's advisable in that case to keep them for a couple of days or so and feed them on fresh vegetation.

Generally speaking with insect cuisine it's the grubs that are eaten though some, when fully grown, tend to begin certain secretions that make them unpalatable even when cooked. As far as beetles are concerned, I personally have managed to survive without eating any and I strongly advise you to do the same!

Choosing and cooking seaweed

Seaweed is another possible source of food, simply because it is so abundant. Most seaweeds cling to rocks and overhanging trees; only a few float freely. Basically most are edible and only a few bitter to taste. Botanically seaweeds belong to a group of

Saw wrack and kelp

Bladder wrack

Above left: Egg or knotted wrack. *Above right*: Fucus (sometimes called sea lettuce) and rockweed

Above left: Green laver – also sometimes called sea lettuce. *Above right*: Pandanus palm and fruit

plants known as Algae. Any seaweed consisting of more than one cell is not poisonous: in fact it tastes a bit like spinach, especially when cooked. But if it's old, stale or clammy to the touch, discard it. Some species contain a lot of protein, all have carbohydrates, are very rich in minerals, especially vitamin C (in some cases more than the amount found in oranges) and all contain iodine: one of nature's antiseptics. As a guide avoid any seaweed that has a thread-like appearance, as these work as a harsh laxative and purgative.

In a survival situation choose only the freshest of seaweeds and never eat any that grow close to human habitats and therefore near sewers, drains etc. Eat little and often; too much of it could make you ill.

Worldwide you will find kelp, pulce, fucus, wracks, green laver (sea lettuce), and sugar wrack (*Amivaria saccarina*) which has exceptionally sweet-tasting stalks. Sea pigweed or purslane, found along the shores of barren atolls, is an excellent survival food. It tastes like watercress. Purslane and water will keep you alive for many months.

While on the subject of atolls,screw pine or pandanus, a native of barren atolls, may be eaten. The fruit looks like a pineapple and is very rich in sugar and starch. Some water can be had by sucking on its long aerial roots.

Cooking

Seaweed is best boiled. If you have any doubt as to edibility tear off a small strip, boil it and then eat it. Wait half an hour. If there is no ill effect go ahead and eat more. Use fresh water to boil it in and remember some take longer than others to cook.

Cooking shellfish

It is wise when cooking shellfish to boil them for at least half an hour. After cooking, remove them and place on a hard surface, perhaps a stone or log. Using a sharp, heavy object such as a rock or chunk of wood, crack down hard on the shell. Once it is split remove the edible flesh: this should be a nice pink colour. Scrape it out onto a clean plate/leaf and eat immediately. Remember, the flesh from shellfish deteriorates very quickly so it must be eaten as soon as possible.

When taking the edible flesh from a large shell (body) take care not to burst the stomach bag and squash the intestines. Gently remove these and use them for bait later.

A warning when handling fish!
Beware of poisonous barbs and where possible descale the fish before eating it.

Any fish, fruit, seaweed etc. that is soft to touch, has slimy flesh and doesn't spring back when pressed should be discarded and used for bait.

Other culinary stand-bys

Survival cake

A simple survival cake can be made by mixing together boiled rice, raisins and groundnuts. If you have any flour handy, mix this in too. When the ingredients are all blended together press the mixture out into a flat pancake and drop it onto a hot stone. Bake for about ten minutes, turning frequently, until crisp and brown.

Survival bread

Ingredients: goat/camel milk, an egg and flour mixed into a dough and rolled out thinly. Place on a hot stone or in a clay oven and cook for 20 minutes. When cooked remove and smear with goat or camel cheese. This is delicious and eaten by nomads worldwide. Honey or butter may be spread as an alternative.

Fish cakes

Simple fish cakes can be made by slicing your fish into very thin strips and mixing with flour and water. A couple of crushed olives, boiled, or the oil skimmed from the surface of the cooking water, can be used to bind the fish cake and prevent it from drying out.

Survival stew

Monkey flesh, rabbit, fish, snake, game birds, waterfowl etc., cooked, sliced and then mixed with rice and manioc or cassava (potato) in a container and left to stew for a couple of hours, make a delicious meal. Chopped seaweed can be added to provide a vegetable base. Monkey meat may be a little strong (peppery) if you're not used to it. It will also need a longer cooking time as the meat tends to be a little tough.

Potato cream

Potato slices or manioc/cassava stewed for half-an-hour in milk cream from the camel, goat or cow, produces a superb meal. After cooking, separate the cream from the potatoes and pour it through a sieve, using your pocket lining for this purpose, and drink the liquid. Keep the cream to spread on the potato slices. The Bedouin use the cream mixed with selected herbs as a medical salve.

CHAPTER 9

Communication

Because it is possible to travel to even the remotest of regions in the world quickly and safely we are able to communicate, if not by common language certainly by signs, with even the most primitive of nomads. The simple gesture of a finger pointing at your eyes signifies 'I'm looking at you'. Equally, a finger pushed inside the mouth and a noise made in the throat will indicate you need food/water or you want to talk. How many of us have gently rubbed our stomachs and shown a sallow face when feeling ill or wiped the back of our hands across the forehead to indicate tiredness or feeling hot?

There are thousands of other body signs used daily worldwide and many have now been adapted for use in individual communication sign language. A classic example is the universal language of the deaf and dumb. Doctors, missionaries, school and other organizations now teach a full alphabet in sign language as part of a daily curriculum to millions of people and in so doing even the most uneducated can now learn to communicate in a matter of minutes.

In Africa the drum is used as a telephone or speaker. In Switzerland they yodel across the mountains to each other and in Alaska they communicate over long distances with clapper boards. Remember the Red Indians in the films? They used smoke signals to communicate. When I served in the Middle East the Arabs used to fire off rifle shots to welcome you and sometimes the women would call to each other using an unmistakable high-pitched yah-yah-yah-yah-yah-yahhhh call, rapidly clicking their jaws.

Today, of course, we don't have to send smoke signals from the tops of hills or yell at each other across valleys. We in the more 'civilized' world have become used to flicking a switch, pressing buttons or turning a knob and in seconds we can speak to someone on the other side of the globe. All thanks to modern technology. Yet, as we all know, even technology can fail, so it's always good to know that if this happens we can still communicate, simply by using gestures or Mother Nature's aids: smoke, noise, colour etc.

Three methods of communication devised by man now commonly in use worldwide are signalling by semaphore, morse code and the already mentioned sign language of the deaf. All three are relatively easy to learn and are excellent ways of communicating.

Morse Code

Morse Code is simply a series of signals commonly known as dots and dashes sent electronically by morse tappers or signalled with a torch, mirror, flashing light and even by drum (remember the Africans). Each dot and dash represents a letter or number, so it is possible to communicate with someone over a great distance, providing the other person can see or hear the signals.

The most common and perhaps the most easily recognizable message sent by morse code is S . . . O . . . S, the abbreviated 'Save Our Souls'. In fact this is not always meant literally. S.O.S. is sent simply because it is very easy to learn and recognize, and the series of dots and dashes can be understood in

A •—	M ——	Y —•——
B —•••	N —•	Z ——••
C —•—•	O ———	1 •———
D —••	P •——•	2 ••———
E •	Q ——•—	3 ••——
F ••—•	R •—•	4 ••••—
G ——•	S •••	5 •••••
H ••••	T —	6 —•••
I ••	U ••—	7 ——•••
J •———	V •••—	8 ————••
K —•—	W •——	9 ————•
L •—••	X —••—	0 —————

any language. Soldiers, sailors and airmen of all nationalities use S.O.S. as the international MAYDAY distress call. Mayday derives from the French *m'aider* (help me).

It is also possible to send messages by colour. Here's how it's done: worldwide, RED is now recognized as a distress signal, GREEN as safe and ORANGE or AMBER as a warning. Just think of traffic lights. RED for stop: AMBER for stand by: GREEN for go. Smoke flares and rockets of similar colour, even flags can be used to communicate the same messages. If using fire smoke for signalling, remember to make it stand out from your background.

Semaphore

Semaphore is a means of sending messages by waving flags and is often used when it's not possible to send messages by radio, reflection or telephone.

It is very easy to learn and flags can be made from tiny bits of cloth or handkerchiefs etc. tied to a couple of sticks. Old coloured plastic bags held in a hand make ideal signalling flags and cut up into squares will serve as marker panels. Material from your car seat cover can also be used, or as a last resort you could simply use your arms.

For semaphore to be fully effective it is best if both you and the signalling flags contrast with the surrounding area. For instance, standing on a hill may sound ideal, but if the cloth of the flags is white and the sky behind you is also white it may not be possible for the other person to see what you are signalling. So, instead of standing on the skyline you may have to use the backdrop of a tree or hill to help clarify your signals. If signalling from a ship or dinghy allow for the swell of the sea. During the night try using two sticks with cloth soaked in oil/diesel/petrol, set alight, with which to signal. Send your message slowly and deliberately – it's all a matter of common sense.

Sign language of the deaf and dumb

Finally, if you are at close quarters with the recipient of your message, you could try the deaf and dumb sign language. The hand signals are shown on page 96.

So, you should never be stuck when it comes to improvising some form of signal, no matter where you are.

Semaphore

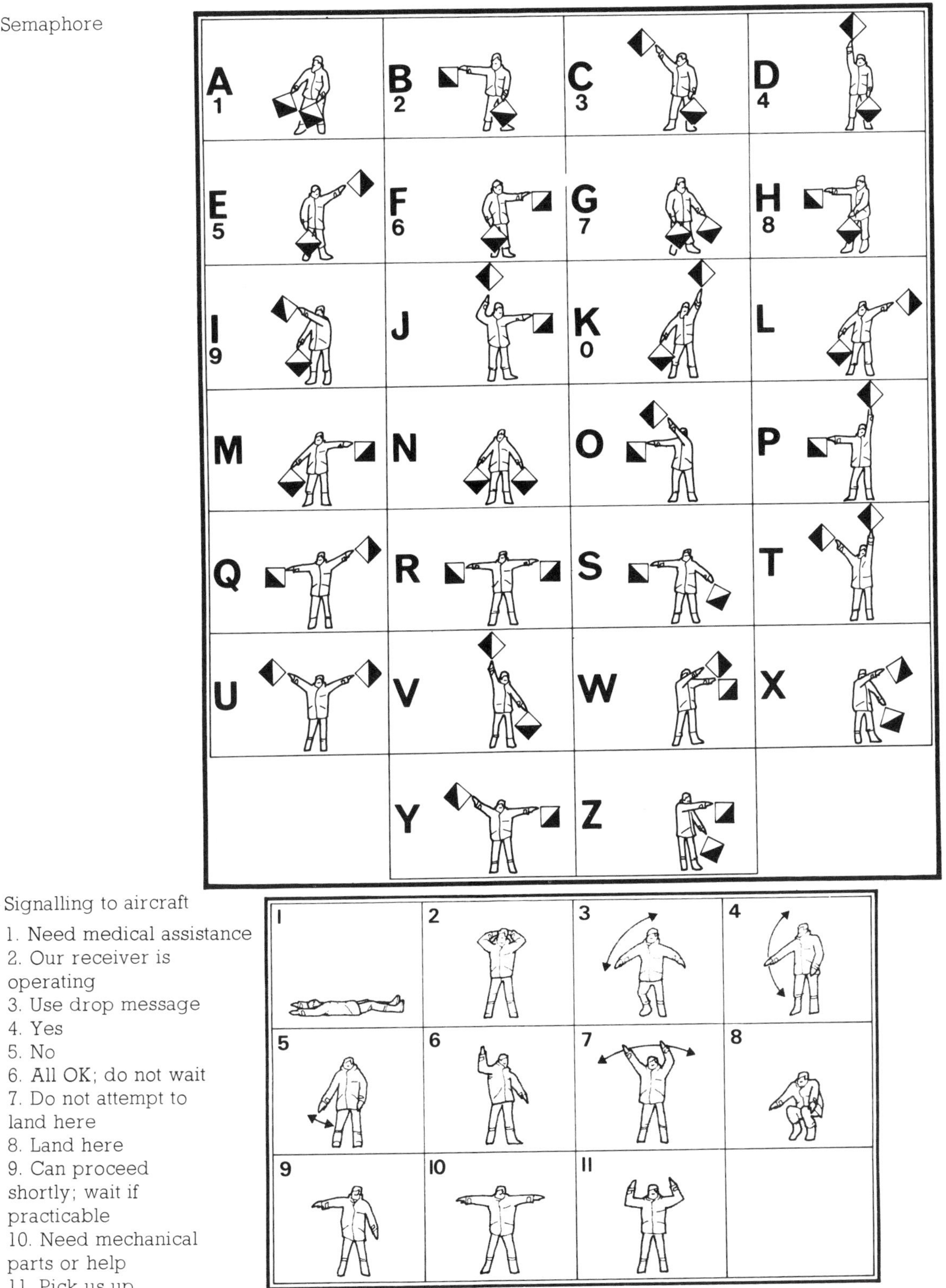

Signalling to aircraft

1. Need medical assistance
2. Our receiver is operating
3. Use drop message
4. Yes
5. No
6. All OK; do not wait
7. Do not attempt to land here
8. Land here
9. Can proceed shortly; wait if practicable
10. Need mechanical parts or help
11. Pick us up

A
B
C
D
E
F
G
H
I
J
K
L
M
N
O
P
Q
R
S
T
U
V
W
X
Y
Z

CHAPTER 10

Personal Safety and Protection

Self defence

Self defence is very much an integral part of survival, and having a basic knowledge can only enhance your chances by making you 'street-wise' and safe. People don't only get attacked and mugged in the streets; in fact statistics show that most attacks happen in the home, hotels, cars, on tube trains and even in cinemas. Wherever the attack happens the rules are the same. Many so-called self defence experts have conflicting ideas as to what you should and shouldn't do when attacked. Women in particular are very vulnerable and are often advised (wrongly I feel), not to take on their attackers. With a little training a woman can easily physically disable her attacker with a well-aimed punch, kick or arm lock. Very often when you do retaliate your attacker is taken completely by surprise and makes a quick exit. If possible try first to walk away from the situation quietly and only retaliate if he puts his hands on you or someone you must protect. The obvious answer is not to let yourself be caught in a self-defence situation in the first place. I know this is easy to say but millions of people have managed to avoid physical danger just by applying common sense.

If someone stops you on the street and threatens you with a knife or gun demanding your purse, give it to him. It's better to lose your purse than risk a beating or worse. You can always get another purse.

Trapped in a house, car etc. different rules must be applied (see *Controlling Fear*, page 104). It may not be possible just to walk away. First, quickly get control of your feelings. If a knife is being held at your throat *do not* struggle. If a gun is being pointed at you *do not* argue or speak until spoken to. If you have to speak, try talking *to* your attacker(s), not *down at* him. Without patronizing enter into a conversation. I know from first hand experience what it's like to face someone threatening you with a gun. Even with all my military and martial arts training I felt scared. Many a person taken hostage has managed to survive simply by keeping calm and non-aggressive.

In the case of a woman threatened with rape, fear, degradation, disgust and distrust will be uppermost in your mind. Remember, after it is over, your helping the police may prevent others from being injured. *Tell the police immediately – don't wait.* But there are a couple of basic survival self-defence ploys you could use should the situation arise.

A technicoloured shirt

Even the thought of someone vomiting all over them makes most people feel queasy, but this is an excellent ploy to use against an attacker if you are trapped in a confined space such as a car or in the seat on a bus or train. In self defence anything goes and pretending to vomit will often give you the breathing space you need to escape, call for help or determine whether to fight back or not.

What to do

If confronted with a gunman, do just as he asks. Talk and move quietly and slowly. Never argue with him; remember, the mere pressing of the trigger and the gun will go off. Don't give him an excuse to shoot you.

The following forms of self defence are appropriate for all other types of standing attack, including the knife attack.

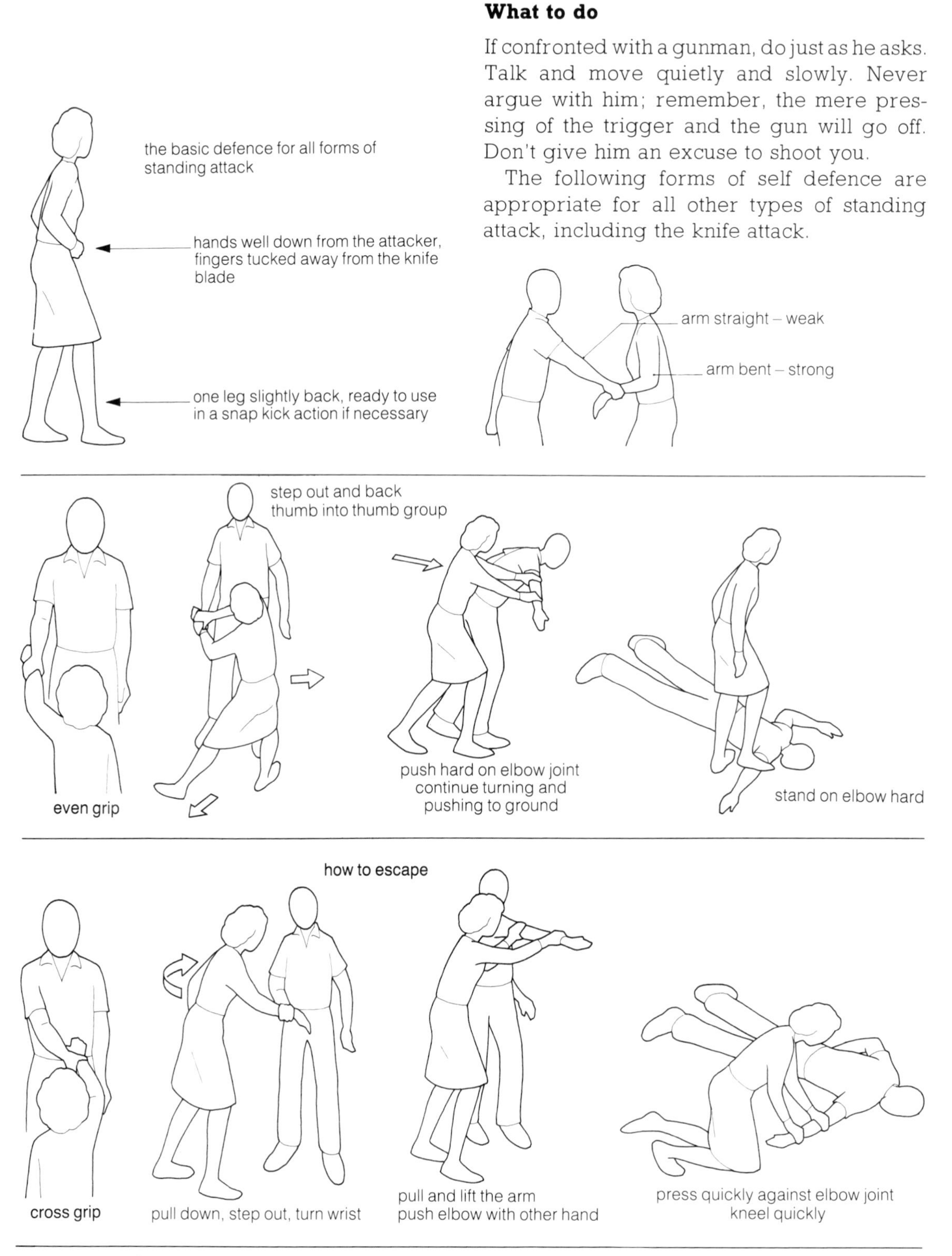

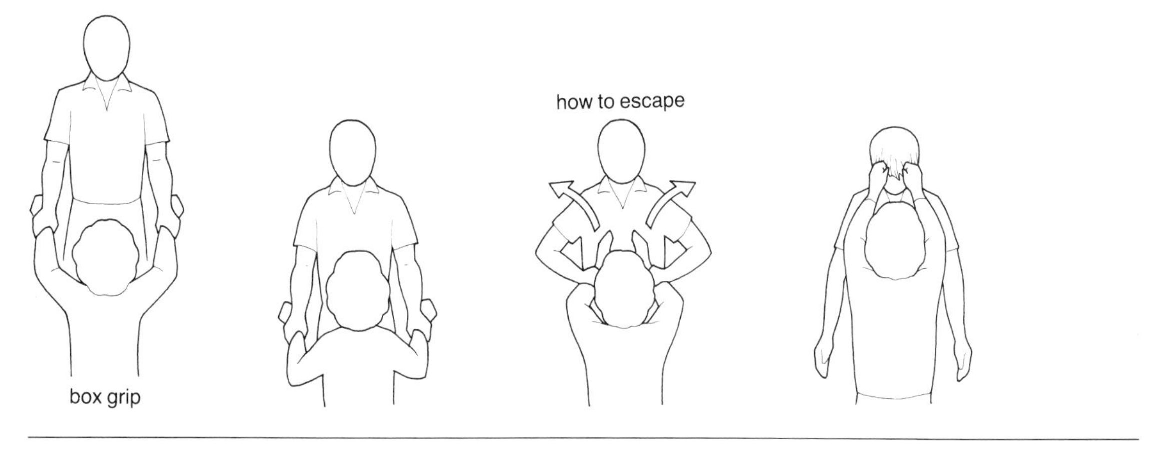

If grabbed from the rear, remember!
HEAD – BOTTOM – FOOT, in that order.

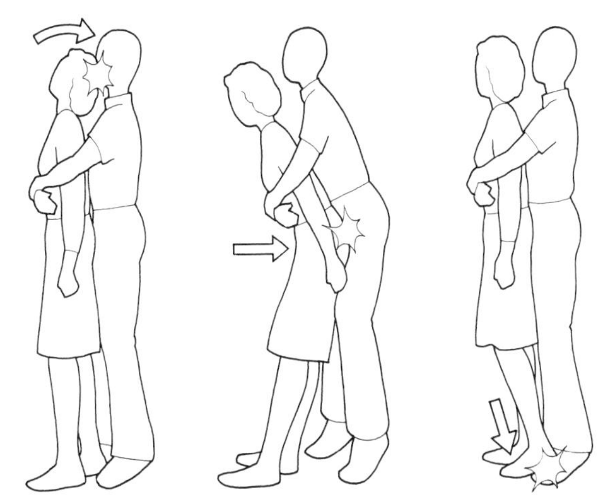

As with any other form of attack, when you are suddenly pounced upon panic will grip you at first, but you will be surprised how quickly it goes. An attack from the rear will have you more panic-stricken than an attack from the front. This, of course, is because you cannot see your assailant. Fight like a wild cat, especially if there is no weapon or stranglehold involved. Never allow him to pull you down to the ground.

Should you be grabbed from the rear and your attacker lifts you off the ground, as with other rear attacks, head hard back first, then simply go for a good, hard running action as quickly as you can, driving your heels into his thighs and shins.

Grip and twist his fingers with one hand while the other hand and elbow can be used to jab and punch him in the groin.

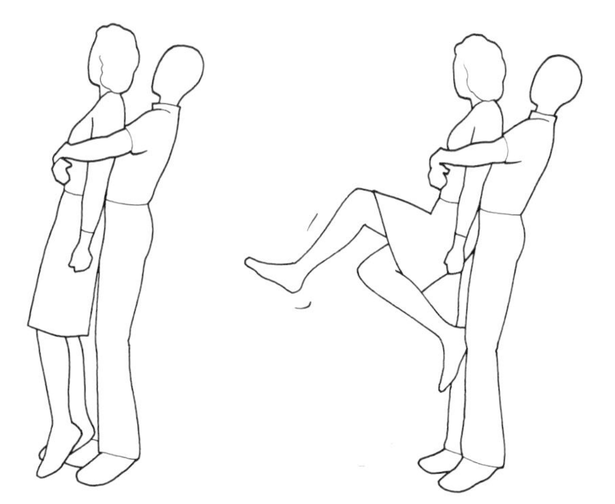

The moment he puts you down on the ground be prepared to run away. A word of caution here: be prepared for him suddenly to drop you, for drop you he will, and quickly, especially if your heels have been driven hard into him.

Self defence against weapons

To tackle anyone who brandishes a weapon at you requires a great deal of courage and appropriate self-defence skills. However, people without any former martial arts training have succeeded in defending themselves quite well and survived. For myself, I always teach the 'softly-softly' rule where possible. Once you decide to take on your attacker you will not only have to remove the weapon threat, but you will almost certainly have to deal with him physically. The choice must be yours. Any weapon held in the hand is an extension, and the longer the weapon, the easier it is to remove from him. How and in what hand he holds the weapon tells you how he intends to use it against you. First get yourself into a basic self-defence stance (see page 98). If it's a knife or club that he intends to use, be prepared for a cut or knock or two.

If the knife is held as in (a) below, the attacker intends to stab downwards. This is a very limited action but a very strong and effective form of attack, nevertheless.

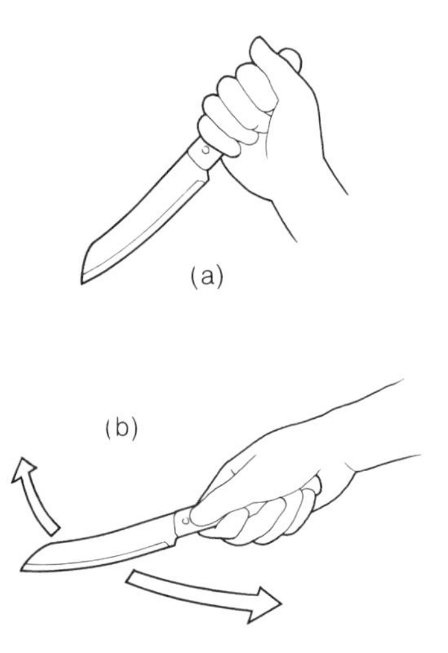

Held as in (b) the knife or other weapon is much more lethal and defence against this form of attack must not be treated casually. Remember to step back, fingers tucked in, hands close to the chest away from the weapon.

Defence against ground attacks

On no account allow yourself to be pulled or pushed to the ground. Fight like hell to remain standing for once down you will find it very difficult to throw off your attacker unless you have had professional training. However, the method shown in the following diagrams has been tried and works. Remember the rules of ground defence. Get onto one hip (never on your back), pivot on the hip, turning quickly to face your attacker kicking and punching.

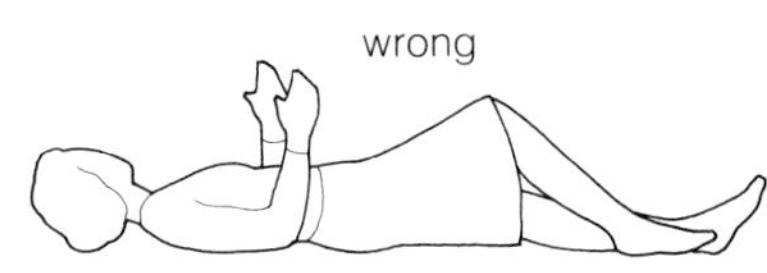

This is very dangerous and awkward for you
Make every effort to get onto your feet as quickly as possible

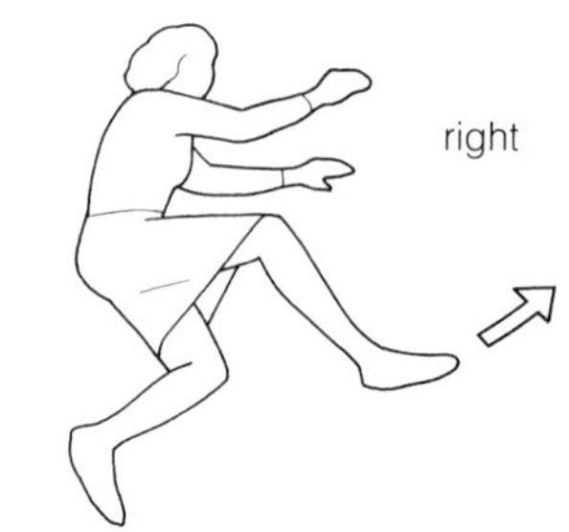

Top leg and arm is used to ward off the attacker

Cross grip thumb hold

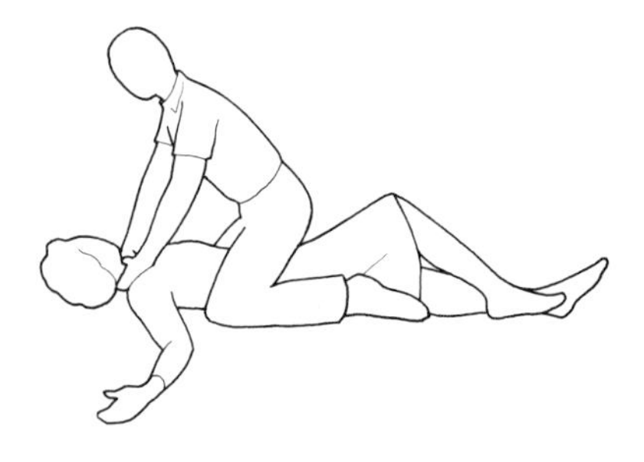

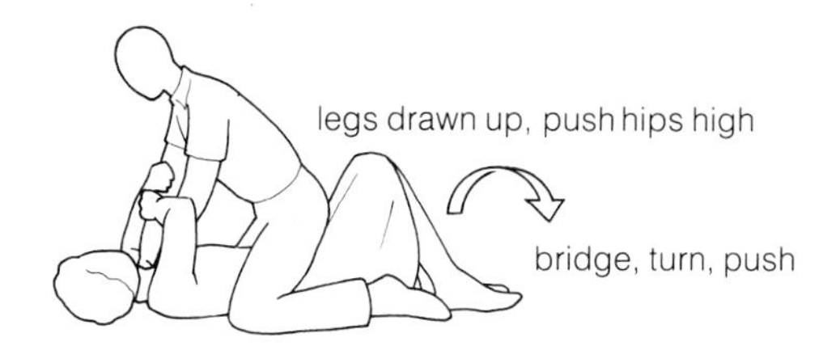

push hands through in prayer action

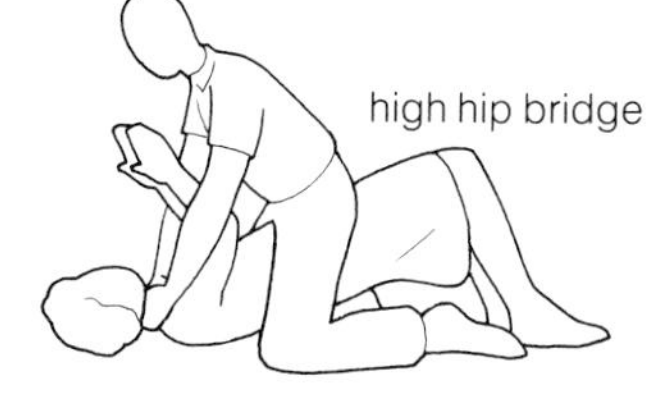

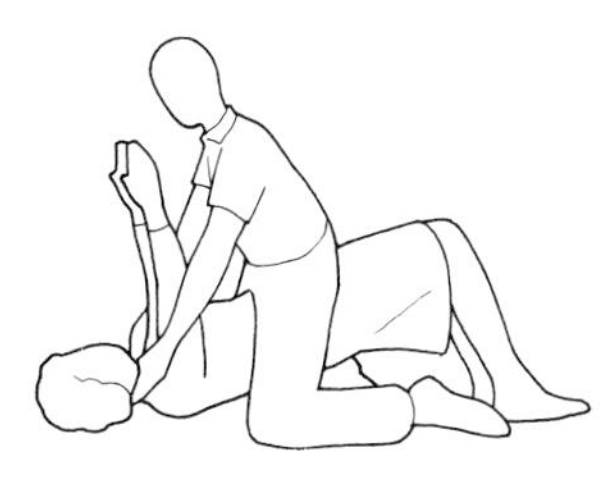

twist and push up hard with your hips
pull down hard on his hair, twisting his head vigorously
keep pushing with your hips and legs

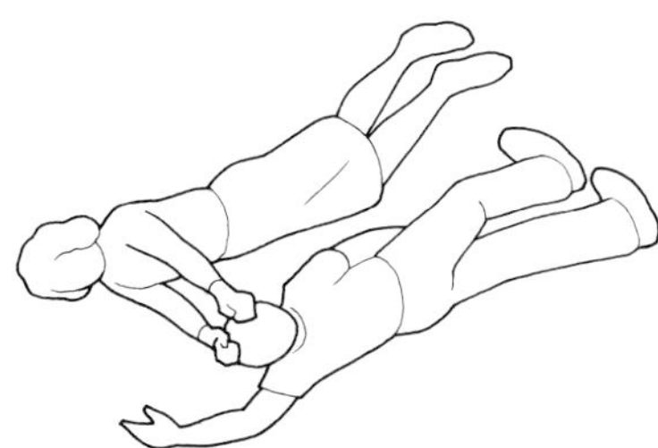

and once you have got him off you, push him away,
then stand up and kick

Kidnap

What should you do if abducted in a car? First, stay calm and quiet. Then use the following guide.

- *Note* how door locks work.
- *Note* where horn and light switch are. Try to get car registration number.
- *Note* number of doors and car colour.
- *Note* which way the window lock moves, and how it slides, presses or locks.
- *Note* how much petrol he has. If there is a clock note the time.
- *Note* colour and state of the car interior.
- Always try to keep your head up if you are being pushed into a car.
- If possible, go into the car backwards or sideways.
- If more than one person is in the car sit directly behind the driver if possible.
- When travelling try to pick out clues as to where they are taking you.
- Take advantage of the *safe area*. Make your break quickly.

Escaping or leaving the car

- Always try to leave the car on the opposite side to your attacker.
- Try to get your attacker to run the longest way around the car.
- Put the car between you and your attacker quickly.
- Try to lock the doors just before you leave.
- Be prepared to jump and roll if necessary if the car stops. Beware of other moving traffic.
- If in any doubt keep hold of the car and move around on the opposite side to the driver. As you move around, close and lock the doors, keeping the car between you. Even if he climbs onto the car, keep close to it and if need be run round it, always making as much noise as possible by shouting and banging on the car.

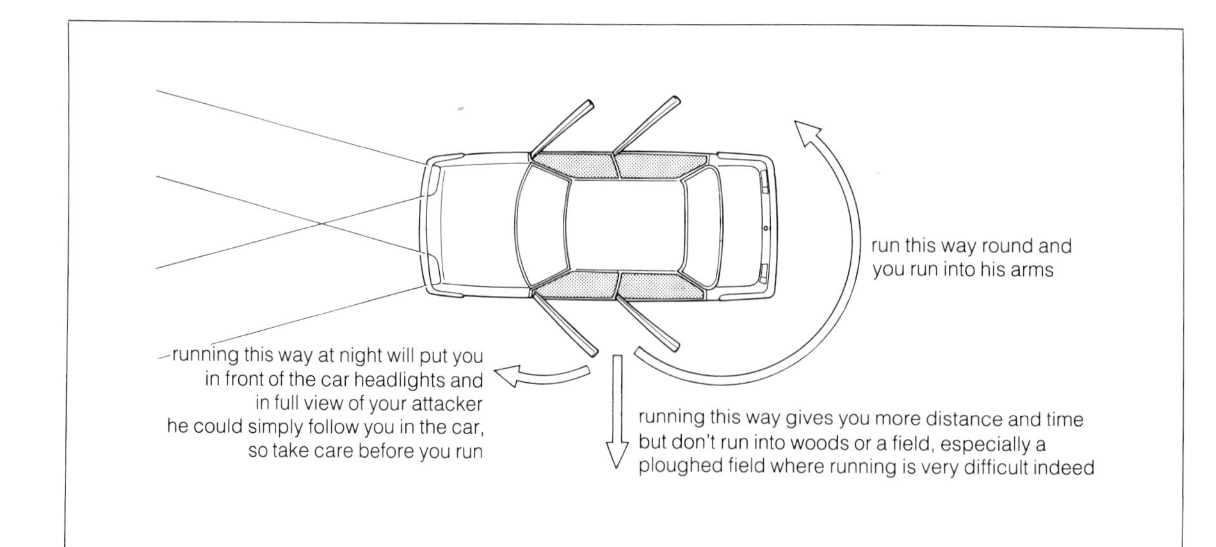

How to escape from being tied up

The following are some safety skills to practise:

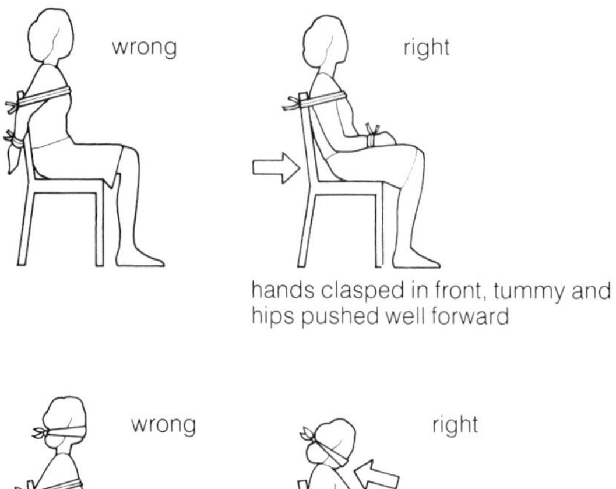

hands clasped in front, tummy and hips pushed well forward

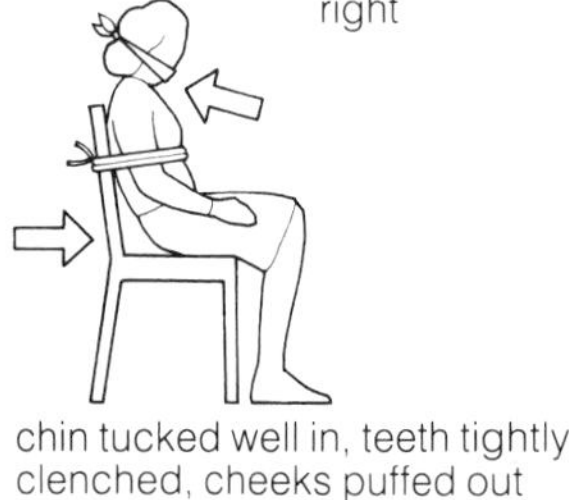

chin tucked well in, teeth tightly clenched, cheeks puffed out

chin tucked well in, hands clasped offset and held high, elbows resting on hips

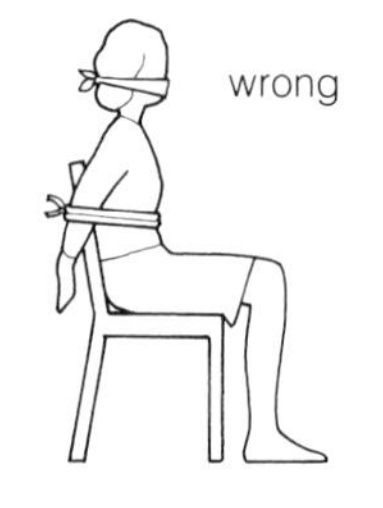

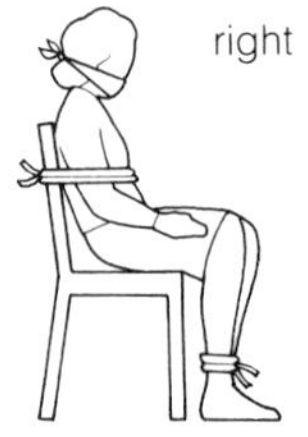

feet offset, legs slightly apart

Escaping from heights

Lowering

Never, never, never jump from a window or indeed any building, wall etc., if there is any chance of lowering first. There would be no point going to such great lengths to escape only to find that you injured yourself because you fell awkwardly. So, look before you leap.

Escaping from a window

Lowering and dropping from heights, although much safer than jumping, still requires a certain amount of skill. Preparation at the window before exit is of the utmost importance. It is well worth the effort and possible frustration to prevent injury to yourself.

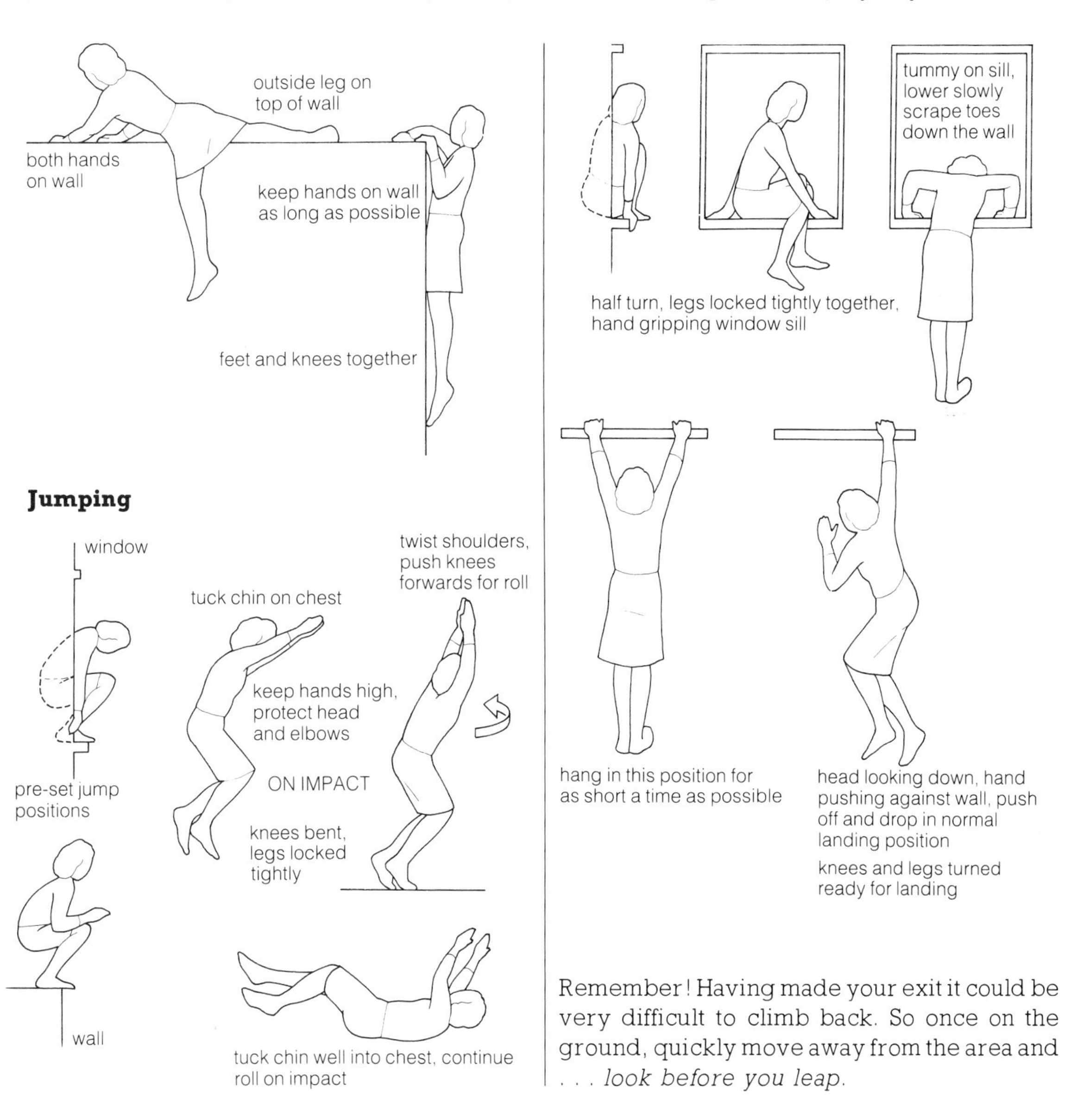

Remember! Having made your exit it could be very difficult to climb back. So once on the ground, quickly move away from the area and . . . *look before you leap.*

Controlling fear

If you are in your own home, or in bed and an intruder enters, keep quiet, calm and don't move. Chances are he is only there for financial gain and unless disturbed will probably never even bother you.

The rule to remember is: *Keep Quiet – Keep Still.*

Remember your observation drills: *smell – sex – colour – age – posture – weight – etc. etc.* To help you control your nerves start counting to yourself slowly. Whatever you do *never* try to take him on physically, even if you have children in other rooms. This is easy to say I know, but you must try for full control. If you're scared of involuntarily calling out, tuck the corner of your sheet into your mouth and bite on this. This is a tried and tested method of avoiding shouting but, as always, the choice is yours and yours alone. Once the intruder has gone, quickly inform the police whilst everything is still fresh in your mind. Write everything down straightaway if you can – even on a mirror with lipstick or felt-tip pen! – so that you can reel off the information as you speak to the police.

CHAPTER 11

Mountains and Moorlands

No need to die

At approximately 8.00 p.m. one October evening in 1980, sixty-five-year-old Mrs Ann Wilkinson had just watched the final episode of her favourite T.V. programme with her pet poodle Benny. Both sat curled up snug and warm in the comfort of her holiday caravan. Outside the evening mist had already begun to drift across the bleak Yorkshire moors.

Mrs Wilkinson rose from her chair, filled the kettle and placed it on the stove ready to make a hot drink. Suddenly she realized that she had forgotten to collect her daily groceries from the local village shop. Fortunately it was only about a mile to the village from the caravan down one of the winding narrow country roads, a road she had travelled many, many times ever since she had been coming for holidays to this spot.

Without thinking she opened the caravan door to peer into the night. As she did so, Benny dashed across to her parked Morris Minor and jumped in through an open window. Earlier that day she had been cleaning the car and had forgotten to close it. On seeing Benny curled up on the back seat, she smiled and climbed into the car. 'Naughty boy,' she scolded him, then drove off, forgetting she had left the kettle on the gas and her coat hung behind the door.

Moments later she arrived at the road junction leading down to the village shop. It wasn't until she had actually arrived at the store that she noticed how cold it was. Already the mist had begun to thicken and a slight drizzle filled the night air. As she put the groceries on the passenger seat she rubbed her bare arms and shoulders to ward off the evening chill. Shivering, she climbed back into the car and made off back to the caravan.

Driving back up the steep winding road through the swirling mist, she had to brake suddenly to avoid hitting a sheep standing right in the middle of the road, oblivious to all around it. As the car came to a sudden halt, all the groceries fell from the passenger seat and clattered to the floor. Amongst the groceries was a bottle of milk and this began to spill out. Mrs Wilkinson saw this, dashed round to the passenger side and in doing so left her own door open. Benny, on hearing the startled sheep, jumped out of the car door and chased after it. She called out to Benny and turned to fetch him back, but in seconds both Benny and the sheep had disappeared into the thickening mist. Mrs Wilkinson ran after him calling his name loudly, but still Benny failed to return.

Stumbling around in the thick bracken and over slippery rocks, Mrs Wilkinson began to feel the cold evening air closing in round her and shivers ran through her body. Suddenly she was overcome by panic. In her desperation to get Benny back she had become separated from the car. Meanwhile the mist had thickened greatly and visibility was now less than a few feet. To make matters worse it had begun to drizzle harder and wearing nothing but a thin dress the chilling mist and rain began to soak the flimsy clothing. Her hair became wet and bedraggled as it fell across her face.

'Benny,' she called, 'Benny, where are you?' her voice weakening with every call. But there was still no answering bark from Benny. Cold, wet and by now completely exhausted, she sat down on a large rock to rest as tears streamed down her cheeks. The cold had now penetrated right through her body and she began to shiver uncontrollably. With constant calling her voice had become nothing more than a croak. Scared, cold and alone, teeth clenched tightly together to try and ease unbearable cold, she lapsed into a deep coma. Half an hour later she was dead. The moors had taken yet another life. Mrs Wilkinson, through a few simple mistakes, became another victim to the silent killer – hypothermia.

Later that evening, as the mist began to drift away, a dull explosion was heard and seconds later a local farmer saw a glow appear in the sky near the vicinity of Mrs Wilkinson's caravan. The farmer immediately called the local police and the fire service. Benny, meanwhile, tired of chasing the sheep and himself exhausted, had returned to the car. Finding the door open he crawled in to rest but not before he had lapped up the remainder of the spilt milk.

When the police arrived they found the car just as Mrs Wilkinson had left it, still with the door open, the headlights on – and Benny fast asleep. An immediate search of the area was carried out and fifteen minutes later they discovered her body still slumped against the rock she had rested on. She was found only twenty metres away from the safety of her car. In her attempt to bring Benny back, she had died.

This case is a classic example of many such deaths that occur every year. Statistically, more people are killed or injured in the mountains and moorlands than in any jungle, desert or arctic region. Even experienced explorers fall victim to hypothermia. It's non-selective and will strike at anyone not properly attired or trained. Weather in the mountains is more unpredictable than anywhere else in the world. In seconds it can change from a warm sunny day to a rainy, wind-driven, silent deadly chill. A not uncommon danger is something called 'white out'. Literally in seconds a freezing snow blizzard can zoom across the mountains enclosing everything and everyone.

Be prepared.

Survival in the mountains and moorlands depends on your ability to prepare for sudden changes. Remember, the **COLD, WIND** and **WET** may creep up on you at any moment. The higher you climb the colder it gets and the greater the possibility of sudden weather change. Be prepared: carry the correct survival equipment and wear the right kind of clothing. Had Mrs Wilkinson simply remembered to wear her coat, she might have survived.

Rough terrain

In mountain and moorland regions you will often find large areas of bracken and forest plantations. As you climb higher the vegetation will begin to thin out until eventually you have nothing but hard, tough grass and rocks, and in higher terrain still, rocks and snow.

Walking on rough terrain such as rocks, marshy ground and hard, clumpy heather will make your legs and feet very tired. If it's possible rest every now and then. The wind chill factor increases the higher you climb so make sure you are fully protected clothing-wise.

In the high moors and mountains, as soon as the sun sets the temperature will drop suddenly, so take care not to be caught out. At sunset you should be resting. Remember, as the body becomes colder so our energy reserves are called upon to keep us going. Without proper food and adequate protection from the cold, wind and wet these energy reserves are quickly used up. High in the hills, even with warm clothing on, if you stand in the wind for just a short while you will quickly notice your body heat falling away.

No matter where you are and in what region, the rules for survival are the same. Improvisation is the key word. Protection from the elements must be considered at all times. Every year thousands of people manage to survive against overwhelming odds simply because they have used their initiative, stayed calm and remembered their survival skills. Only a fool will try to battle it out with the elements without the right clothing, equipment and shelter.

If you find yourself caught out in the hills, trapped in a sudden weather change, STOP. If you have spare clothing, put it on, keep warm and dry and if possible get down out of the wind and look for a natural shelter. Sheep, hardy as they are, can often be seen sheltering under rocks, curled up beneath land overhangs and in hollows. These places tend to be dry and out of the wind. Many times I have found myself in such a situation, so I can tell you from experience that it is possible to survive, if you have the will and determination to do so.

Weather in the hills

A couple of useful tips in reading the weather is to look at the mountains or hills. If you can see quite clearly and the picture ahead is sharp and crisp the air is almost certain to be cold. As the mountains warm up a slight haze or mist will take the sharpness off the picture.

Remember the following:

A. Cloudless sky in the mountains means a dramatic drop in temperature.
B. Cloudy skies may mean rain, hail, sleet and even heavy snow.
C. Lightning can be extremely dangerous. If possible get deep inside a cave, old mine or rail tunnel. Do not sit on your rucksack or shelter under your bicycle. Do not sit beneath a loose tree. If there is nothing to shelter in, sit it out on the side of a grass covered hill, away from anything that could conduct the lightning. A tent is quite safe providing there are no metal poles etc.

Shelters for survival

People who attend courses at my survival centre often say that they learn more about nature in a couple of days than in the years spent studying books. From the moment we go outside I emphasize how nature will provide everything we need in order to survive. If necessary use natural foliage with which to build your shelter. If it is to be just an overnight stop, build only a small shelter; save energy. Decide the next day whether or not you wish to remain where you are. If you do decide to stay you'll have a lot more time to build a safer, warmer shelter for your protection. Don't expect a good night's sleep; chances are that you will get very little, if any, sleep, but at least you'll be alive next morning and that's what survival is all about.

If you have to spend the night out in the hills without overhead protection, it's better to wear your jacket as a blanket rather than keep it on. If the jacket is worn tightly round the body (especially the back) heat from this area will quickly evaporate. Worn as a blanket it will help trap the warmth from your body. Sit crouched, pull your legs close and drape your jacket over your head and shoulders. Water running down a slope will seep through your clothes, so if you have something dry and waterproof to sit on, use it. If you have decided to curl up close to a rock for shelter, take care that when it rains water doesn't settle at the base of the rock, leaving you sitting in a puddle. Also, damp or wet rocks quickly absorb body heat so try not to rest up against them. If you are fortunate enough to be able to find some sticks or branches, use these to ward off the wind. Lean the sticks up against the rock or ridge and cover them with bracken, grass or moss.

Large clumps of moss stripped from the rocks, draped across a couple of sticks and overlapped like slates on a roof make an excellent shelter and if built correctly, a waterproof one. Even if there are no sticks or branches around you can still improvise. Once you've learned the techniques of building a shelter using rope made from grass or bracken you'll feel confident enough to build a shelter anywhere.

If travelling by bicycle a rough shelter can be made simply by leaning it against a tree or rock and covering it with bracken or your cycle cape.

Dry bracken or grass stuffed inside your saddle bag will make an excellent pillow or foot warmer. Most saddle bags are made of plastic and can be used for collecting water. Spokes from your bicycle wheels make very good spear prongs, fish forks, skewers and even needles. Inner tubes make good slings and if cut into strips may be used as a catapult or tourniquet. Brake cables can easily be adapted to make snares and the torch used for signalling. Remember, everything must have a multiple use in a survival situation.

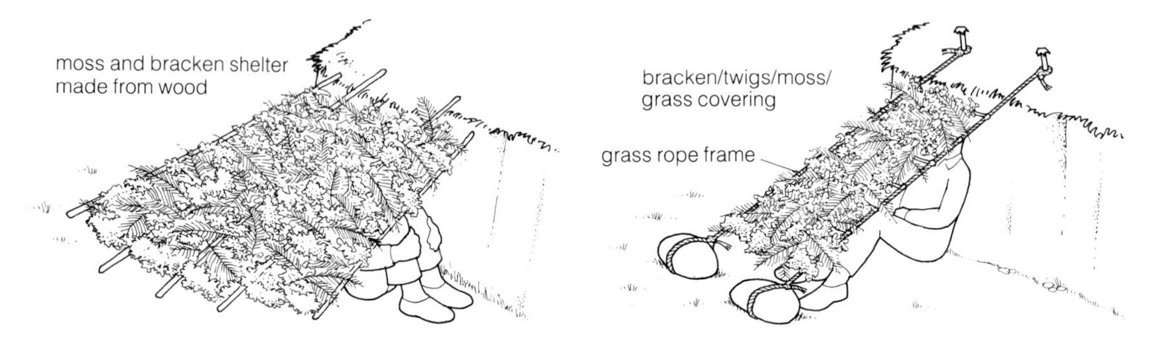

Building a shelter from peat and moss

A very simple, weatherproof shelter can easily be built by stacking dried peat blocks to form a wall. This method of building and the materials have been around for thousands of years and even today you can still find nomadic hill tribesmen building shelters just as their ancestors did. Peat, when allowed to drain off most of its moisture, makes first class building bricks and these, when stacked on top of each other, form a superb weather insulating wall. With lots of moss and marsh reeds placed on the floor, the shelter will be extremely warm and comfortable and a roof of sticks, moss, peat and earth will make it almost waterproof.

Where peat has been removed for industrial use, e.g. as fertilizer or fuel, there will almost certainly be some kind of track to transport it down. If this is the case, it could lead you to safety.

In Australia peat bogs provide home to many species of animals including crocodiles, turtles and large lizards. In Alaska, local people cover themselves in peat mud to help ward off the bites of insects.

Hair washed in gooey peat water takes on a superb shine and softness when rinsed in clear water, and if you suffer from tired feet try soaking them for a while in hot peat water. You will be amazed just how much it relieves them. The water in the peat marsh will almost certainly be dark and will taste very brackish if drunk, but as a last resort it may be drunk without purification.

So you see, even something as basic as moorland bog or peat marsh has its uses! As I have emphasized so many times before in the book, use what is available to help you to survive.

Boggy marshes and quicksand areas

Moorlands and mountains are very likely to have bogs and marshes, so it is inevitable that you will end up with wet feet. If you have to remove your shoes and socks to ease your feet, try to dry them. Remember, the wind will make a much better job of this than the heat of a fire. The latter is much quicker, but very often dries them too much and they end up splitting.

If your feet have been subjected to constant wet, give them a good wipe then a little light massage and finally wrap them in some loose dry clothing. Some water can be got out of your boots by scraping a knife over them, and hot stones placed inside will also dry them. Wherever possible keep your feet warm and dry.

I shall say something in a moment about crossing rivers and the dangers involved. The same applies when crossing boggy marshes and quicksand areas. If possible skirt around them but if you have to cross, try to disperse your weight over the surface. Silly as it sounds, depending on the thickness of the quicksand (or mud) it might be safer actually to try either to swim or crawl across it rather than walk on it. Walking on thick boggy marsh requires a certain skill. Tread only on the thick tufts. If the surface is thick gooey mud and you find it impossible to drag your legs free, rock forwards and backwards to create an air space around your legs. If necessary create the space with your hands or a pole and when ready to move put your hands under your thighs and ease the leg free. It's a slow, laborious way, but very effective. A couple of long poles are invaluable when crossing such an area, and so of course is a rope.

Water trails

As all water flows down to the sea, by following mountain streams you will eventually come to a river – and then to human habitation, whether on mountains and moorlands or following rivers in the jungle. As you descend so the foliage and animal life increase, and so too do your chances of survival. Take care, though, when using tracks alongside the streams and rivers, as many are nothing more than animal trails. Most mountain rescue teams are trained to search close to water, knowing how dependent on it we are.

Crossing rivers and streams

The same rules apply here as when crossing rivers and streams in the jungle. First, select a suitable crossing point, then test the depth and river bed before setting off. Always face upstream so that the force of the water pushes your legs back, locking them at the knees. Move only one foot at a time and try to cross diagonally upstream. *Do not cross in a straight line.* If there are more than one of you, put a safety rope across. If you're carrying a rucksack make sure it can easily be slipped off your shoulder in the event of an accident. When crossing rivers I always make sure that at least one shoulder strap is clear. Use a pole and work your legs and pole in a triangle.

Remember the following rules:

A. Move the pole first to test the river bed, left to right.
B. Next, move the right leg whilst pressing on the pole.
C. Now move the left leg. Do not try to walk. Lift a foot, feel the river bed, put the foot down firmly.

Never dive or jump into water. Lower, probe, test and then cross. Check both up and downstream before finding your crossing position. In cold climates DO NOT REMOVE YOUR BOOTS.

In an area where there is ice: an ice platform can be improvised to get you safely across. To support the average adult it will need to be about 12 in. thick and at least 10 ft. × 6 ft. If you have a rope, tie a weight to one end and throw it across the river into a bush or behind any thick ice and gently pull yourself across letting the flow of the water guide you. Fortunately ice doesn't form on fast-flowing rivers so you should have no problem with currents. The bigger the ice raft, the safer it is. The bigger it is, the slower it becomes. The choice is yours.

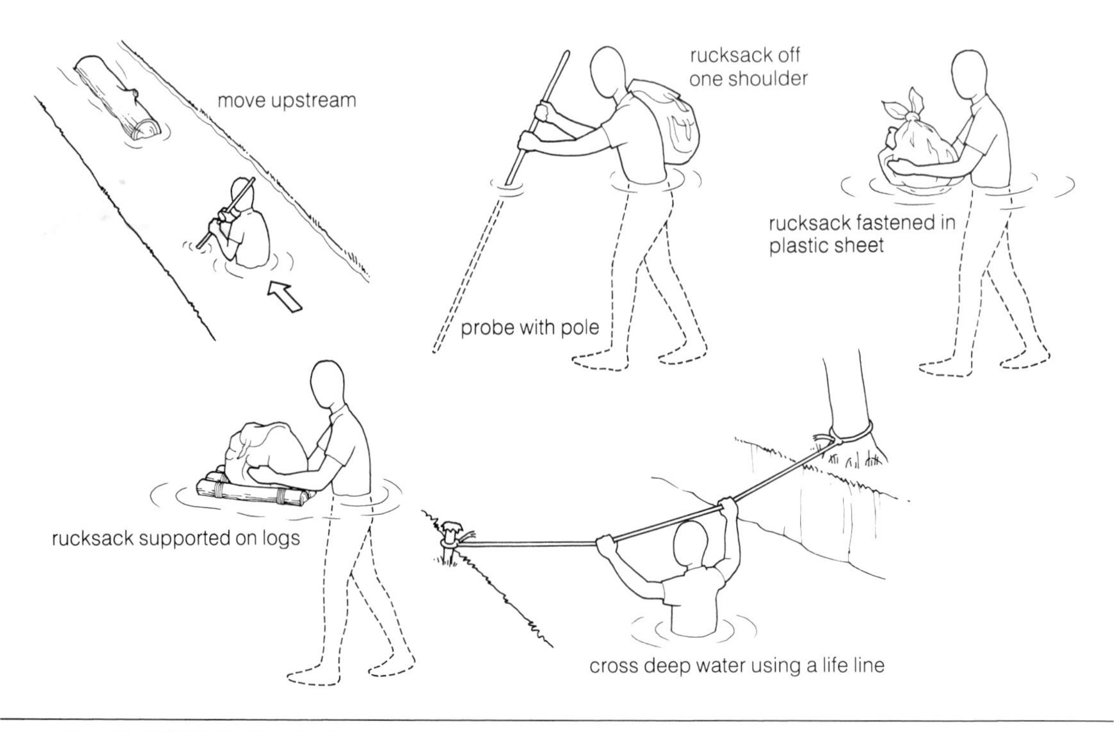

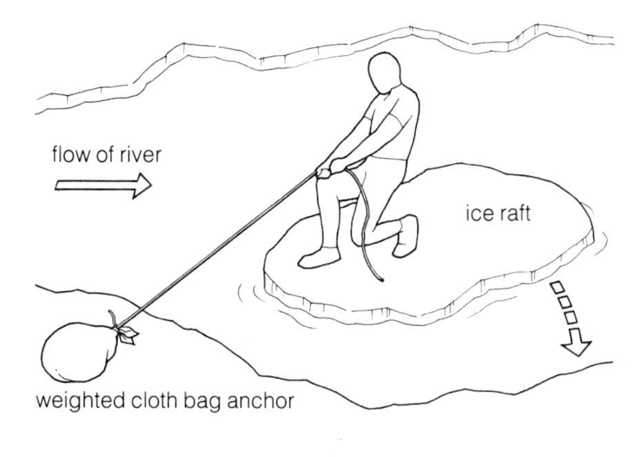

Crossing a river by ice raft

Building an improvised bridge from logs

If it's not possible for you to cross the stream/river by wading or using stepping stones it may be necessary for you to build an improvised bridge. This can be done quite simply by straddling the gap with a couple of stout logs or poles. Providing they reach the other side, to get them safely across without too much effort is not a major engineering task. In fact it can literally be done in a couple of minutes without any help.

First, push one end of a log out approximately halfway across the stream at roughly forty-five degrees to the flow of the river. Then secure the end left on the bank with a couple of stake ties as shown.

Take up the other log and place this over the first. Push it out across the water until it engages the far bank. Lift off the log and square it up.

Now release the first log from the stake ties, lift one end up and place this onto the one straddling the water. Push it along until it also rests firmly on the opposite bank. Then lift it off and place it alongside the other log. All that remains is for you to fasten the two logs together firmly and you have your instant bridge.

A similar bridge may be built to cross rivers in the jungle, and if you need to, you can easily build yourself a safety rail or simply fasten a rope across for support.

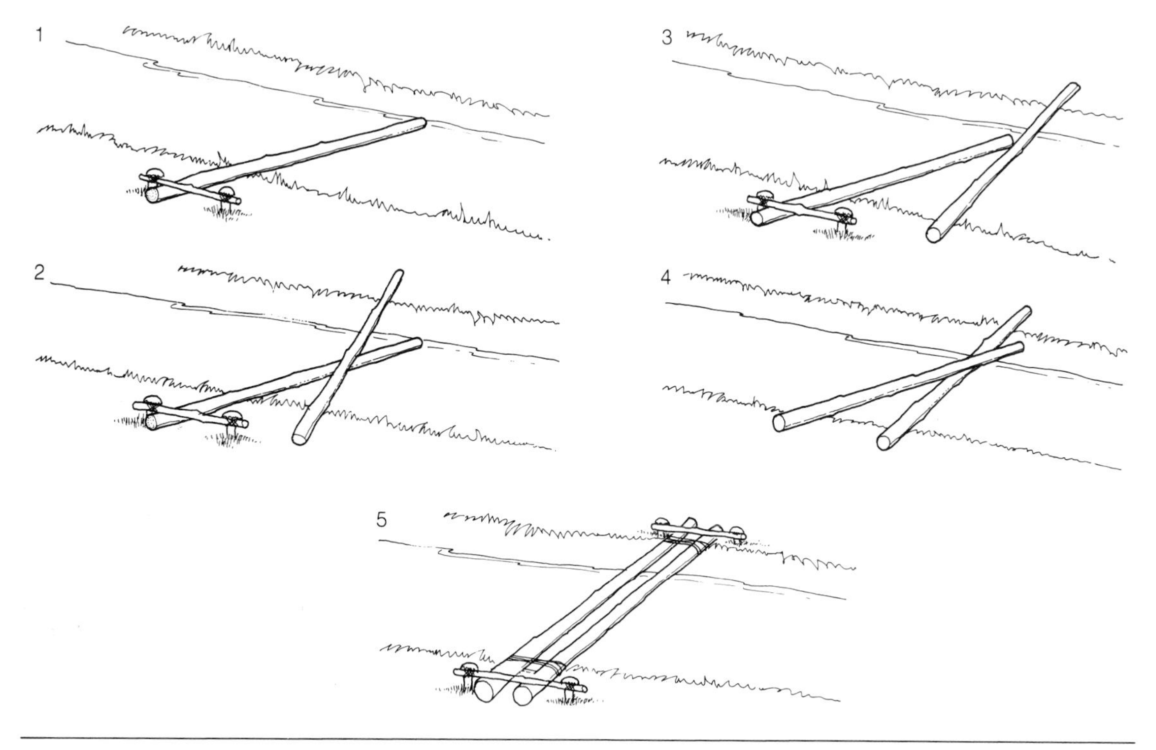

Traversing (zigzagging)

Staying alive in the mountains and moorlands requires just that little bit extra from your survival training reserves. Knowing how quickly the terrain can change in just a few metres and how rapidly the weather can deteriorate draws upon your mental and physical stamina. One minute you can be making good time walking along a trail on firm ground and the next you could be up to your knees in a bog or marsh. For this reason some experts claim it is both wiser and safer to traverse the high ground as much as possible. Others say keep off the high ground and exposed regions, and use the lower trails, making use of the terrain and natural shelters. Each method has its own merits.

For rapid travel, once up high stay high and come down only if the weather and terrain demand it. On the lower slopes it can be very tiring and time-consuming walking continuously up and down hills. Providing you have the right clothing and equipment and move sensibly you shouldn't come in for too much trouble. Of course it would be nice to be able to cross as the crow flies, but you can't without wings, so a little upping and downing is a must, I'm afraid.

Changing the angle of your walk – leaning forwards to climb, walking on the edges of your feet to traverse a steep hill or leaning backwards to avoid toppling over on a steep descent – can and does cause havoc with your body, especially your poor old feet and legs. Many people who have to live in mountainous regions quickly develop a method of conserving energy and walk great distances in unison with the terrain. In other words, they simply stroll along casually as modern ramblers do.

When they want to climb a particularly steep section they simply zigzag up the hill following old sheep or deer trails. It takes a little longer to reach the top, but it's far less exhausting.

Where the moorlands or mountains have been taken over by humans you will come across many trails, stone walls, fences, hedges etc. Use these to help guide you to safety. The wider the trail, the more it's in use.

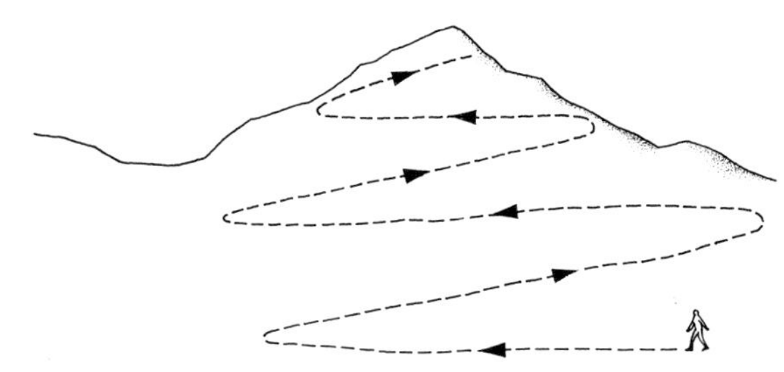

Zigzag up a hill following animal trails

Stone walls tend to run in straight lines and apart from giving obvious protection from the weather they can indicate a way down. For instance, very few stone walls actually go right up to the summit of the mountain: most stop halfway. All stone walls join others. Use these junctions to rest and re-orientate. If it's foggy and you come across a wall, simply follow it to get down. Keep the wall constantly on either your left or right shoulder as you descend; this way you will know whether you're climbing back up or not. If you find you are walking in a circle, mark and cross over the wall, change shoulders and continue downward.

Improvisation with a plastic bag

Because I live on the edge of the famous, bleak Yorkshire moors a lot of my teaching is carried out there. Very often I ask my students to improvise with anything to hand, and more than once one of them has picked up an old plastic fertilizer bag. It never ceases to amaze

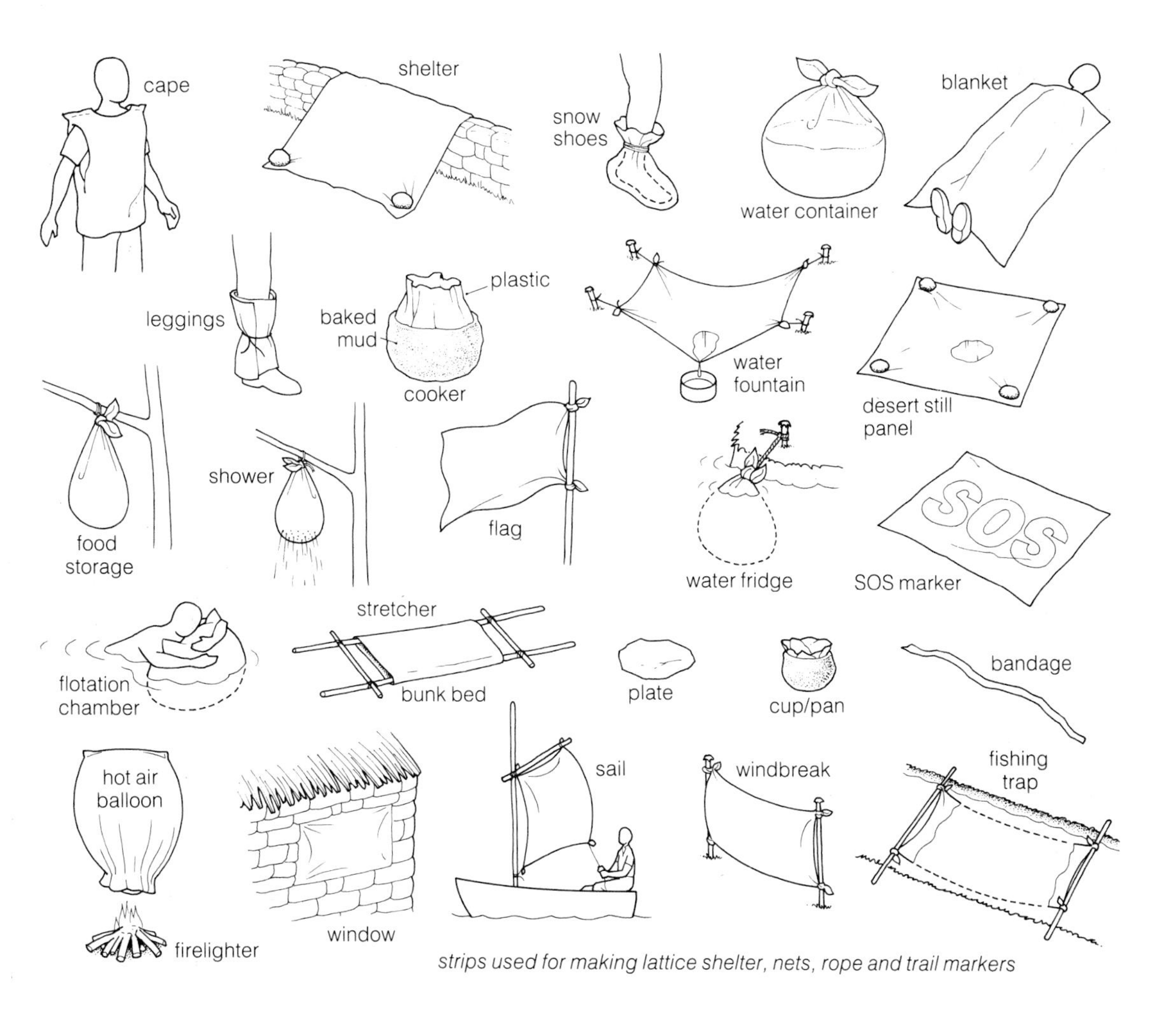

strips used for making lattice shelter, nets, rope and trail markers

me what they come up with. Above are but a few uses for the plastic bag.

Anything with which you can improvise to aid your comfort you must use; only a fool stays uncomfortable. Plastic bags tied to the feet help keep out much of the wet and equally a piece of plastic sheeting draped across the shoulders will ward off most of the damp. An old plastic fertilizer or waste bag may also easily be improvised as a pillow or even a mattress.

Finally, remember! The higher you climb, the colder it gets. Foliage is sparse and protection is practically nil. If you're fit enough, use the highest of terrain to cross the country or signal. For a good night's sleep and safety seek out a shelter early. Any sign of nausea, vomiting, loss of energy or drowsiness and you are probably suffering from either hypothermia or altitude sickness.

Cure: get down off the high ground. Get WARM and DRY!

CHAPTER 12

The Jungle

Jungles, or tropical rain forests as they are more properly known, are to be found within the world's natural green belt known as the 'tropical zone'. This is a wide, lush belt circling the earth, stretching from the northernmost regions of the Tropic of Cancer to the southernmost limits of the Tropic of Capricorn. Halfway between these two lines lies the equator, and it's more or less along the equator that the world's jungles or rain forests are to be found. To most westerners the image of the jungle is a vast, hot, steamy, humid forest, crawling with poisonous snakes, crocodiles, man-eating animals and impenetrable thorns, bushes and vines. Let me assure you that nothing could be further from the truth. Of course there are wild animals and it can be hot and humid. There are also poisonous snakes, crocodiles and areas infested with swamps and disease-carrying insects, but fortunately these areas are very few. The chances of seeing any of the large animals, let alone being eaten by them, are very remote, unless you go looking for them.

I have had considerable experience living in the jungle and tracking animals. When I took part in the Zaire Expedition in 1975 I spent some time 'living' with the Pygmies in the tropical rain forests there. These forests are incredibly dense and dark. I saw virtually no signs of wildlife apart from a couple of rats and one or two birds. At one stage, after I had been out hunting with my hosts, I hadn't been able to spot any animals of the region because I was unfamiliar with the habitat. However, once my hosts began pointing out where the animals and birds were I quickly learned the way of the forest and then I began to see what had been there all the time.

Rain forests need a constant supply of water and heat in order to flourish. Given the frequent tropical rain storms and the regular sunshine, it is usually only man who puts a halt to the rapid growth of jungle territory. The fast vegetation growth in turn creates hot air and humidity, and the humidity speeds up the decay of dead vegetation. In turn this provides the jungle with its own source of natural fertilizer. All of these actions working in harmony cause jungle vegetation to grow extraordinarily fast.

It would be true to say that some regions *are* very inhospitable to man. There are jungle areas in which, even with an abundance of animal and plant life, the chances of survival are pretty slim. Mangrove swamps for example, found flourishing along the equator, are very difficult to live in. Yet, there are people who can, and do live there.

One thing that virtually all jungles and rain forests have in common is an abundance of lush green foliage. You will find every shade of green imaginable. To the survivor this foliage will provide an unlimited supply of shelter-building materials. Whereas in the desert we had to guard against the intense heat of the day and against the bitter cold of the evening, the temperature in the jungle tends to remain pretty stable. It does get cold at night, but nowhere near as cold as in the desert. Elementary science can explain this. In the desert there is very little, if any, cloud and the evenings are usually completely clear. Without cloud cover to hold in the heat it

The Amazon jungle – the tallest trees reach 130 feet

Note the trailing lianas, invaluable to the survivor

quickly dissipates. In the jungle it's just the reverse. The thick canopy of trees holds in the heat so jungles are permanently bathed in mist caused by the constant combination of warmth and humidity. What hot air does escape meets up with the clouds above and simply falls back down into the jungle as rain.

However, having said this, what we gained on the swings we now lose on the roundabouts. Instead of the freezing temperatures we have almost nightly rainfalls to contend with, and these can be just as energy-draining as the cold in the desert. When the body is cold it burns up energy to keep us alive. When the body is cold *and* wet it burns up energy even more quickly. Remember the three environmental killers:

COLD . . . WIND . . . WET.

Because of the denseness of the jungle, when storms blow they don't penetrate the foliage, so the chances of your shelter being blown away are very remote. Even so, the mildest of breezes which do penetrate will increase the body chill factor so it's very important to try and keep as dry as possible.

In the desert during the day one tries to get off the ground so that cool air can circulate beneath. In the jungle where the ground is always damp and wet it is imperative to build your shelter off the ground for both day and night comfort. Not only is the ground damp, but also very much alive with insects, snakes and rodents. (For improvised 'off the ground' shelters, see pages 128–9.) The first thing you have to do is look for somewhere suitable to build your shelter, and then something suitable to build it with. Because the sun very rarely penetrates to the jungle floor, most of the material lying around will invariably be old and rotten.

Basically jungle foliage can be divided into three sections. The upper layer, consisting of very tall trees with thick interlocking foliage, is called primary jungle. These trees, often standing some 130 feet high, will usually have taken up to 100 years to grow. Then you have secondary jungle. These smaller trees, about 80–100 feet in height, also form a canopy over the jungle floor. Finally closer to the ground you have shrubs, palms, ferns and so on, with herbaceous plants, mosses and fungi. Linking all three are vines and creepers, and the combination creates the density of the jungle and its dark, forbidding gloom (see photographs on page 115).

Experts tell us that about a fifth of normal sunlight manages to break through this thick umbrella. However, when it does manage to penetrate, plant life flourishes and can be a pleasure to behold. It can provide ample food as well as material for shelter.

The abundance of vines and creepers in all jungles deserves special note. In South America they are called *lianas*. These attach themselves to a host tree and wind their way right up to the top of the canopy one hundred feet off the ground, and then send off shoots back down to the ground. This same action is then repeated on most other trees. As a result, when you enter into the denser parts of the jungle, you will see hundreds of vines hanging down like cables. Some of them are exceptionally strong and will easily bear the weight of three or more men using them as ladders.

The thinner ones can be woven to make rope bridges, and the much thinner ones can be used as string or rope. They can also provide fresh cool drinks. When cut into, a sweet-tasting liquid drips from them and many survivors have lived off this. To the jungle dweller these vines or lianas are the truest of friends.

The jungle tap

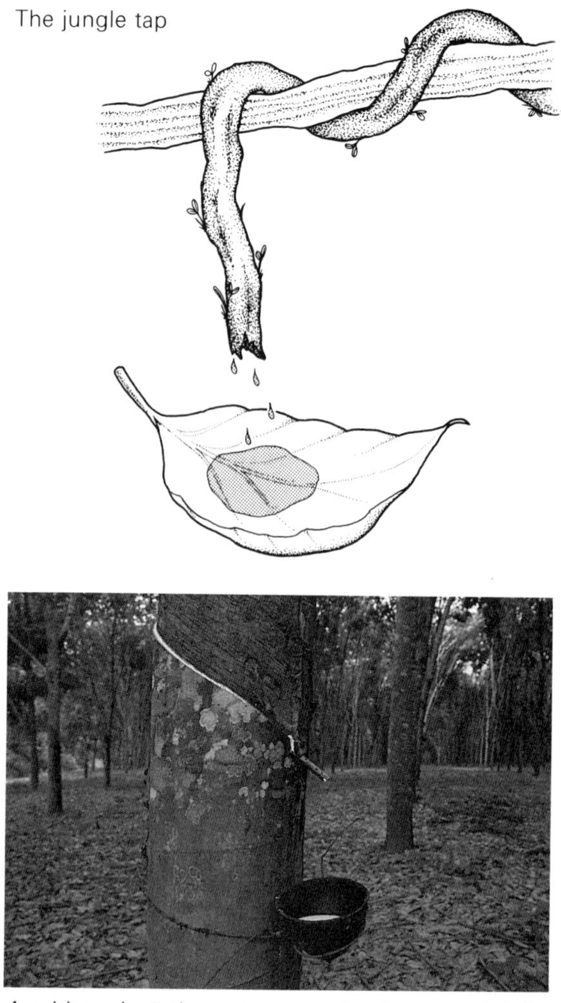

A rubber plantation – trees need to be tapped daily

However, they can also be a hazard. Where they have taken a very strong hold, so many may hang down that they form an almost impenetrable wall and walking amongst them can be virtually impossible. Because they are so strong, hacking your way through is particularly exhausting.

If you arrived in a jungle on foot, with any luck you will have maps and a compass to identify your direction of travel. As you move around look carefully for any evidence of cultivation: rubber or tea plantations for example. These indicate the likelihood of human habitation – as will plantations of coconut

Cultivated coconut palms

palms. Rubber trees need to be tapped daily so people may not be too far away. As you make your way through the jungle be sure to leave well-marked trails and don't forget: if you have crash-landed, always check yourself first before you set off and treat any injuries you may have immediately. In tropical areas infection can set in very easily and a few minutes taken before you move off will be time well spent.

Junglecraft

Before looking at specific types of shelter we should consider basic junglecraft – the shelter only differs from other forms of construction because of the different materials that are likely to be at your disposal, notably bamboo and vines or creepers. Even a sketchy knowledge of knots and lashings will enable you to construct a basic shelter from what's lying around. A bonus, of course, would be to have some string with you to fasten your shelter together. Fortunately there are plenty of vines and other materials available that will do equally well.

How to make rope

The ability to produce improvised rope from natural materials is a must for any survivor and rope, twine or string will become an essential part of your survival kit.

In the tropics and areas where there is abundant green vegetation there are always useful materials to hand: vines, lianas, roots, tree bark, grasses, reeds, nettles, brambles and ferns etc. The list is endless. Even the husk from ripe coconuts, the outer bark from banana trees, bamboo and the bark of the bread fruit tree all provide excellent fibres for rope-making. The fibres of the banana tree

Corn fibres are ideal for making rope

are strong and thin enough to be used for fishing nets. Vine or fern stems are usually completely water resistant and no matter what material you use the process of making rope is the same. For instance, a grass rope is very easy to make and if plaited correctly is exceptionally strong.

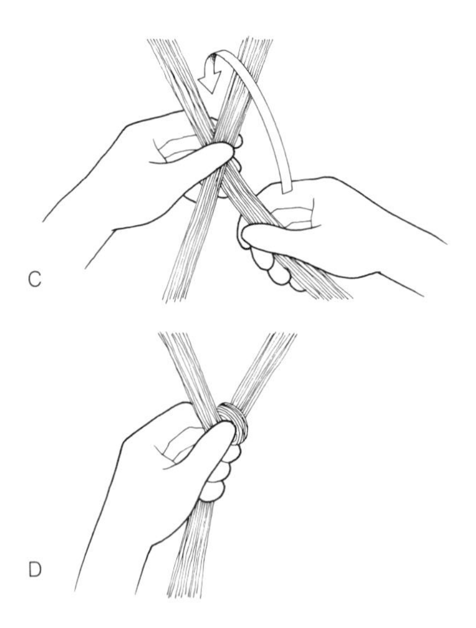

Grass rope

Gather a large handful of the longest grass you can find.

A Take hold of equal amounts of grass in each hand, holding them between your thumb and fingers.

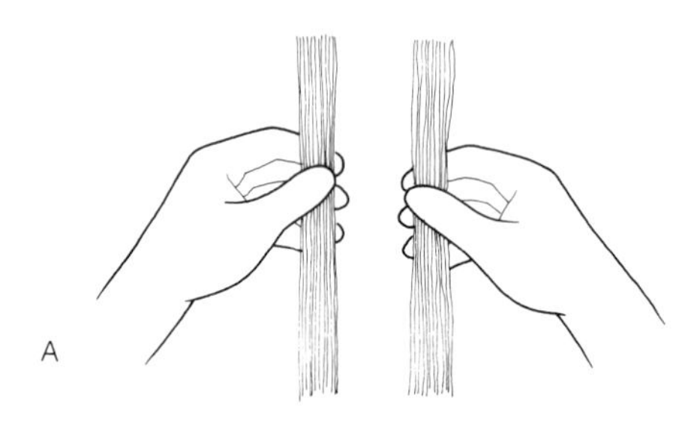

B Place the right hand bunch of grass across and behind the left, forming a cross. Hold the centre of the cross in your left hand between the thumb and finger.

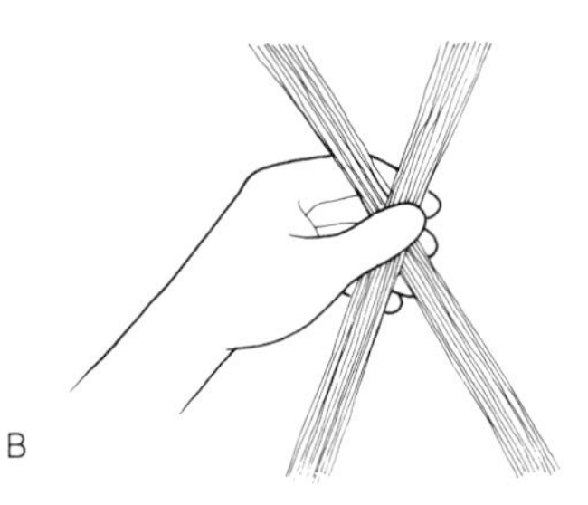

C and D Take hold of the bottom right-hand section and pass this over and through the centre of the cross and hold it with the forefinger and middle finger of the left hand. Hold both bottom sections as if holding a catapult.

E Place your right hand on your left wrist and slide it forwards until you can take hold of the right hand section of the grass as shown. This means you are holding the grass at the best angle to make a good tight rope.

Now twist the grass away from the body as indicated by the arrow.

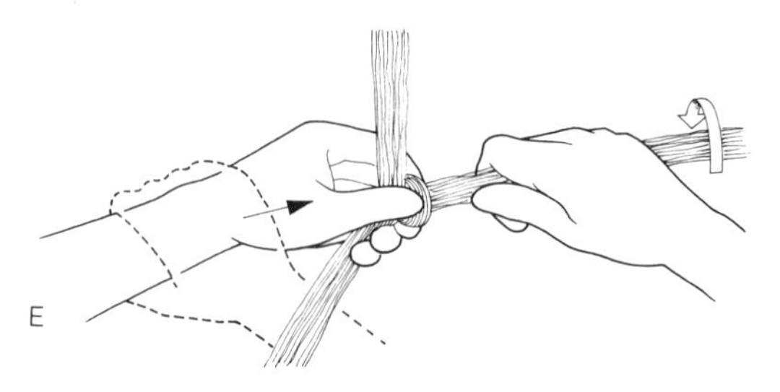

F Keeping the twists taut place the rope between the left forefinger and middle finger, holding it tight. Now repeat the movements of diagram E with the left hand section of grass and replace the twists held between your fingers.

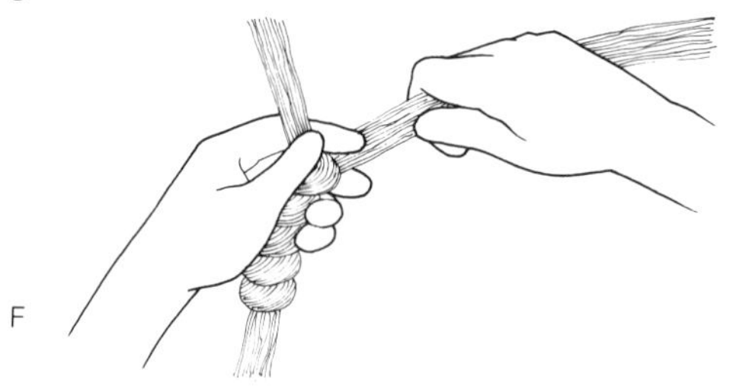

G Continue with this plaiting until you begin to run short of grass. You will now see that the grass rope is beginning to appear. You can let go of the catapult stem. This is the crown knot and won't come undone. All that is needed now is to add further grass to make the rope longer and this is simply a repeat of C. Twist in the grass as explained and you can make the rope as long as you wish.

In the beginning whilst learning how to make your rope use strong, long, fresh, supple grass – about a dozen strands in each hand to begin with. When it comes to adding more grass to make the rope longer, remember to limit yourself to the same amounts, otherwise the rope will get thicker and thicker and then you'll not be able to hold it. Remember, to stop the rope unravelling it is important to keep the tension on the twists as you place them between your fingers. When I am teaching grass rope making it normally takes about two minutes for the students to grasp the technique. An excellent way to practise and educate your friends is to use two-inch-wide strips of cloth. This way you will be able to see your rope appearing quicker, and without much fuss.

Knots and lashings

A survival skill you can practise easily in the comfort of your own home is how to tie knots and lashings. There's no point in being able to make rope from grass and other materials if you don't know how to use it. You never know when you may quickly have to lash some things tightly together.

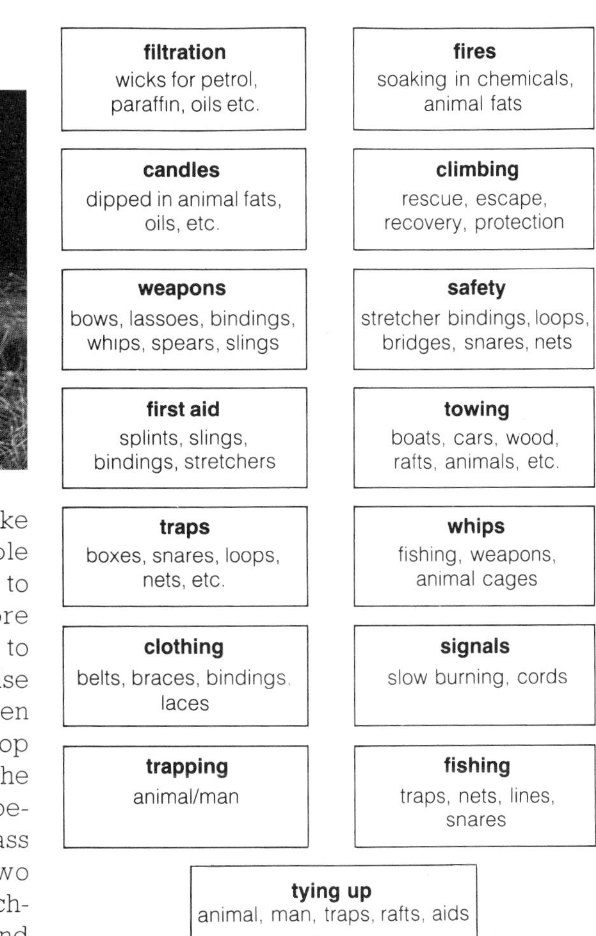

Just as with everything else in the survival world, knots and lashings have multiple uses. Apart from the obvious use, i.e. fastening things together, a knotted rope makes a very good escape ladder to climb up or down and even when crossing a fast-flowing stream by rope a few well-placed knots ease the ache in cold, wet hands.

Those of you who were scouts or guides have a head start, but for those who have never even bothered to learn about knots and lashes, now is the time. Probably the simplest to learn is the *granny knot*, similar to the *reef knot*, a knot used for joining two equal thicknesses of rope together. The former, under pressure, will come undone but will be almost impossible to untie, especially if your hands are cold and wet, and you *have* to untie a knot in an emergency. The latter will not come undone under pressure and nor will it tighten to the extent that it cannot be unfastened.

The bowline knot is used for tying to a belay point – fastening yourself to a rock or tree or something equally solid.

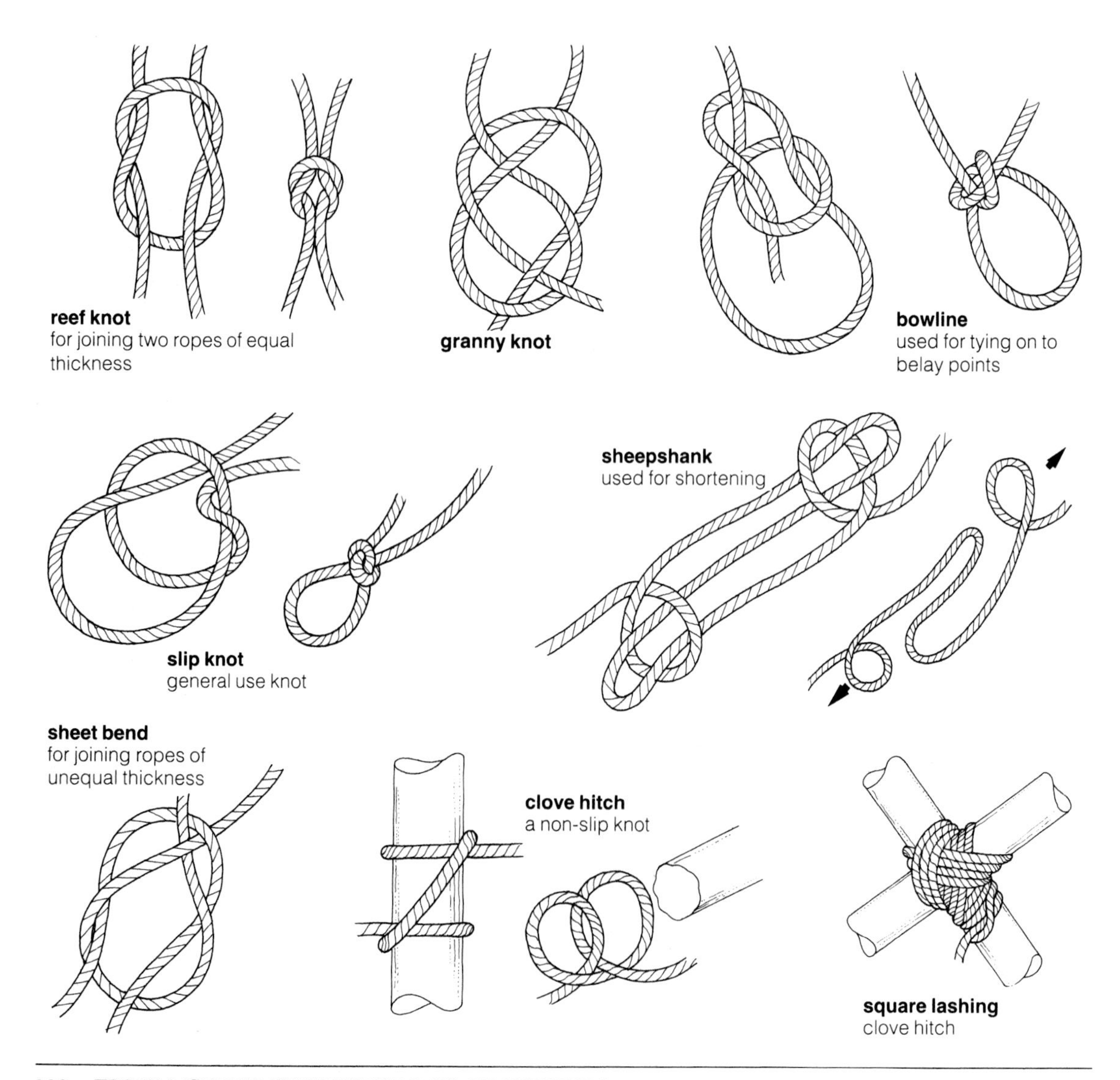

Rope stretchers

A stretcher can be made quite easily from a long rope, in such a way that it can be carried by four people or slung beneath a rescue helicopter and even suspended from another rope when lowering the patient.

There are many variations but the one I've chosen is probably the safest and simplest. It is called the *Alpine basket.*

Firstly the rope needs running out in a straight line and a loop tied at one end to support the feet.

The second stage is to form the rope into a series of 'S'-shaped loops.

Next the patient is placed onto the loops and the foot loop secured around the feet.

Leaving the arms free the loops are then drawn across the body and laced up with the remaining rope, ending with a harness preferably gathered in the centre of the chest.

The Alpine basket

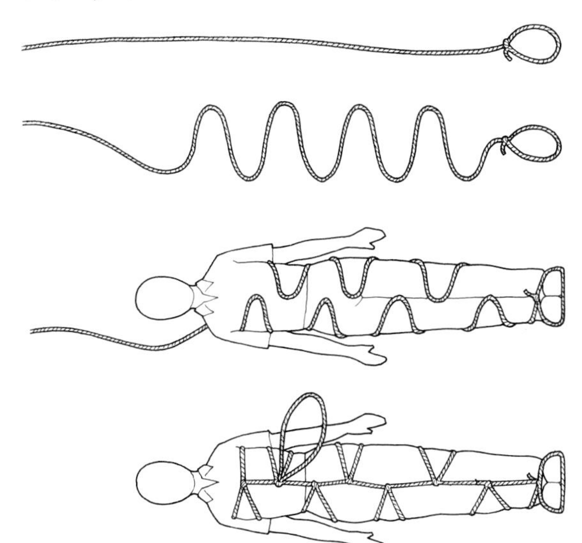

Spinning wool

Clothes may be made simply by spinning the fur of an animal, or flax or cotton, on a dolly spinner. This is nothing more than a thin piece of stick with a dried blob of clay fastened to the bottom.

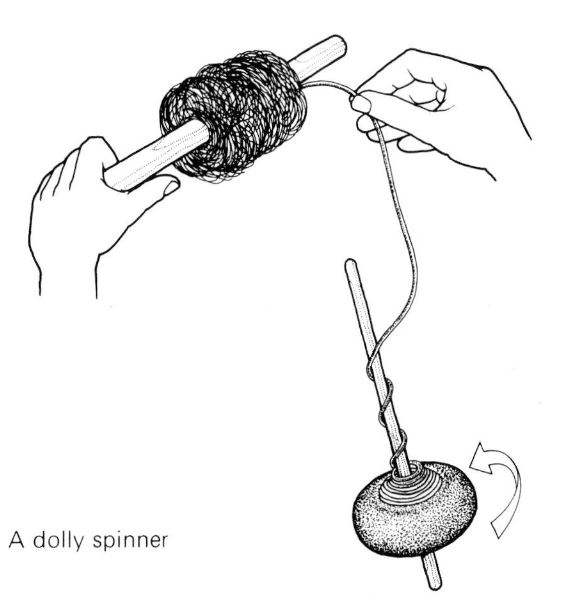

A dolly spinner

The fur or wool is held by the left hand around a bit of wood (above). Fibres are then pulled out from the wool and twisted around the dolly spinner. A gentle spin of the dolly will twist and wind the wool onto the shaft as you gently continue easing more wool from the lot held beneath the left arm. As the dolly spins the strands of wool form. When you have sufficient on the spinner remove it and wind it into a ball.

Bamboo

Because of the likelihood of your finding bamboo and because of its usefulness, let's look at some of the ways it can be adapted. It's worth remembering that bamboo shoots are edible and that the leaves may be boiled to make them edible too. The base of the green bamboo, once the hard outer skin has been removed, may also be cooked and eaten. The roots may also be boiled and used for food but they need to be cooked several times and the water changed each time, otherwise they will taste very earthy.

Hollowed-out sections of bamboo may be used for cooking vessels as well as more obvious things such as water-storage, but always be careful when you work with bamboo because the outer skin may be very

A bamboo plantation

Green bamboo

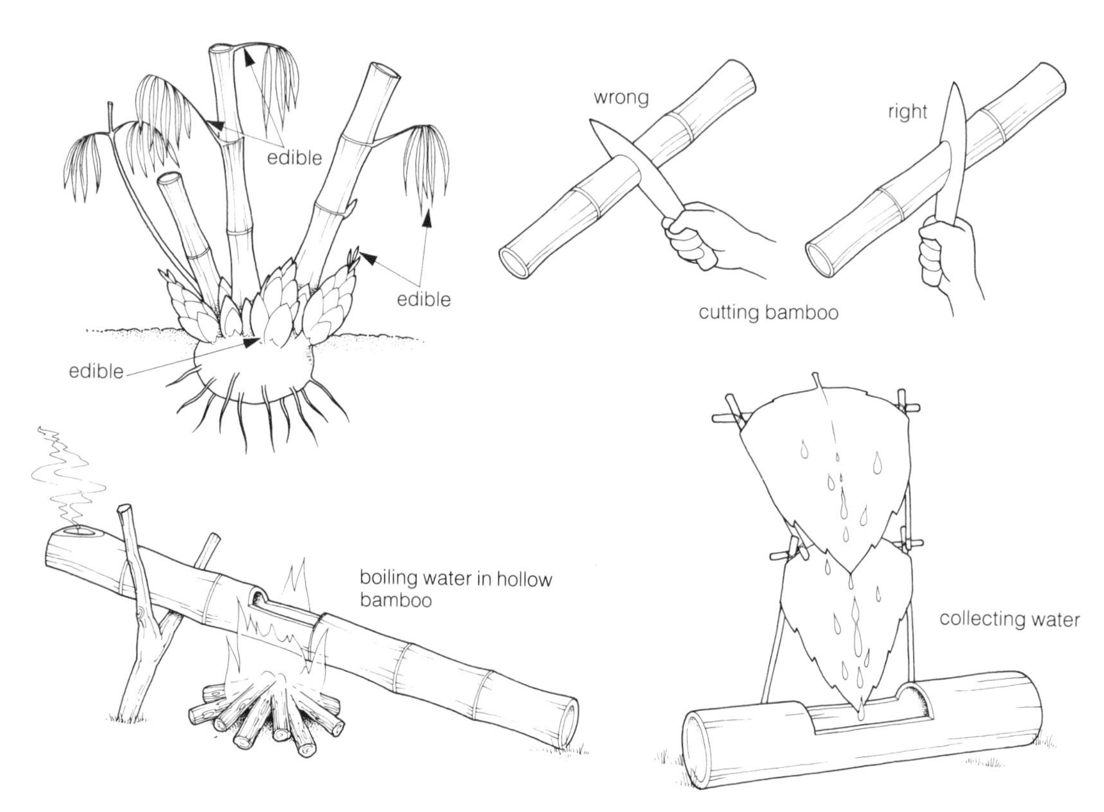

hard, and slivers may be extremely sharp. A cut in a tropical jungle is very likely to become infected unless it is properly treated. If you have a sharp knife, cut the stem of bamboo at an angle of 45 degrees, which will usually prevent the stem from splitting. It's much more difficult to cut bamboo at right angles but if you're going to, lie it on a hard surface and start cutting into the skin, rolling the bamboo gradually so that you cut a groove around it. You can then make this deeper and deeper until you have cut cleanly through it.

Bamboo is often used for lean-to shelters, rafts and furniture such as tables, chairs and beds. It may also be used as the basis for cooking utensils or drinking cups. Hollowed-out bamboo may be used for drum signalling. It is often used as a musical instrument and it can be particularly valuable for making tools and hunting weapons such as harpoons. Green bamboo is difficult to burn but if dried it makes easy-to-use tinder.

Where to camp

In the chapter on deserts I shall be covering the advantages of staying with your vehicle or crashed aircraft and using it as a base camp. The same applies in the jungle, the only difference being that circumstances may force you to live elsewhere. For instance, you may have crashed high in the jungle foliage or landed in some mosquito-infested swamp, so you will have to move, and if that is the case, choose a spot higher than the nearby swamps or streams. You'll find that there are fewer mosquitoes and it will obviously be drier. Jungles tend to be very wet so there's usually water on the ground, humidity in the air and frequently larger drops coming from above. So it's very important to think carefully about your location in relation to water and dampness that could spoil your comfort.

If there's fresh water nearby then there are obvious advantages to being *reasonably* close to it. In the desert, you *have* to be close to water, but here it's usually better to keep a safe distance. If you're near large rivers there could be a danger of crocodiles.

Crocodiles

The salt water crocodile has an average length of between ten and twenty feet (maximum) and can be found as widely spread as India, the Philippines and the northern shores of Australia and Ceylon.

Over land and for short distances the reptile can move very quickly. When stalking it is guided by sight only, and after catching its prey it pulls it beneath the water, continues to spin and twist until the victim drowns, and then rips it to pieces. Crocodiles are not fast, though very powerful, swimmers and over a short distance a fit person using the crawl could easily outswim one.

Crocodile flesh can be eaten and crocodiles are often caught on hooks or by traps. In fact decoy ducks are often used to draw the croc into a net.

Though large and very cumbersome in appearance a crocodile can emerge from water in almost total silence. Another reason for not making camp close to water!!

Other dangers

Rivers also tend to be used for drinking by large animals such as buffalo and rhino, and at night hippo frequently come out of rivers to graze. If the water nearby is shallow and stagnant it will almost certainly have an impressive number of insects buzzing around it and these may carry disease. Perhaps the most dangerous single nasty is the malaria or yellow fever-carrying mosquito. More on insects later.

Under no circumstances camp in or right by a dry river bed. Flash floods can be as much a danger in the jungle as in mountains or desert areas. Another reason for staying away from river banks is that during heavy storms trees destroyed by high winds or lightning can be swept down river. They become entangled with the river undergrowth to form a crude dam and as the water rises behind them it builds up until it breaks through and then sweeps down river, taking everything on the banks with it. So if time allows, choose an area a safe distance away from the water supply, as high up as possible and not over a game trail – more than one jungle traveller has had to vacate his sleeping quarters in a hurry because he forgot to avoid this.

If you decide to settle some distance from fresh water you may be able to 'pipe' it closer to your camp using bamboo stems split longways into two halves. Alternatively you may simply have to carry water which might mean using your junglecraft to create storage containers, which incidentally need to be well covered to prevent insects from getting in.

Piping water to your camp

In swampy regions where there is very little foliage other than thick reeds, it's still possible to build yourself some form of shelter. Pull up large handfuls of the reeds and pack them tightly into bundles, using individual reeds to tie them. It may be worth making very small bundles initially and then tying them tightly together. Place them alongside each other until you form a platform and then add another layer on top at right angles to the first ones. After a while they will become strong enough to support you and should be quite dry.

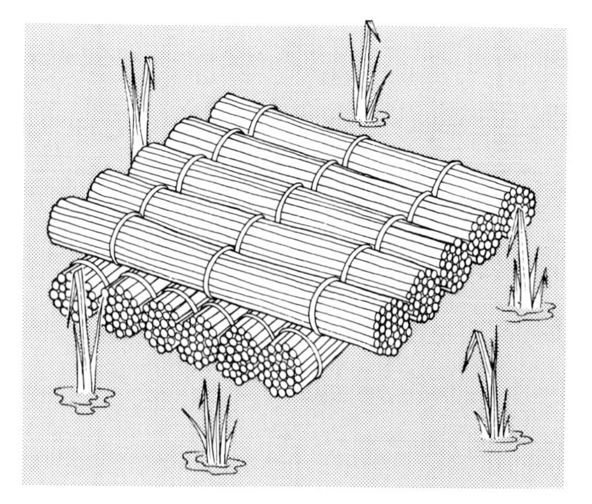

Floating marsh reed bed

In Egypt, along the banks of the Nile, there are vast areas of reed marsh, covering thousands of miles. Whole villages live on platforms made in this way and some of the 'houses' are as big and grand as those you would find in cities. Boats, as well as carpets and baskets, are made from reeds. Bound tightly together they become excellent bouyancy aids.

Logs or boulders can also be used to help you raise your base off the ground. Whatever you do, remember that damp is a permanent danger, however mild and harmless it may seem at first. If you are exposed to it for any length of time, it seeps away your energy. Everything you need to survive, Mother Nature will provide, but it's up to you to use the resources available to the best of your ability.

Clearing a space

You should do this both below and above where you intend to site your camp. Avoid overhanging branches especially if the trees look as though they are dead or dying. Falling branches are not fun and coconuts also have a bad habit of dropping down on top of you. The reason for clearing the ground covering vegetation, which is rotting and smelly, is because it will be home to thousands of ants and insects, leeches, tics and other nasties.

Even if you are hot, light a fire as the smoke will keep flying insects away and the ash can be used to keep ants and crawlies at bay. It's actually worth making a fire simply to produce a supply of ash which can be spread in a circle around the camp. You'll find it effective in keeping out all forms of crawling insects. All of this obviously takes time, so start early in the day if possible. In the jungle night comes very quickly and the last thing you want to be doing is blundering around in the dark trying to construct your shelter. It's also important to remember to try and get a certain amount of rest to keep your strength up. Jungle heat and humidity sap your energy reserves so try to work slowly and methodically and don't get in too much of a panic. If possible choose an opening in the jungle foliage where the air is less humid.

Insects

If there are lots of mosquitoes around try hanging your clothes in the smoke for a while, then when you curl up for the night, the smell of the smoke helps drive them away. It may also keep *you* awake, but that may be preferable to slapping yourself every five minutes to squash the mosquitoes.

You must take precautions – such as wearing long trousers and long sleeves, tucking trousers into socks, tying string or a piece of vine around your cuffs and your ankles thus helping prevent insects such as leeches and tics from climbing your limbs. In fact, you need to take more precautions against smaller jungle creatures than against the large ones. Although monkeys, apes and other animals make terrifying noises, they aren't likely to attack. The real dangers tend to come from infection and disease, which can be caused mostly by insects. Mosquitoes are probably the single greatest danger, together with fleas. The *Anopheles* mosquito carries malaria and if you haven't taken precautions you may be in trouble.

If you come across a wasp or hornets' nest,

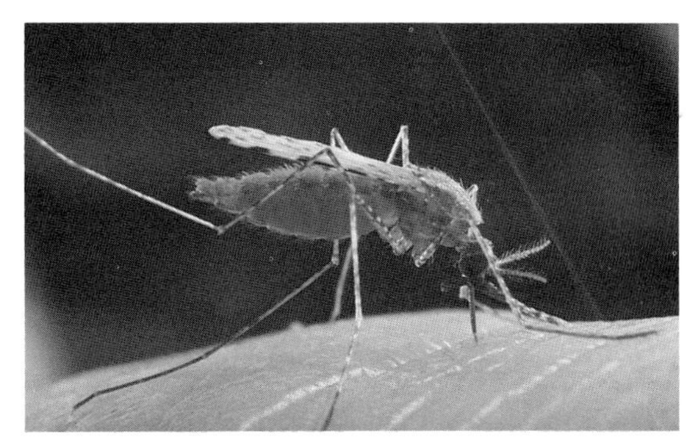

Female anopheles mosquito

or you suspect a swarm is in the area, evasion is the best defence. Quietly withdraw and detour round them. If they are swarming and there is water close by you, gently submerge until they have passed – making sure the water is safe first, with no crocodiles etc! Thick smoke may drive a swarm away; even crouching in dense undergrowth helps, but the best advice I can give you is to quickly, but quietly, put some distance between yourself and them, even if it means moving camp. One species of African bee, now found worldwide, is particularly dangerous. Keep your camp area tidy and leave nothing exposed that will attract them – sugar, jam etc.

Leeches

Leeches, which live on fresh blood, are quite easy to deal with but make sure you don't pull them off leaving the head embedded in your flesh. The juice of raw limes, or from a fresh

Blood sucking leech

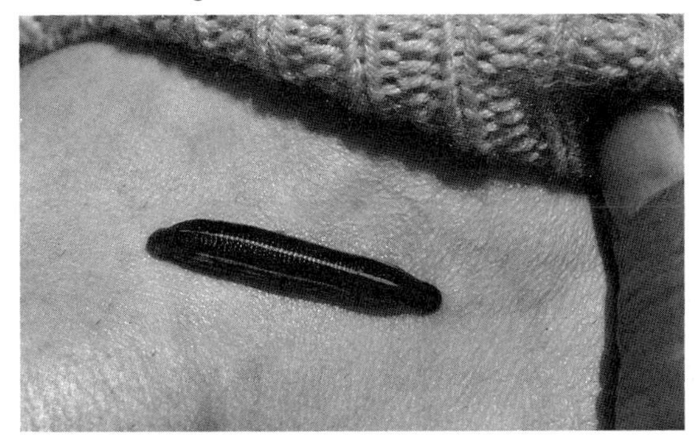

tea bag, or salt if you have any, or ash whether from a cigarette end or the fire, may be used to make the leech open its jaws and you can then remove it. There may be a small blood clot which you should squeeze gently to clean the wound.

If you intend to spend a lot of time in the tropical jungle it's well worth looking into the range of insect life you will find and taking precautions beforehand.

Other jungle nasties

One particularly nasty little nasty is the Sand Flea. Its bite is very similar to that of the itch mite. After a biting you come down with a fever, called sand fly fever, with symptoms very similar to malaria. Without antibiotics there is very little you can do. When you feel the fever coming on, rest and have all your needs handy – spare blankets, fresh water, firewood, matches etc.

The temptation to scratch the bite is overwhelming at times but you must resist. Scratching only induces further infection. One flea can bite several times so should you be lucky enough to catch it in the act either throw it on the fire or roll it in your fingers to kill it (a simple squeeze will not do the job). Remember to wash your hands afterwards.

Protection is obviously the answer but this can be difficult without the right clothing and footwear. You can get some relief from the itching by soaking a clean cloth in hot water and applying a poultice or, if there are any available, rubbing it with a slice of onion or garlic. In the tropics natives use limes or lemons.

While on the subject of insects it might be worth mentioning an ingenious method of getting rid of ants from your camp site. While I was living in the Congo Basin of Central Africa amongst the Pygmies, the camp was situated deep inside the equatorial rain forest and as you would expect the ground was very damp and covered in lots of decaying foliage. During the day hundreds of mosquitoes buzzed around, along with lots of other insects. On the ground centipedes, snails, leeches and even scorpions were quite common. In fact it was one of the most insect-infested regions I'd ever been in. Worst of all, though, were the ants. Day and night they were on the move – large black soldier ants. At night they would stream through our camp, often in ranks two to three inches wide, like a giant black snake or hose pipe on the loose. As they scurried across the decaying foliage, eating anything edible in their path, you could hear the noise of their talons snapping the air.

When they did eventually pass, a thick, dark brown, acrid trail would be left in their wake. This trail took my attention. I noticed that no other insect, beetle, slug or even snake would cross the line: all came to it and turned back immediately. The problem was: could this somehow be used to keep creepy-crawlies out of my shelter? It seemed not. No matter where we attempted to pitch camp or stored our supplies, the ants managed to find us. Worst of all was their nightly scavenge up the support poles of our shelters. We tried everything to stop them but they still managed to crawl all over us. Eventually, in desperation, I went along to speak to the local head man. He listened as I tried to explain and smiled as I scooped up some ants to demonstrate. The answer was so simple.

A young guide was summoned and told to go back to our camp and help. Before we arrived back he took me to a nearby tree and made a deep cut into the trunk. Then we went back to my shelter. At the base of the pole supporting it he scooped out a small hole and using some water began to mix the earth into a muddy substance. This he fashioned into a crude bowl-shape around the base of the poles. Eventually he formed two cups, one on top of the other.

The bottom cup he baked hard by using hot embers and ash from our fire. Once dried he poured water into the cup up to the rim. Next he returned to the tree and removed the soft gooey resin that had been secreted and moulded this in his hands to make it pliable. He then smeared it all around the inside of the second cup and a little up the poles and tie-ropes of the shelter. Finally he sprinkled some of the remaining hot ashes from our fire on the ground around the shelter. Then disappeared into the jungle and returned carrying a large leaf filled with hundreds of seething ants. Quickly he demonstrated his trap by spreading the ants around the shelter and on the poles above the trap. In seconds there was utter confusion. Those on the ground wouldn't cross the cup traps and those he had placed on the poles above wouldn't go down the poles.

The principle was very simple: ants don't like water and fire. The hot ash held them back, any attempts to climb into the water-filled cups would result in drowning and if they got past that, the sticky, sweet, pungent-smelling resin held them fast. From that time onwards whilst in that camp I was never again bothered with ants or other creepy crawlies climbing into my shelter – since the acrid trail left by the disappointed ants beneath the water trap also deterred all the other insects.

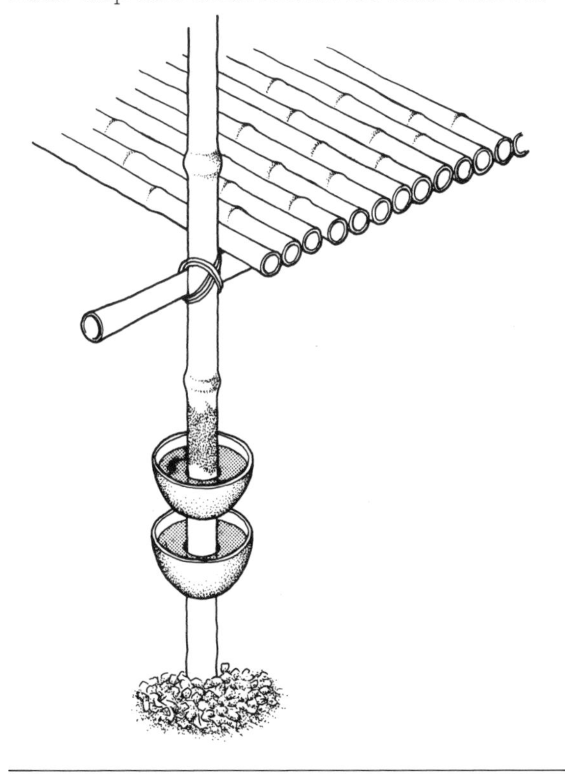

Building and siting your shelter

There are a number of general rules which are worth taking into account:

1. In the first instance you shouldn't make your shelter any higher or larger than necessary or you will have to collect much more material to build it. Make it big enough for you to be comfortable and for it to include any material or equipment you have with you for an overnight stay.

2. Wherever possible, always build a shelter big enough to keep your feet inside. Don't let them stick out – always keep them covered and warm.

3. If you have to build a shelter in a hurry the first day, go over it on the next day and make sure that the leaves are properly secured and tied down and will not easily fall off. Added foliage will help form a fairly impenetrable barrier so that, should creepy crawlies climb over it, they will just keep going rather than make their way inside.

4. Always make sure your shelter is a safe distance away from your fire. Leaves and branches can become dry and sparks can easily set a shelter alight.

5. As I've already emphasized, however valuable water may be, build your shelter and your camp a safe distance away. Remember about the dangers of insects and animals. Once on an expedition in the Congo a young scientist working with us built his 'basha' right across a hippo run! He soon learned that it is not wise to argue with a hippo when it is charging through the undergrowth. That night he spent a miserable few hours perched in the branches of a nearby tree.

6. When siting your camp near, although not too near to water, a point worth mentioning is that in the case of a jungle or savanna rescue, searchers tend to use the water routes as

The river is easy to see from the air; near it you are more likely to be seen by rescuers

marker lines. They fly up and down them looking for signs or signals from lost travellers. Jungle rescue teams know that water travel is probably the only way you can reach safety. So again the importance of water to our survival is emphasized. A marker stretched out across a river, or marker die sprinkled on the water, is often far easier to see from the air than smoke, which is dissipated by the dense undergrowth.

Immediate shelters

Probably the most basic shelter you can build is to place some branches across a couple of fallen tree trunks. Cover the branches with a layer of ferns, moss or leaves. You'll be able to sit on this, raised off the ground. To keep off the rain, tie several large leaves from palms or ferns over a pole support, rather like an umbrella.

If you came down by parachute it's very unlikely that you will have crashed all the way to the ground through the dense foliage. More likely you will have had to lower yourself to the floor and in doing so you will have left most of your parachute entangled in the canopy above. However, if it's possible try to get the parachute, or pieces of it, down with you. To a jungle survivor the parachute is an invaluable item of equipment. Because of the density of the foliage any rain that does penetrate tends to fall in a drizzle and a taut parachute shelter will ward off most of the rain. Strips torn off make excellent hammocks, sleeping bags, bandages, mosquito nets, face veils and so on.

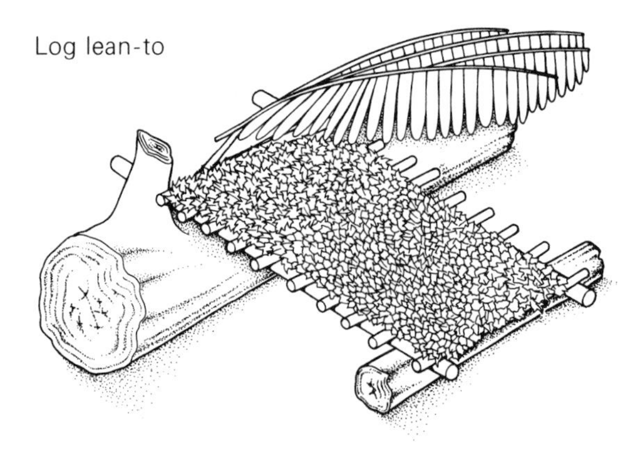

Log lean-to

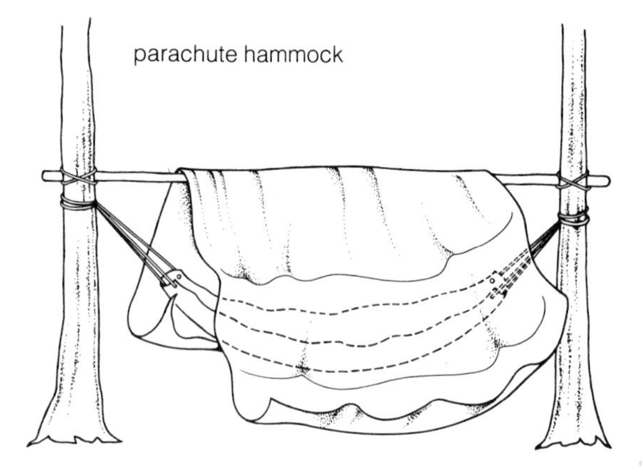

parachute hammock

Off the ground

All jungles or tropical rain forest floors abound with creepy crawlies: ants, leeches, scorpions, snakes, termites and many, many more. Some will be harmless, but others will be either a great nuisance or a positive danger, so make the effort to get your 'floor' off the ground.

Long leaves from the palm tree, split down the middle and placed over bamboo poles, or sticks or branches taken from trees make excellent overhead cover; they also make a good bed. The more you put down the more comfortable it will be.

Vine hammocks

Vines or lianas make excellent hammocks. Simply string a couple of loops between two or better, four strong trees, lay a series of long poles or logs across them and you have a first-class bed.

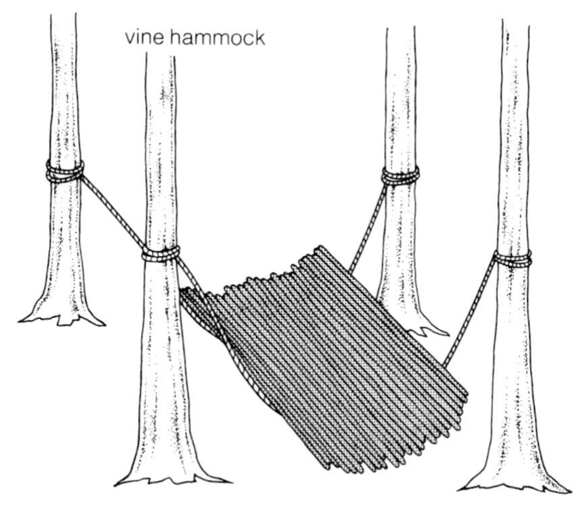

Other simple shelters

Another very simple shelter to build if the materials are available is a variation on the earlier lean-to. For this you'll require four strong poles about one-and-a-half metres long and sharpened at one end.

Tie two of the poles together at the un-sharpened end, then do the same with the other two poles. Place the two sets of poles over a bed of logs and press them firmly into the ground on either side of it. To help support them you can lash another pole across the top, or you could use a survival rope.

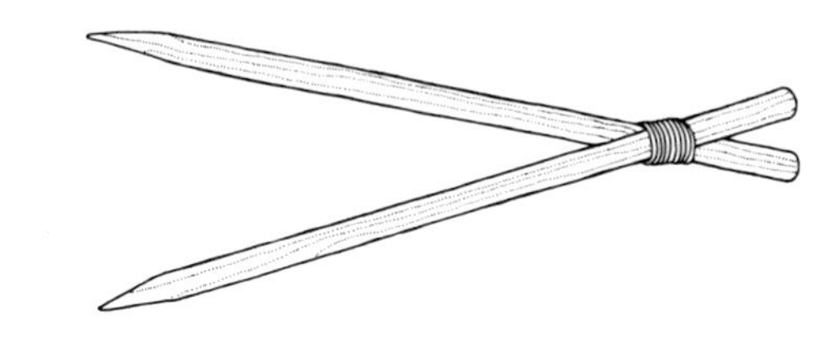

All you need now is something with which to cover the frame to keep off the rain. As before, sticks, moss or reeds will all do, but to ensure that it's waterproof these will have to be packed tightly. They can be held down with more survival rope or turf clumps. The thicker the shelter cover, the more effective it is.

An alternative is either to thatch or 'tile' your shelter. To do this the A-frame itself will have to be built much firmer, and this is done by simply weaving long thin branches in and out of the frame.

To 'tile' the shelter gather large vine leaves, make a notch in the stems and hang them onto the frame. While I was living in a tropical rain forest in the Congo the locals advised me to light a small fire beneath the shelter of leaves I

A simple A frame

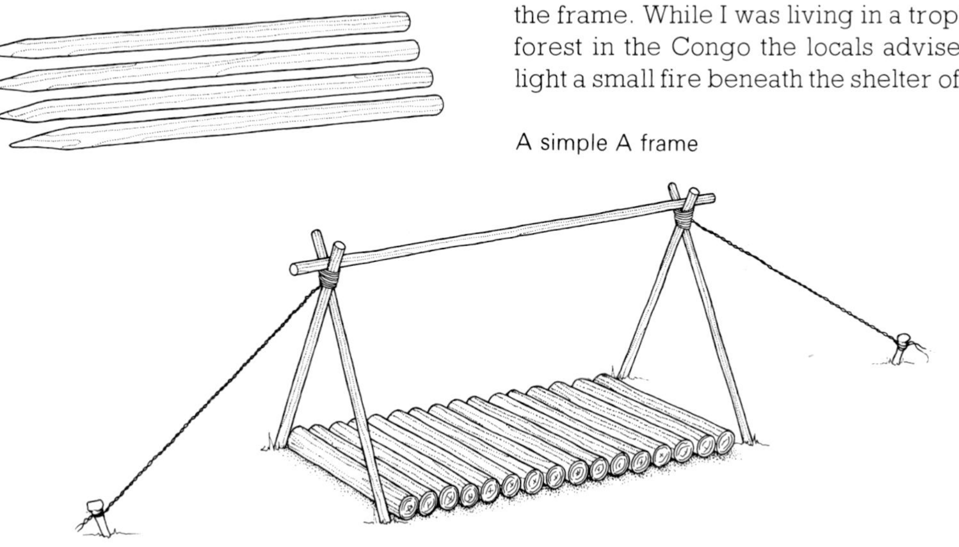

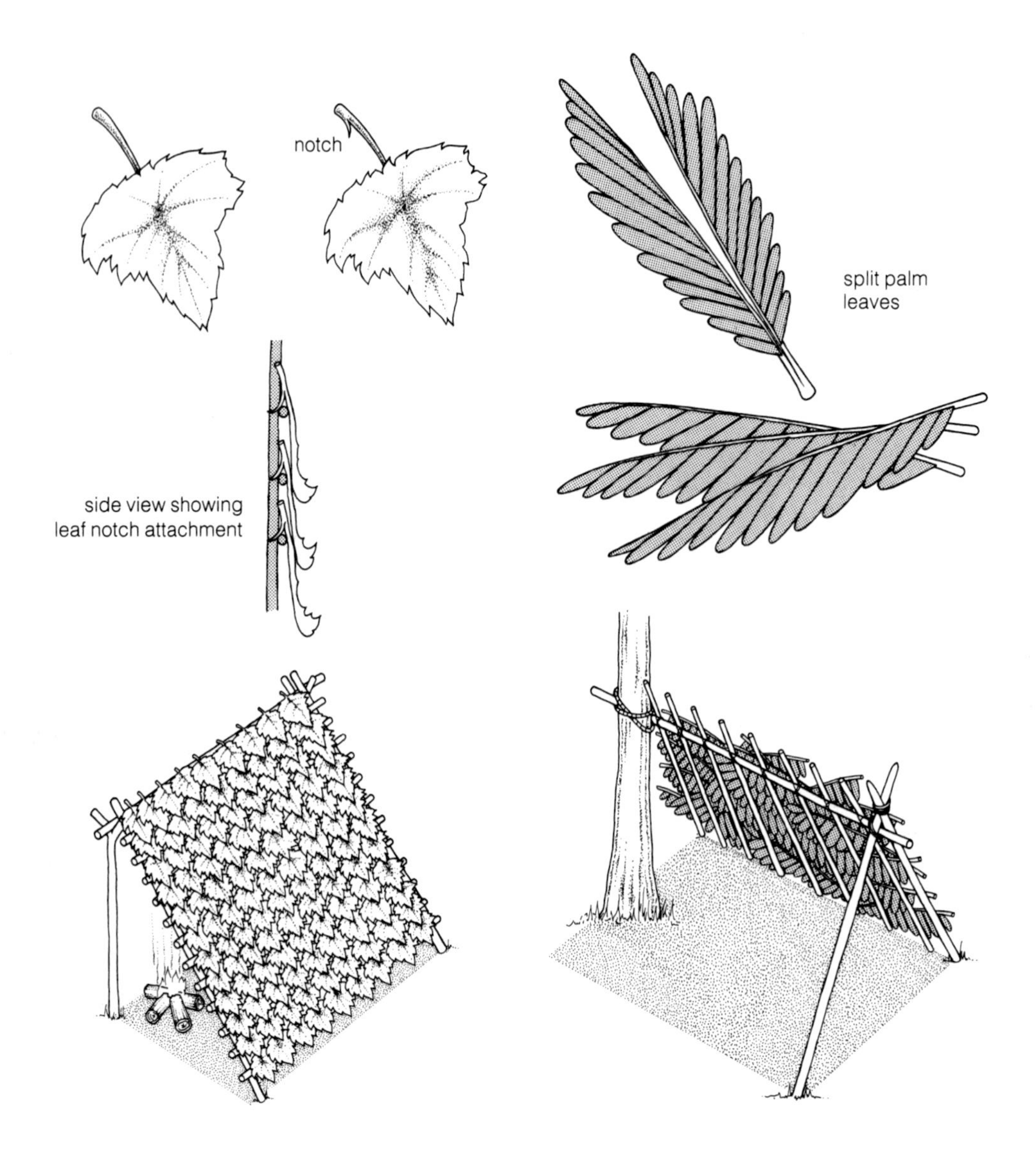

Tiling the shelter with vine leaves

had built because the heat and smoke make the natural oils in the leaves secrete and fuse together to form a crude waterproof blanket. To thatch your shelter gather lots of long-stemmed grass and cut yourself about three dozen small fastening spriggots, 30 cm. or so long, from supple green twigs. Sharpen these at each end, then, starting at the bottom corner of the frame, secure the grass with your spriggots. Work along a tier at a time. When you get to the end start on another row, until you reach the top. To secure the top, press the grass over it and fasten the thatching down using more spriggots. Done correctly this should last you about a month and will be completely waterproof.

If you make the woven frames strong enough you should be able to transport them around without damaging them. This means that if you have to move house you can simply take your shelter with you, or if you go off hunting for the day and you don't want to leave it open to invite in any passing animals or snakes, you just tie the sides together and hang it on a tree. I carried one such shelter with me for months, and even when I travelled down river on my raft I took it with me. Like fire, having your own shelter with you is a great morale booster. It's a simple matter to lean in against a fallen tree or large rock, or over a small indentation in the ground and 'hey presto' – an instant house.

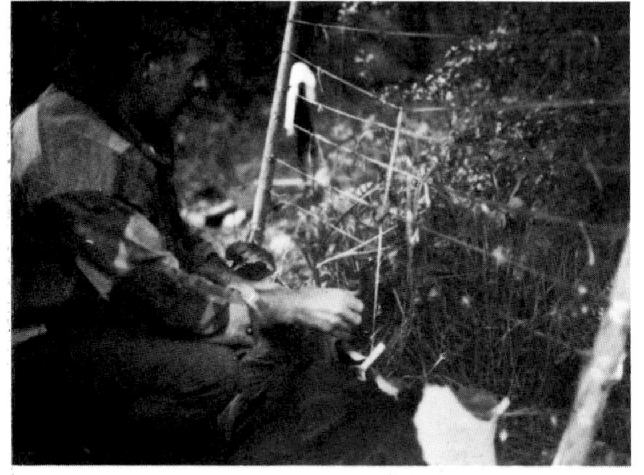

Practise tiling a shelter with large leaves

Cut a notch in the stem to hang it on the frame

A practice shelter (built at my training school)

A palm-leaf shelter I built in Zaire

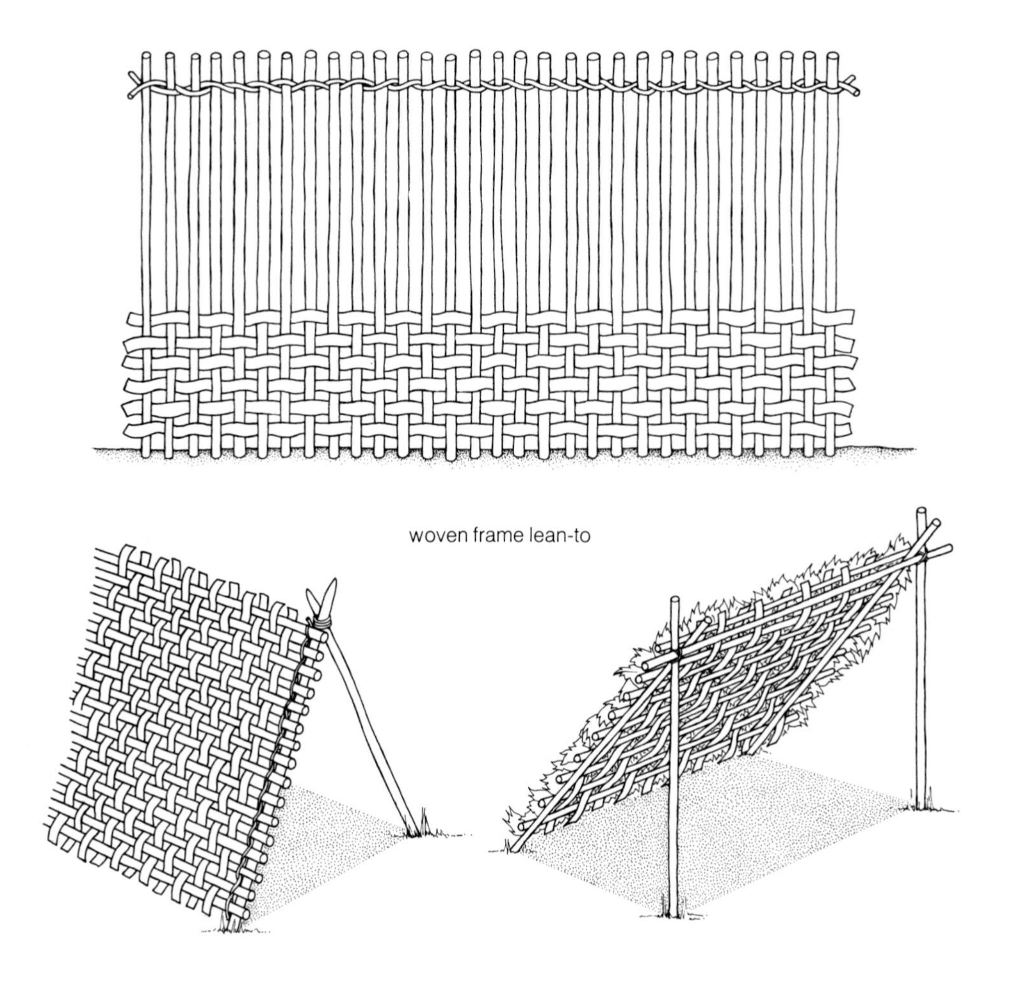

Woven frame shelters

There is another simple method of making a woven frame without having to use any ties whatsoever. Gather about thirty long thin supple sticks, just a little taller than yourself. Then cut a dozen thicker stakes, which you should sharpen at one end. Mark a straight line on the ground and leave a space the width of a clenched fist between each stake. Press the thicker stakes firmly into the ground then, working from the bottom, weave the supple sticks in and out of the stakes. As the weave begins to take shape press it down using your hand or a small log to make it firm and compact. Once you reach the top, tie off the frame with a length of survival rope or one last length of stick. You now have a very strong and portable wall. A woven wall of grass makes an excellent shelter and if crafted correctly it, too, will last a very long time.

Beds

There are various, simple beds that you can make, from woven mats to hammocks. I've already described the vine hammock. If you've no fabric from a parachute or no car seats with you, you may have to make do with twigs, branches and leaves. If circumstances demand it and you have to sleep on the ground, clear the area carefully.

Sanitary arrangements

Whether in a jungle, desert or indeed anywhere else, it's important to make sure that proper sanitary arrangements are made. It's best to dig a refuse pit some distance away from the camp. At regular intervals throw earth or leaves over layers of waste deposited. This will keep insects and animals away and will prevent the spread of infection. Personal hygiene in jungle conditions is very important. It's so difficult to keep yourself completely dry and, apart from the physiological problems that can arise, the constant decomposition and humidity that surround you will, as I've said, quickly sap your energy reserves and will often cause severe depression. Clothes will decay rapidly and fall apart; your skin will also begin to suffer badly. Without exposure to the sun and fresh air your skin becomes waterlogged. Minor scratches and sores may fail to dry and heal due to the humidity and continuous sweating. Then infection will set in. So wash frequently, and build a proper toilet.

A rather elaborate jungle loo! But proper sanitary arrangements are essential

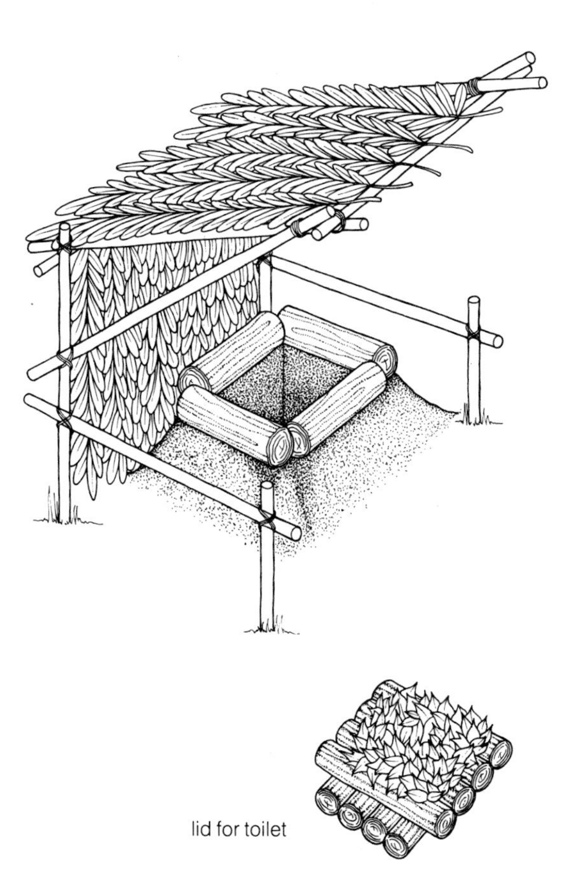

lid for toilet

Fires

A fire is the focal point of any camp. For obvious reasons the siting of the fire is very important. Built in an exposed place most of the heat will be blown away, and your valuable tinder used up very quickly. Also, there is of course a danger of your starting a forest fire!

Important as it is, the fire should only be lit after you have made your shelter. Lighting a fire, especially without matches, can be very time consuming and your first priority should be to protect yourself from the elements before you set about sorting out your camp. You may have to search round for suitable tinder and a safe place to light it. Dead and decaying foliage will probably be too wet. Bark from trees, or layers of leaves covered by other leaves, may be dry enough but avoid wet bamboo as it splinters when heated quickly. If you're going to stay in the area for any length of time you should make it a priority to collect a supply of firewood. If you intend moving it may well be worth collecting some tinder to take with you. This will help you to start a fire each night as suitable material is unlikely to be readily available. During the day burn green wood – this will give off a lot of dense smoke and will help any rescue party out searching for you. At night burn dry wood as this gives off more heat and light.

Conclusions

As in many survival situations it should only take you a few days to become acclimatised to the jungle. Soon you will find yourself moving around quite freely as your confidence grows. Because it may be some time before you are rescued you should try and make yourself as comfortable as possible, perhaps concentrating your energy on building a more permanent shelter.

Generally speaking, jungles provide an abundance of materials for you to build a very sound structure; or if you are in an area such as South America where there are very large trees like the giant Sequoia, whose roots spread out widely and stick high above the ground, you may find it relatively easy to build a roof between two of these and you'll have a very solid shelter.

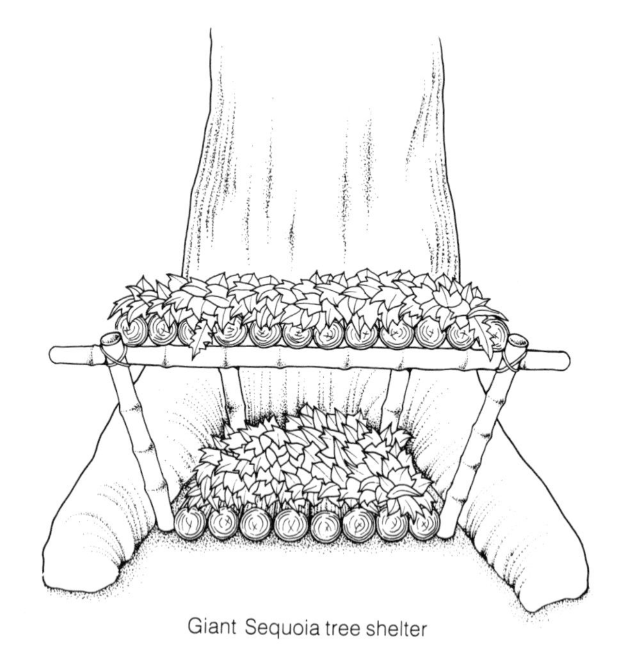

Giant Sequoia tree shelter

CHAPTER 13

The Desert

In the chapter on psychology I emphasized certain priorities essential for anyone's survival, in particular the importance of gaining control of fears and emotions as quickly as possible. Having done this you must concentrate on protection against the elements and any other dangers. Now that you are in a survival situation you should start to formulate a plan. Don't do the first thing that comes into your head: stop and think, decide on your priorities. Assume that for the time being the chances of being rescued in the next twenty-four hours or so are pretty slim. To protect yourself from the elements a crude shelter will have to be found or made. This will mean some physical effort, which may be the last thing you feel like doing, especially if you are still recovering from shock, but you *must* make the effort. Shake yourself out of your depression and search around for somewhere to shelter or find something to build one with. Psychologically it will be a terrific morale booster for you, and as small and skimpy as it may end up, to you it will be a home – somewhere to feel safe in, not only from the elements but also from other possible dangers.

Obviously the building of any shelter will depend on the type of terrain in which you find yourself, but even in very sparsely covered areas like the desert, where it may seem hopeless, it's usually possible to build yourself something. You may not realize how wonderful a small shell-scrape in the ground can be; but once you crawl into it, it will almost certainly make your labours seem worthwhile. However, before we look at shelter building in desert conditions, it will be helpful to know a few general facts about these wastelands.

Desert terrain

Every continent has at least one desert. Twenty per cent of the land surface of the earth is covered by them and just under five per cent of the world's population actually lives in them.

The biggest deserts are: the Sahara (3 million square miles), the Libyan Sirte (600,000 square miles), the Arabian (500,000 square miles), the Gobi (380,000 square miles) and the Kalahari (225,000 square miles). Deserts vary from those which have very extreme climates (the Sahara, the deserts of Arabia, Iran, Iraq, the Gobi and the smaller ones along the west coast of South America) to the deserts such as those in the south western USA, Northern Mexico and Western Australia, which are far less extreme.

The main hazards are heat and cold, and the lack of water, food or shelter. Add wind to these conditions and you have a lethal combination. However, there are simple and sometimes surprising ways of dealing with the elements. They may not always work but as I emphasize frequently throughout this book, being prepared is halfway to surviving. If you find yourself in a desert you will probably see the following:

1. rocks and sand
2. cloudless skies, sometimes thick mist and haze

3. little vegetation or animal life
4. little or no evidence of water

Conditions can vary widely. In many deserts you will come across vast expanses of barren, rocky plains and great mountain ranges. During the monsoons or winter season it is quite common for the desert to be shrouded in a thick mist or haze, often lasting for weeks.

Sandstorms

Then of course there are the infamous sandstorms, lasting for anything from a couple of days to weeks. During a sandstorm it is very easy to become disorientated.

I spent a great deal of time soldiering in the desert, often working behind enemy lines and this obviously placed restrictions on my movements. Many is the time during a sandstorm that I have simply lain down on the sand, curled up and gone to sleep with no protection. Sometimes I needed to tie myself to a small bush or rock to prevent being dragged off during a severe storm.

Generally speaking, during the night there is very little wind as the sun sets and the earth cools. Early morning and late evening is when most sandstorms blow. The wind can whip up a storm against which you will certainly need protection. One thing is for certain: you don't want to be wandering around during the storm – just curl up and sit it out.

An approaching sandstorm

On one occasion in the Middle East I was caught out in the desert during a raging sandstorm and I had to shelter for nearly two weeks. Sand dunes were magically formed by the wind whipping up loose sand and reshaping it. At the end of the storm I climbed out of my shelter, tired, stiff, dirty and a little scared to say the least. Before the storm I had been making my way towards a nomad village at the base of a mountain range. Sensing the storm coming on, I had tied together the legs of my camel, Sally, to prevent her from straying and quickly set up my small tent.

As the storm continued to blow I huddled beneath my blanket trying to sleep. I woke only to go to the toilet and make myself something to eat. Sally carried her own built-in survival kit. Before setting off from base I had made sure she had a good meal and was topped up with water. On her back I'd tied bundles of green foliage for her to chew on as we crossed the great plains. When the storm eventually died down, I stood outside the tent and was amazed to see just how much the terrain had changed.

Before the storm I had been crossing a large rocky plain with the odd sand dune here and there. Now, all around me were hundreds of dunes, some well over fifty metres high. Later, when I got back to camp, I was told that I had survived one of the longest and most ferocious sandstorms ever recorded in that region. As I came plodding over the hill towards the Bedouin camp they came out and stared in disbelief at this creature singing loudly, spurring his camel on. Dressed as I was, in full Arab attire, when I stepped down from my camel I must have been a puzzling sight. Having been out in the desert for a long time my skin had become as brown as that of the locals, but I have bright blue eyes and I became known as 'El Blue'. Having a reasonable grasp of their language and being able to live close to their way of life, we all quickly became friends.

I carried with me, as I always do, a well-stocked medical pack, so at each camp where I stopped I took over the role of doctor. As a result my full Arabic name became 'El Blue Tabeeb' – the blue-eyed doctor. On that particular occasion I ended up delivering a baby and stitching up a very severe wound in the backside of a young Arab who had fallen onto a broken Coca Cola bottle.

Back to the sandstorm: it's not generally true that people and animals get buried alive. Elementary precautions – body shelters, cover for the face and the back of your neck, sitting or lying with your back to the wind, moving about – all ensure survival. However, there are some vital steps to take before settling down to sit the storm out. Mark the direction of your travel using stones or bushes weighed down with other stones, or sticks deeply stuck into the ground, if you have them. Take note of any outstanding landmarks, because the surface scenery will change as a result of the waves of sand deposited by the wind.

Mark your direction of travel before sheltering from a sandstorm

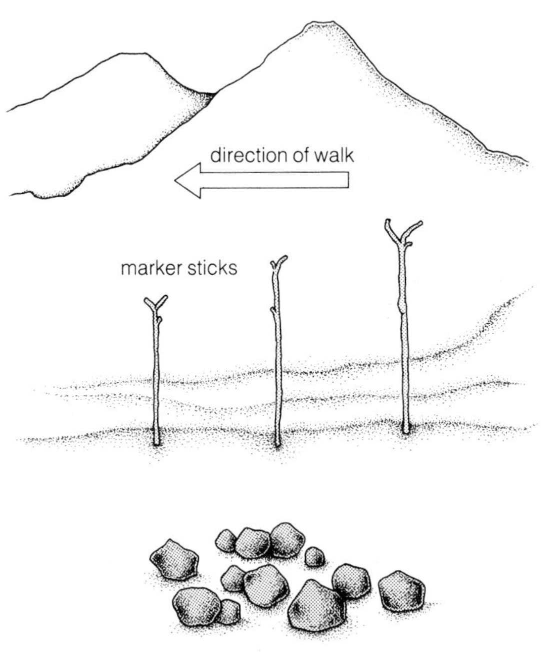

If you're in a vehicle, park with the engine facing *away* from the wind, unless you can park in the shelter of a tree or cliff. Block the exhaust pipe, being careful if it and the engine are still hot. Cover or seal the petrol cap, the air filter, the carburettor and the distributor. If you have a spare blanket, parachute fabric or anything else suitable, try to cover the engine, or possibly the whole vehicle. Close the doors and windows except for the window on the side *away* from the wind, which should be left open to allow air to circulate – it can be very hot during a daytime storm. Once the storm is over remove all the coverings and check the vehicle carefully before trying to start the engine. For more information on sandstorms, see page 142 'wind'.

General conditions

The desert may seem an inhospitable place in which to survive, but if you want to live and you have the will to, you can. It's as easy as that. As well as knowing something about desert conditions in general you must have an understanding of the main dangers that will face you. As I have stressed, the three most common environmental killers we know are COLD . . . WIND . . . WET. In the desert, add to these HEAT. You may be surprised to know that in deserts the cold and wet can be as lethal as heat. Saturated from a heavy dew, lying curled up beside or beneath a rock with a strong breeze blowing, you could soon become a candidate for hypothermia. Unless you are physically completely exhausted, always remember to make the effort to protect yourself from the cold, wind and wet before settling down for the night. If you are preparing your night shelter during the blazing heat of the day, this can be difficult to remember, but simple precautions such as hanging up a coat or shirt over the entrance to a shelter, or piling rocks, sand or brushwood will often do. You will, of course, need to protect yourself against the sun and heat. Heatstroke, exhaustion, cramps and sun blindness are all real and

A desert scorpion

frequent hazards in desert conditions, but you can avoid all of them with a little ingenuity.

There are other hazards with which to contend as well; surviving in a desert is never easy. Scorpions, snakes and insects can cause you terrible problems. Your shelter-building plans should take into account as many identifiable hazards as possible and never forget the importance of the psychology of survival. You may have decided to stay where you are and wait for rescue but you must still keep yourself highly motivated. If you're going to try and walk out of the desert it is essential to keep yourself reasonably fit and this means getting proper rest and sleep.

The decision to move from the shelter you will build, or from your vehicle, needs careful consideration. Whatever you decide, when tired and near exhaustion you may make mistakes; even the most experienced and expert amongst us have done so. Use a rule of thumb: when simple mistakes turn into minor accidents, stop and rest. Otherwise you'll end up making one mistake too many and then it will be too late.

If there are no materials around with which to build yourself a shelter, look for a sand scoop or shell scrape. Better still, look for shade under a bush, rocky overhang or small cave. Even in an area of only sand dunes it is possible to find or make some shade. Many sand dunes have large cornices (overhangs) that offer shade – just dig further in to increase the shadow of the dune. But remember, as the sun moves, your precious area of shade will move and disappear.

Finding a shelter

When travelling down wadies (or valleys) or crossing mountains, before I decided where I would sleep, I'd poke around under a suitable-looking rock or ledge to make sure there were no scorpions or snakes lurking there. If the cave or shelter is being used by an animal or by creepy crawlies, tell-tale signs will be identifiable. Look for droppings, tracks, discarded feathers etc. Animal dung and the smell of urine should be easily recognizable if the shelter has been used for a long period. Many animals seek shade during the heat of the day and move on during the night. Another simple shelter you could try to build, providing the materials are to hand, is a desert sangar. These are quite frequently used by desert nomads. Gather as many stones as possible and lay them out in a half-circle. Pile the stones on top of each other until you have them stacked about a metre high. Remove your shirt or jacket, untie your laces and fasten them to the cuffs of the garment. Anchor them with a stone and you have a crude but effective shelter from the blazing sun.

Alternatively you could cover the roof with some desert gorse or bushes. Flimsy as they are they really do help ward off the burning sun. Remember to site the entrance to the sangar so that you can trap any breeze that may be blowing. Also, take into account where the sun rises and sets. You will need to be in the shade as much as possible. Trenches may be dug or used if a suitable site cannot be found – such as in a dried up stream bed – though this can be a dangerous place to sleep

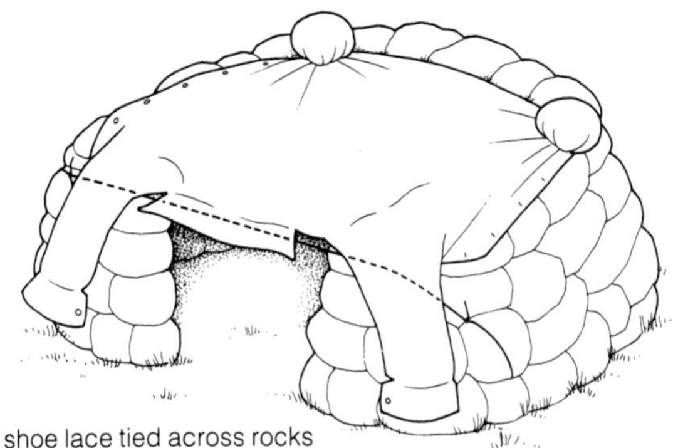

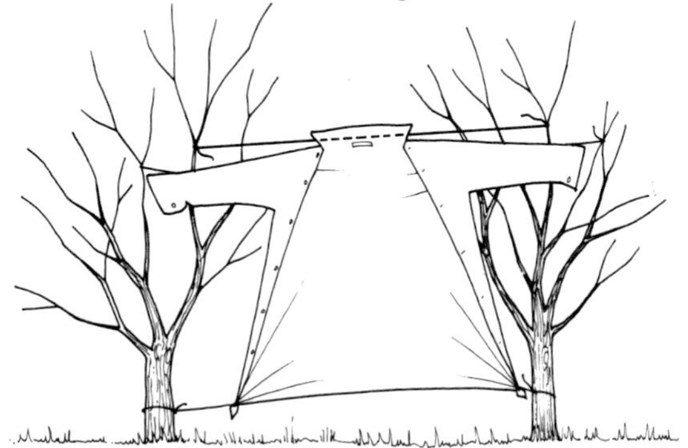

A desert sangar (*top*) and, (*above*), another way of creating some shade

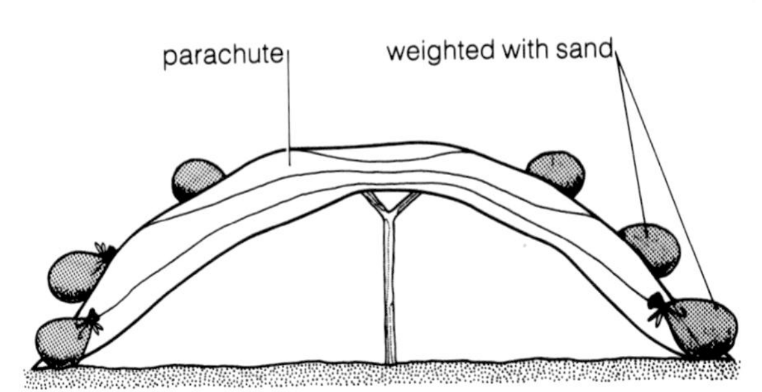

Using parachute material to make a shelter

because of flash floods. If you dig about six or so inches deep you will notice that the temperature of the sand will be pleasantly less than the surface temperature on the ground. If the ground is too hard to dig deep enough or if it's rocky, make the trench deeper by placing rocks along the sides and putting branches, clothing, blankets, parachute material or whatever over the rocks, anchoring the material down if possible. If you have a choice use white or light-coloured fabric to reflect the sun's rays. It's essential to allow air to circulate within the trench so make sure there are spaces for it to get in and out.

A palm thong blanket

A very effective and simple mat or blanket may be made from palm thongs. Just strip these from a fresh palm branch and cut yourself some long, thin strands from the stem. Lay the thicker thongs out on the ground and tie them with the strips as shown below.

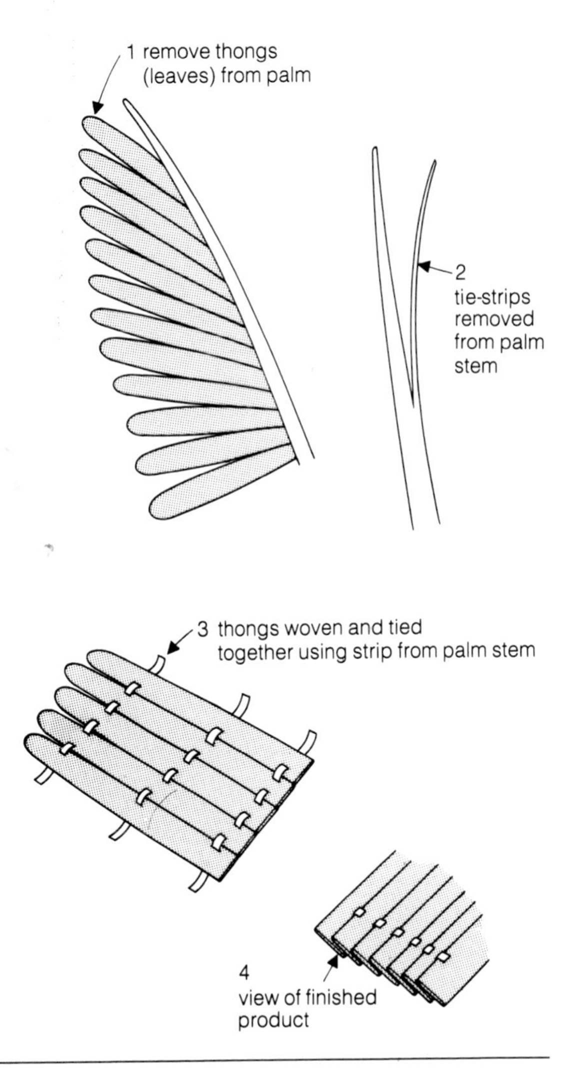

Using your surroundings

If there are any rocks and sticks available and the ground is too hard to dig into, try and use these to make a raised platform rather than lying on the hot sand.

During the day in most deserts there is nearly always a slight breeze blowing and the traveller needs to make this breeze work for him, so when resting try to have your bed or shelter slightly raised off the ground. This way the breeze, even though it's warm, is flowing beneath it. A hammock, of course, is ideal for this providing you have somewhere to sling it. Leaves from any bushes or palm trees often make very good shelter material and once while travelling in the vast plains of Kenya I came across a shelter built from the bonecase of a buffalo. The skeleton was the main structure and grass had been heaped on it to make a very dry and comfortable hide.

In South America where the giant cacti grow, I have even seen these used for shelter. It's all a matter of improvisation, ingenuity and the will to survive. It's amazing what you will come up with.

A very simple but extremely effective way of warding off some of the heat and glare from the sun is to build a lattice-slat shelter. This consists of strips of wood, sticks or even lengths of cloth placed over a couple of supports. If you haven't any wood or strips of clothing a small gorse bush held above your head will suffice. You could tie the bush to a stick and drape your shirt over the bush. Hold the stick to support the bush over your head like a parasol.

In certain areas you may come across lush green pastures, large lakes of fresh water and lots of fruit trees. These are mostly at the edge of the deserts, mainly along wadies or river beds. Occasionally it's possible to find a similar area out in the hot sands called an oasis, and it could be your only means of survival when crossing large expanses of desert.

It isn't only the sun's heat that tires you; the glare and reflection from the rocks and sand are equally exhausting. Therefore, unless you take avoiding action quickly to combat this, you will suffer from eye strain and severe headaches. Nature has so many ways of providing you with materials with which to improvise: the important thing is to know how to use them. Don't just sit there feeling sorry for yourself. I always say 'nothing ventured, nothing gained', because in my many years of desert experience I've never failed to find a way of providing myself with some form of protection when it has been needed.

Natural shelters

There are several obvious ways of using desert material to build shelters. I've already mentioned gorse bushes, stones, cacti etc. But before you waste precious energy and moisture why not have a look round for any natural shelters? You won't be the first or last person to sleep beneath a rock overhang or inside a cave. Primitive though they may be, these natural shelters are often ideal. Often along the banks of rivers you will come across both caves and overhangs and it may surprise you how cool they can be. Caves, particularly where the sun is unable to penetrate, can be very dry and comfortable and give you all the protection you need. Remember though, there are others in the desert seeking the same refuge, so again check for unwanted tenants. Most rocks in the desert are coarse and as you would expect, sand stone. They do get hot during the day but not blisteringly so. However, the harder the stone – granite, marble, flint etc. – the hotter it becomes.

As always, you can make your stay that bit more comfortable if you are prepared to improvise. However, because vegetation is very sparse, to venture out and find it during the day could expose you to further dangers from the heat, so if possible move around either first thing in the morning or late in the afternoon when the sun has lost most of its glare. Wear the right amount of clothing to suit the temperature. You can also move around during the night. I've done so hundreds of times, but let me assure you it does get very cold. Many times I've crouched down in the early hours of the evening with just a blanket wrapped round me for protection, only to be woken up later literally freezing. The blanket would often be covered in heavy dew and sometimes ice. That's right – ice! Without overhead cloud protection it can get extremely cold in the desert. More than once I've managed to collect almost half a cupful of dew from my blanket alone. At times the desert can be very soft, quiet and peaceful. At other times, when the sun's beating down, or the wind's howling, blowing hot stinging sand into your face and eyes, it can be the most inhospitable place on earth. If you read and work with the desert and use it as the nomads do, you will survive. Let it get the better of you and you will die.

Burrowing in sand

If the only available protection from the sun is soft sand, try burrowing down into it. I've done it and it works. Remove your jacket, drape it over your head and cover your legs and body with a good layer of sand – the thicker the layer the cooler it will be. Aborigines use this method all the time and simple as it may appear, it does help to reduce excessive sweating and can prevent some water loss. Above all it could save your life.

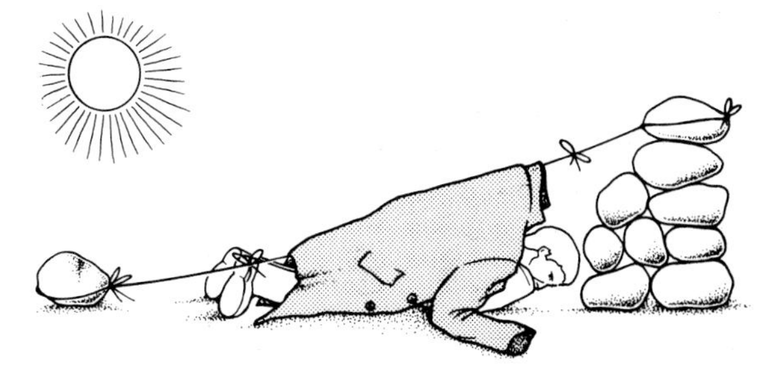

Finding natural shelters doesn't come easy. In all probability you will need to improvise, and use whatever you have with you. If necessary remove your shoe laces, tie them together and gather some stones to pile up. Fasten the laces to the top of the stones and the other end to a small rock on the ground. Drape your shirt/jacket over the lace and crawl under into the shade. If possible, build it over a small scoop in the ground; this will give you more room.

Alternatively, you could simply spread your shirt or jacket over a gorse bush. This obviously is less demanding and can easily be altered to catch the shade as the sun rises and sets.

Temperatures may get so high that paint may blister, and vehicles or empty petrol cans may burst into flames (petrol vapour is combustible). Fires have been started with the sun's rays striking a dew drop, creating the effect of a magnifying glass. So think about the implications of anything you do.

Desert clothing

Next to shelters to protect you from the elements, clothing is vitally important. Sometimes it may be the *only* protection you will have if you decide to leave your vehicle or camp. Your clothing will play its part in saving your life, or at least making you more comfortable. In general, desert people such as nomads or the Bedouin wear light, cool clothing during the day, mostly of a white material to reflect heat and glare from the sun, but in the evening after the sun has gone down, the locals will cover themselves with warm blankets and as much extra clothing as they can. They often sleep on thick camel-wool carpets. Very few desert people sleep unprotected. At night, when temperatures drop dramatically, stomach chills may result, so keep your midriff covered.

Some tribes do wear black even during the day. Black does absorb heat and it's as well to remember that these people were born in the desert and have learned to adapt to it. You and I will only acclimatise slowly. Clothing, therefore, needs to prevent water loss from sweating and to protect you from insects, scorpions or snakes. Don't ignore the possibility of injury from thorns and sharp stones. You must always remember that in any survival situation special attention must be paid to your head, eyes and feet. Above all, *keep covered*. It is better to wear long sleeves and trousers than short ones, even though you may feel like taking everything off. In the heat of the day the body will sweat and with no clothes evaporation will be much faster. Vital body fluids will be lost.

Local tribes wear loose-fitting robes. This keeps heat down because the layer of air between the clothing and the body acts as an insulator (just as it does in the cold to keep the warmth of the body in). Clothes shouldn't be tight, so remove belts and undo any elastic restraints such as waistbands etc.

Wind

Clothing should also protect you from the wind. Desert winds can kill by causing hypothermia as well as by whipping up blinding and stinging sandstorms, so never throw away spare layers of cloth or coverings. In a sandstorm you may have to cover yourself entirely with everything you have. Be sure that there's air in your tiny tent or shelter and move about from time to time to prevent sand from building up and submerging you. Before the sandstorm hits you, tighten your clothes with string or shoe laces, particularly around wrists and ankles; do all your buttons right up to the top. If you have nothing else except the clothes you are in, try to cover your face with a piece of cloth or garment, even if it means removing it from somewhere else. Always try to avoid getting sand into your nose, mouth, eyes and ears. If there's nowhere else to go and nothing else you can do, lie down with your back to the wind. Check the back of your neck and your waistband to make sure both of them are protected as much as possible.

Your head

The head – which loses heat so fast in cold weather – needs to be covered to protect you from sunstroke. Treat the back of your neck as you do your head, and protect it at all times from direct sun. Use whatever hats or caps are available. If there are none, try to fashion a face covering or an Arab type headdress. A simple face covering could be like a mask you might see on a bandit: a handkerchief tied around the bottom half of the face covering the

pieces of parachute cloth used as improvised Arab headdresses

shoulder and head protector

nose and mouth. The neck can be covered by draping a cloth in a similar way at the back of the head so it hangs down. A neck cover can be secured with a hat or a piece of string or plaited grass.

The eyes

Eyes are particularly vulnerable to very bright sunlight, reflected glare, dust or sand. If you have sunglasses they may help, although most conventional sunglasses are not strong enough for desert sun. Use a peaked cap or make a peak from paper, cardboard, plastic (which could get hot) or leaves. This will provide some shade for your eyes. A cloth hung over your face with slits, no more than one inch wide and a quarter of an inch deep cut in it for the eyes, is another way. Glare can be reduced by darkening the skin under the eyes with soot or mud (you may have noticed American football players doing this), but do not use oil. In a sandstorm it's probably advisable to cover the face and eyes completely with some cloth or leaves.

Your feet

Your feet are vital to get you out of the desert. They always need particular care. Because of the extremely hot ground surface your shoes may be inadequate. If they have very soft rubber soles the heat may soften them and make the shoes unwearable. Soles can be reinforced by using tyre rubber. You can add to your footwear by wrapping cloth or paper round your feet or shoes. Carrier bags, even small boxes may be used.

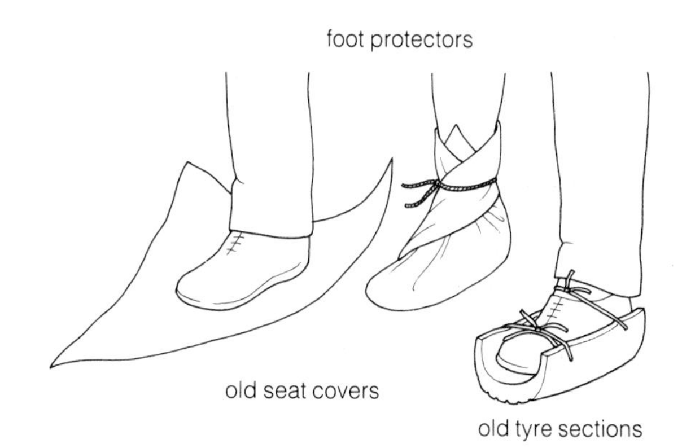

It's important to take off shoes and socks *frequently*. If you don't, after three or four days sand will get between your toes and literally rub the skin off. Change socks often if possible. Wash them out if you have any water, but if you don't let them hang up in the air and make sure they dry. To prevent sand getting in, tie leggings of cloth, paper or leaves around your ankles. In the army, soldiers are supplied with 'puttees' – strips of cloth wound in a spiral around the leg which cover the calf down to your shoes. If you make some, don't wind them too tightly – you could affect your blood circulation.

Be warned! When you remove shoes and socks and it's hot your feet will swell, making it difficult to put them back on again. Walking barefoot may cause blisters which need careful tending to avoid infection. Because initially a blister may not seem very serious do not ignore it. Bits of wool or very thin strips of soft cloth loosely wound around a blistered toe will help prevent rubbing. Plaster or bandage, if you have them, will of course be ideal. If possible, avoid breaking blisters and exposing the skin beneath. When exposed the skin is very tender and susceptible to infection.

If you have to, blisters may be pierced carefully with a pin or knife blade using a flame or boiling water to sterilize it. Gently squeeze the liquid out and place a built-up circle of cloth around the blister, then lightly bandage the area. A needle pushed into the blister and cotton pulled through will help the fluid gently seep away without damaging the skin beneath.

Insects

Before putting on clothes or shoes shake them vigorously first to check that no insects, snakes or scorpions have taken up occupancy.

In general try to keep clothes as clean as possible. If water is available then wash them frequently. If they get torn or worn out, try to mend them. A thorn and some cotton or fibres from a tree may be used if more conventional means are not available. I once used a prong from my comb as a needle.

Approaching a village

In many remote regions of the world the local people, nomads, natives etc. tend to be very clannish and many resent intruders, even though you may need their help. Fortunately most nomads and Bedouin are friendly people and will readily offer help to you, but do remember that to win over their hospitality you must be prepared to live as they do.

Here are a few rules you must follow for your own safety:

1. Approach their camp (wherever possible) from the front.
2. Act in a friendly manner and smile.
3. Under no circumstances speak to, touch or even look at the women unless asked. In many nomadic camps women are given severe punishment if they, or you, break the camp code. So a simple wave from you could cause a young woman/girl to suffer a severe thrashing or worse – be thrown out of the tribe. Women who are outside, unattached and have no children are generally ridden with venereal disease as the only way they can survive is by prostitution.
4. If you have to describe something then do so with your hands. Never use your foot as in many camps this is considered an insult.
5. Never throw sweets or offer cheap gifts to the children.
6. Unless asked, never gamble.
7. Never, never, never swear or ridicule someone in front of others, especially a person of high honour.
8. Don't be impatient and even though you may not like or want what refreshment is being offered, take it and either eat or drink it slowly, as to refuse may offend.

Animal attacks

When approaching a village beware of the many dogs that live there. More than once I've had to make a hasty retreat up the nearest tree to avoid being bitten. Most tend to bark and snap as you approach. If the dog continues to rush you, stop. If there is a stick close by, pick it up. The dog will sense this is to be used as a weapon and probably bark more but the stick, if used correctly by you, is very effective. Prod the dog away rather than swing at it. If necessary, kneel down and hold the stick in front of you firmly. Dogs, like many animals, are colour blind and because they will be unable to distinguish the colour of the stick/knife due to the shadows of your body they will rush forward onto it. If you don't have something to push them off with, wrap a cloth around your arm, and use this for protection. Then if the dog does attack it will bite the protected arm.

Most land animals fear being pushed under water, so if there's water around jump into it and let the attacking animal swim to you. Just before it reaches you, sink below the water's surface and pull it under. If you sink, submerge it and then reappear behind it, the animal will get confused and panic. As you swim beneath the animal, if you have a knife or sharp stake, thrust up at its stomach. Even the tiger, which enjoys splashing around in the water, fears being attacked from beneath – many a land man-eater has become a meal to the ubiquitous crocodile.

If a wild dog or other animal comes into your camp, use a lighted stick to ward it off. All animals fear fire. Or throw any hot water, soup etc. into the animal's face.

While we are on the subject of animal attacks, although not found in the desert both the grizzly and the polar bear are tenacious hunters and a few prods with a stick or a little hot water won't deter them. However they do fear fire and loud bangs as both have very acute hearing. Contrary to popular belief they are not very fast swimmers, so you could avoid them by swimming away. On land they can move far more quickly over short distances but they soon become disinterested. Both can and do climb, so beware.

Wolves tend to hunt in packs and will only attack under extreme conditions – probably to protect their young or if driven by starvation. Use the same evasion techniques as for warding off dogs. If you have to, swim off or climb to safety, but be prepared for a long wait. A pack of wolves may hang around for hours. If it's possible to kill or injure just one of them the rest will turn on it and satisfy their aggression.

Making bread

A must for any desert traveller is to be able to make bread in a simple desert oven. Before setting off on my travels with Sally my camel I spent a few days living with a tribe of nomads. Whilst I was there they taught me how to make desert bread. This comprised flour, water, date juice and camel milk, all mixed together in a bowl to form a dough. A fire was then lit in a hole scraped from the sand. When the fire had burnt down to embers they would be scraped out and the dough dropped into the hole. The embers were then put back over the dough and a final covering of sand was added

Making bread in the sand/earth

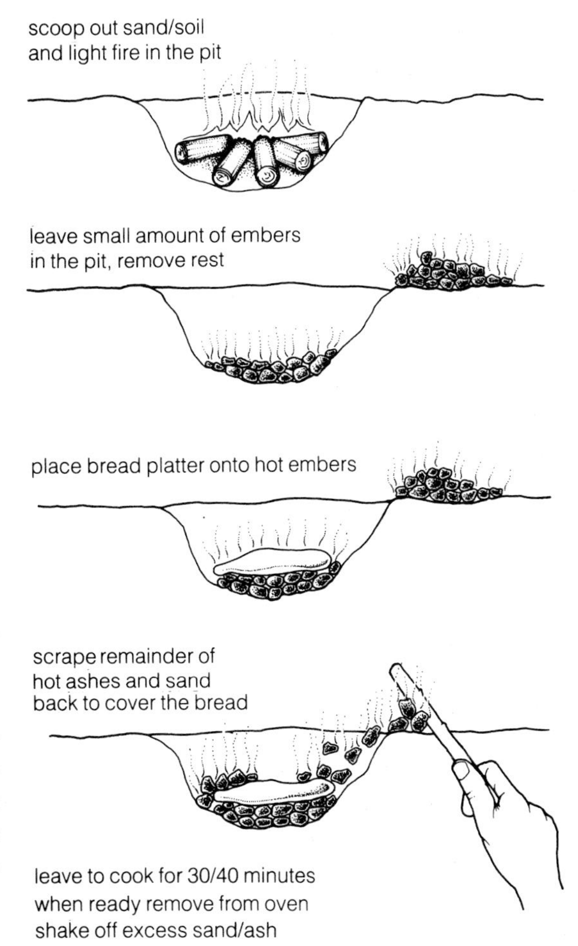

to seal the heat in. Generally, depending on the thickness of the dough, it would be left to cook for about an hour. When cooked it was simply removed from the sand oven, the embers and ashes shaken off and you were left with a beautiful fresh baked, brown cob. Eaten with a little of my cheese made from camel milk, I can tell you it was delicious.

The problem is that, as the bread is cooking, a tantalizing aroma wafts from the ground, so there is a great temptation to remove it from the oven before it's ready. The young Bedouin girls would use the same oven continuously: as one roll came out, another went in.

Sometimes, if the camp was to remain in one spot for any length of time, an above-ground oven would be made. This was simply a dome of mud and rocks with a small fire hole set below. The top of the oven would be open to enable cooks to slap the thin dough cakes onto the side of the oven. Normally once the fire was lit, this method would only take a couple of minutes to cook the bread. Sometimes the oven used would be slightly different, with the fire inside the dome instead of below. Both are excellent ways of cooking and I strongly recommend that anyone interested in learning about survival should make an effort to try each method out for him or herself – if necessary in the comfort of their own back yard.

Making fuel from animal dung

To get the best out of burning dung for fuel, try mixing it with some leaves or grass. This way it will burn better and will give off more heat. You can burn dry dung on its own providing it *is* thoroughly dry. When rained on it takes ages to burn and gives off little heat. Dung alone is ideal if you just want the fire to smoulder, but for quick heat to cook on it will have to be mixed.

Away from your camp (you don't want to attract flies) mix the dung, leaves and grass into a gooey mess using a little water. Where do you get the water? I knew you'd ask. Well, why not do as the Bedouin do – use urine. Mix all the ingredients together using a stick, then take out small handfuls and pat them down into pancakes to dry in the hot sun. Once dry – and only the outside will dry quickly – as soon as you have your fire lit, place a couple on. At first they will smoulder, but eventually they turn a bright red and work just like charcoal.

Remember, you are in a survival situation, you can't afford to be squeamish!

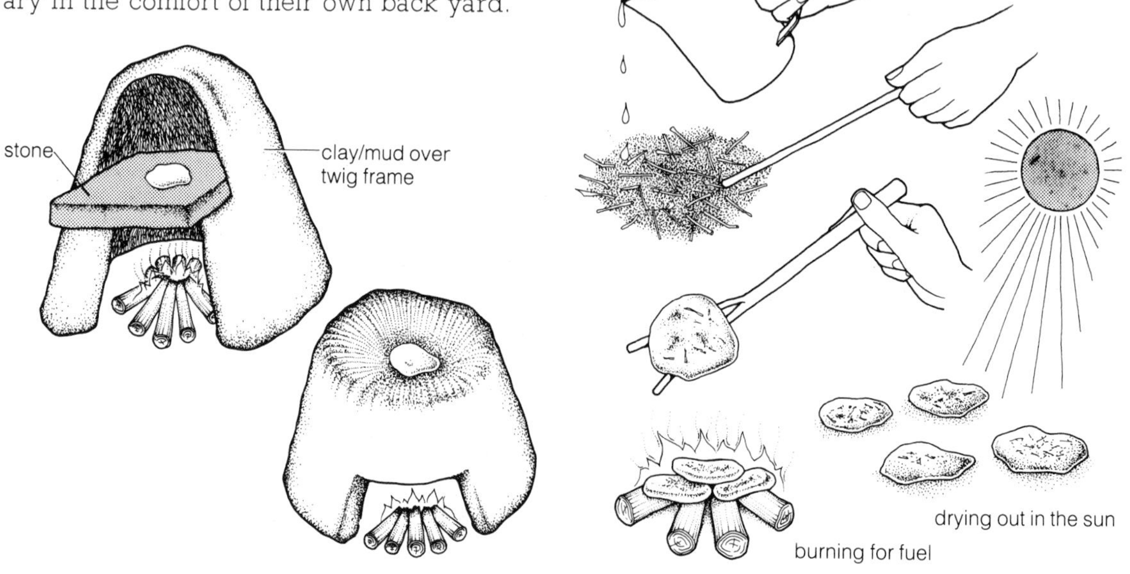

CHAPTER 14

Surviving an Air Crash

Probably the simplest way to get you thinking survival is to go through a hypothetical survival situation. Let's assume that you're in a small aircraft travelling with your family to visit some friends whilst on holiday. Everything's going fine and you are just crossing a remote stretch of desert. Suddenly the aircraft's warning light comes on, the engine splutters and then cuts out. Fortunately you are flying at about 5000 feet so you have plenty of time to look for a landing space before bringing the aircraft down. But, first you call up control and use your MAYDAY distress call. As you lose height, check the skyline for possible routes out of the desert and take particular note of the compass heading and position of the sun! Everyone is told to get into the safety impact position and you swing the aircraft around to run into the wind.

With a lot of luck and skill you or your pilot manage to bring the aircraft down safely, though some damage to the undercarriage has been done, making it impossible to fix the fault and take off again.

impact position

I've deliberately not mentioned the possibility of bailing out or leaving the aircraft by parachute as I'm assuming there wouldn't have been sufficient time. Nor have I mentioned anything about loosening the seatbelt so that you can make a quick exit to avoid being trapped in the aircraft if there were a fire. Some private air services advise loosening your seatbelt, but my own preference is to remain strapped in so that the belt will take a lot of the impact. But whatever the case, let us assume, after a bumpy landing, that you are now on the ground.

A few minutes ago you and your family were happily winging your way across the clear blue sky, looking forward to your holiday visit with friends. Now, here you are, suddenly thrust into a real life-or-death situation. Now more than ever you're going to need all your skills, stamina and control of your emotions to keep the family safe and alive.

Seconds before you crashed you managed to turn off the ignition and thus avoided the possibility of starting a fire. Fuel may have sprayed over the engine or a spark from the electrics set it alight. Apart from a few bruises most of you managed to survive safely.

After the crash

Leave the aircraft quickly, get everyone well clear and assembled together, keep close and console each other. If there are any fires smouldering around the aircraft, quickly cover them with sand or use the aircraft fire extinguisher. Once you are satisfied that the aircraft is safe, one of you may move forward to remove quickly all luggage, food, tools and the first aid box.

If it's safe to do so, remove the compass from the aircraft, then you can re-check the directions from down on the ground. Remembering the time of day, the aircraft's approach path, the position of the sun, moon or stars will all help you to work out your present position. When you switched off the engine and radio you probably prevented the aircraft from exploding on impact, and you now have all this equipment to use for your survival. Only after you have checked that there are no injuries and that no one needs immediate attention, and you have gained control of your nerves, venture back inside the aircraft, but not until you're absolutely satisfied that it has cooled down and there is no possibility of a fire, especially around the engine. When you do eventually approach it, do so from the tail section. Then if it does suddenly blow up you will at least be clear of any spraying oil or petrol. Walk towards it slowly and cautiously. Smell for the tell-tale aroma of petrol fumes.

IF IN DOUBT . . . STAY OUT!

Before entering the aircraft try to remove the door or at least make sure it can't close or lock behind you. You may need to make a quick exit so make sure that the path to the door is clear. Having carefully checked conditions on board the aircraft you may now make full use of it as a survival aid.

This of course is how you would like it to end. All you want now is for the rescue party to come and collect you all safely. Alas, this isn't always the case. Things happened so quickly in the air, now down on the ground after all the noise and panic, the only sound heard is the gentle breeze or the sighings of those in the party. As you sit and stare, slowly the reality of what you have just been through will begin to dawn and many of you may now succumb to shock. This can be just as frightening as the actual crash. One of you will now have to take full control.

Remember the advice given in chapter one on survival psychology: you may feel dazed and confused as you try to take in the ordeal you have just experienced. Your whole body may begin to shake uncontrollably and you may shiver, not with cold but with fright. Here's what you should do: place your hands around your shoulders, tucking your head into your chest, draw up your legs and crouch there. To get the shock and shivering under control breathe slowly and deliberately. It may be necessary for you to wrap a garment around your shoulders to ward off the cold.

Many people at this point may find themselves wanting to vomit: this is nature's way of easing the safety valve. After vomiting you'll feel cold and clammy even though you may be sitting in the hot sun. This is where covering yourself up and keeping warm becomes invaluable. Remember that convulsive shivering after an accident is a normal reaction. In such situations people who are not able to control their fears and emotions quickly break down. During these bouts of shaking, suffering from cold sweats and shivering you will quickly burn up a great deal of vital energy and in the desert lose a lot of valuable fluids. You can prevent fatigue, or at any rate minimise it, by keeping a check on yourself and letting nature take its course. The sooner you get these fears under control the better your chances are of survival and the sooner you will stop shivering. Having your emotions under control is important whether you are on your own or not. If you feel like a good cry, have one. If you feel like shouting and cursing, do so. Get it out of your system.

Before the crash you may have managed to get out a MAYDAY signal, but unfortunately it wasn't acknowledged so you have no way of knowing whether anyone heard your call for help. If the radio is still working, using proper radio procedure you can call up control and give them a fix on who you are and what your bearings are. Now it's up to them to come and rescue you.

What can you do to help your rescuers – for help is what they are going to need if they are to rescue you quickly? The longer you spend in a state of shivering and panic, the longer it will be before you can start to assist those who are perhaps going to save your life. The first thing you must do now is to set out some sort of signal marker, burning oil on the sand, or setting out aircraft bits and pieces, mirrors, footprints, flags or anything that will aid the rescuers. If you have any parachutes spread them out as markers.

Shelter

During the day you can obviously shelter beneath the aircraft and at night you can shelter inside it as the temperature drops. If, on impact, the aircraft hasn't broken up, you can use the wings, doors or even parts of the fuselage to build a shelter. Some of the superstructure may also be useful, as will the seat covers for awnings during the day. They can double as blankets at night.

With the covers removed, use the seats to rest on. Sitting on the hot sand will make you perspire and you're going to need all the liquid you can save. From the moment you step outside the aircraft dehydration will begin: conserve your energy and water evaporation.

These same survival rules apply if you have been stranded in a car. Switch off the ignition, conserve the battery. You may need the lights and horn with which to signal. During the day rest up inside but leave the doors and windows open to allow any breeze to circulate. At night close the doors but leave one of the windows slightly open to allow fresh air in. If necessary remove the seat covers and use them as blankets. Don't waste time and energy ripping the door or bonnet off for shelter.

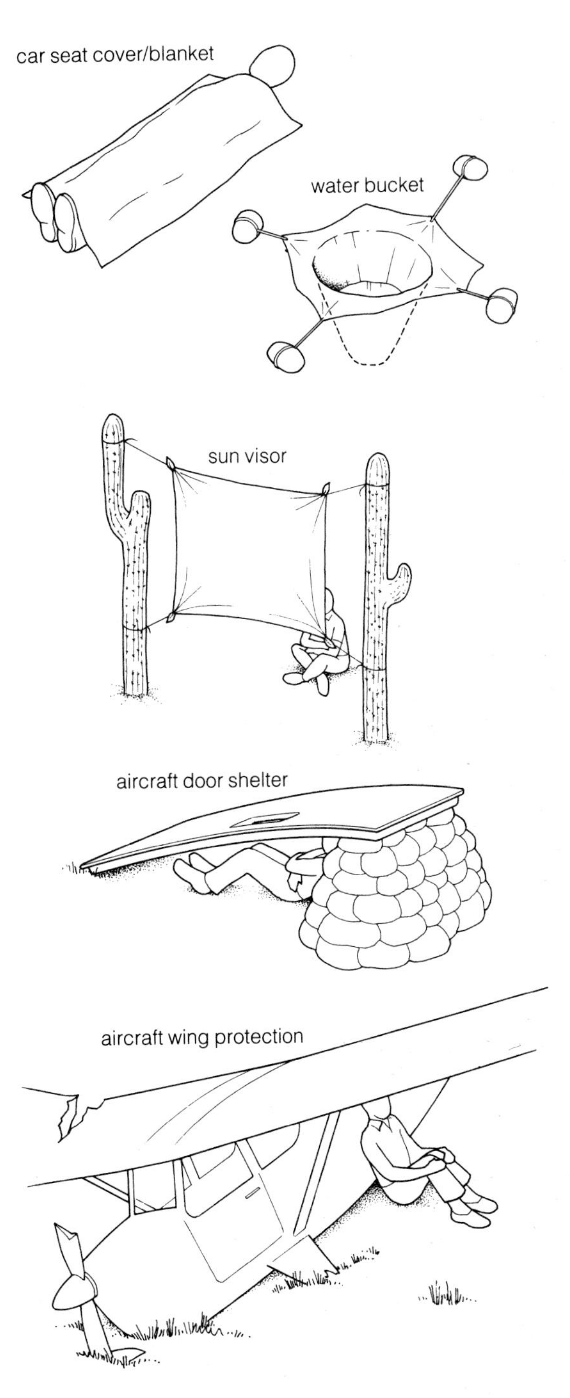

Using parts of the crashed aircraft for shelter

Improvising for survival

There are dozens of survival aids that can be improvised from parts of the aircraft or car. Here are but a few:

1 Parachute

As an airborne soldier, one of the many skills taught to me was the practical use of the parachute as a survival aid. To a paratrooper the parachute is simply a fast, silent, efficient way of getting into battle. Once on the ground the paratrooper leaves his chute behind and moves off to fight. But as every soldier knows the parachute is not only his lifeline during descent but also very often after he has landed. Parachutes can be used to make shelters, bandages, sleeping bags, a signal-marker panel, water filter bags, ropes, hammocks, fishing nets, carrier bags, rucksacks, clothing, firelighters and traps. A chute has even been used as a signals pad for writing messages on. Every single part of the parachute, including the harness and metal dee-ring attachments, may be used. Dee-rings make excellent climbing carabiners and winch pulleys. Improvisation is the name of the game.

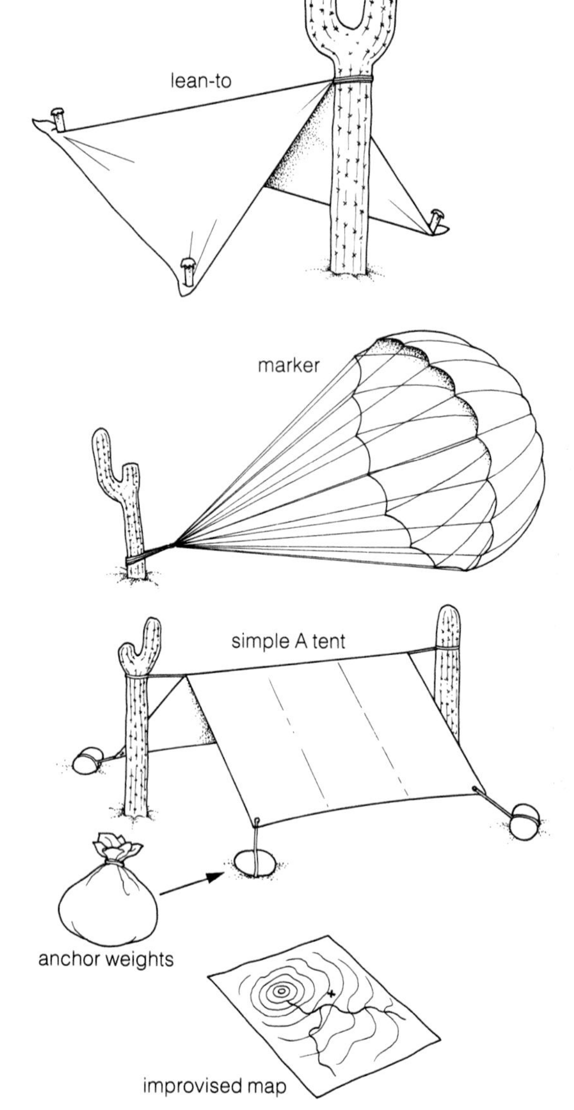

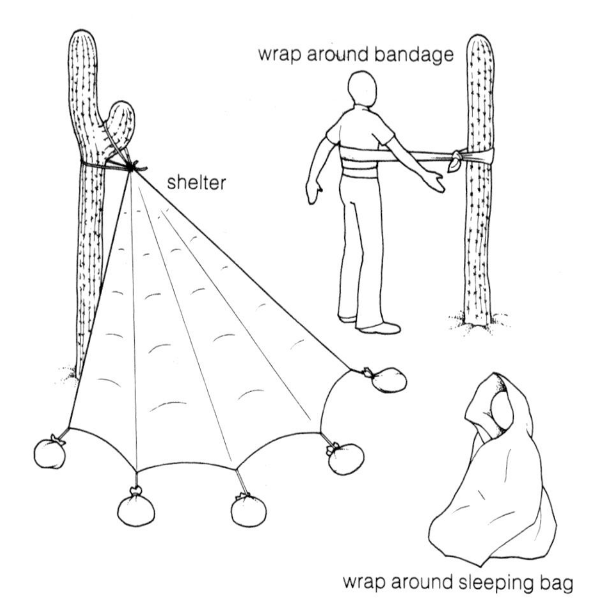

Uses of the parachute as a survival aid in the desert. See also pages 139 and 142 for shelter and Arab style headdresses

2 Oil

This should be collected from the aircraft (or car) and can be used to start fires, for cooking and also for signalling. Mixed with sand it makes an excellent cooker.

3 Rubber piping

This can be taken from water hose radiators and can be used for burning, storage and improvising other survival aids, such as traps. Rubber hoses make superb splints and shoes.

4 Electric wire

Useful for making traps, snares or tying other materials together. Also for rope, shoelaces, belts or harnesses.

5 Battery and bulbs

The lead from batteries can be used as sinkers; the acid to burn through rope. Batteries and bulbs may obviously be used as a source of light. Bulbs make useful fishing floats and a surgical knife can be improvised by using a broken bulb. I know, I've used one!

6 Petrol and diesel

Both can be used for signalling and lighting fires. Black smoke (from diesel) is easily seen against clear desert skies. Droplets of diesel or petrol flare up when sprinkled on a fire. Diesel is also good for killing jiggers (infected flea bites on the foot) and dropped in water makes a good reflective colour marker like a rainbow.

7 Old tyres

Can be used for collecting water, or cut up to make into shoes, or burnt for signalling (rubber gives off dense black smoke). Also for rubber bungies (loops), raft supports and improvised hammocks. A section of tyre may be used as a leg or arm splint.

8 Inner tubes

Can be used for making traps, burnt for signals, used for supports for beds or in strips can be employed as tourniquets, catapults, loops, water bottles, life jackets, rafts etc.

9 Car or plane seat covers

These can provide warmth as blankets. They can also be used to keep the sun off, to make backpacks and other storage containers, or for clothing.

10 Tools

These have uses in almost everything you may wish to do and can also be particularly valuable in making weapons such as spears, knives and axes.

11 Hubcaps and seatbelts

Hubcaps can make water collectors and signalling devices, improvised plates and even trolley wheels. Seatbelts can be used for hammock slings, rucksacks, waist belts, shelter ties, climbing harnesses or firelighters. The buckle on the end of a seatbelt can make a useful weapon for self-defence.

12 Paper salvaged from the wreck

Useful for insulation, fires and even to give yourself something to read. In an emergency chewed paper pulp helps to settle the tummy and as a makeshift bandage may be used to stop bleeding.

13 Mirrors

For signalling. Also if broken the glass edge may be used as a knife, to collect moisture, or to attract fish.

14 Lining from car/plane roof or from seats

Can be used for sleeping on, making foot and hand comforters, backpacks, clothes, hammocks or water filters.

15 Carpeting

Excellent as ground and sleeping insulation or overhead protection. Also for hammocks.

16 Underlay

Useful as thermal insulation in snow holes – see Chapter 15, *The Arctic*. Underlay is also good for shoes, gloves and even hats. Very good for burning – gives off dense black smoke.

Care must always be taken when improvising. Remember to think about the changes in temperature when using metal for protective covering; it conducts heat and cold. In extreme temperatures it can either burn or freeze the skin if there is direct contact.

CHAPTER 15

The Arctic

The very word Arctic conjures up images of intense cold with vast regions of dense freezing fog and never-ending snowstorms. Temperatures are so low and inhospitable to man that without the proper protective clothing and shelter, even to be exposed to the elements for just a few seconds could result in almost certain frostbite and possible death. Man is very adaptable and can survive, even in the harshest of regions, but the most hardened and experienced of explorers will be the first to admit that to survive in arctic conditions requires just that little bit more effort at self-preservation.

For thousands of years Eskimos have learnt to survive in sub-zero conditions so hostile to the outsider, that without proper training and survival experience they would die. Eskimos learned their survival skills by trial and error and many of these aptitudes have been taught to the outsider. As a result, thousands of lives have been saved. Basic skills needed to survive in the Arctic, apart from staying warm and dry, include how to hunt or fish through ice, how to build shelters to ward off freezing snow blizzards, and how to build with animal skins, construct snow houses and use underground caves.

In Mongolia when the harsh winters come, all the inhabitants and livestock take refuge in their cave houses, which are often as deep down in the ground as twenty or thirty feet. This means the animals have to be lowered by ropes. Whilst the livestock winter at the bottom of the cave house, the family live on the floor above them, and all cooking and heating is done by using animal dung as fuel. This means the whole family and their cattle can stay down in the house, often for up to three or four months.

In the very remote regions one thing you will notice is the eeriness that seems to creep over the area (unlike the jungle or desert at night where there are lots of insects and birds buzzing around all the time). Sometimes you might catch sight of a large wild animal but they are more likely to avoid you than attack you. Other than that, the only sounds will be howling winds and the occasional passing bird.

As you come further south from the polar cap both animal and vegetation life increases. The snow becomes more manageable and not as powdery as that in the extreme north. Days become longer and thaws set in much quicker. Your chances of survival improve greatly.

Igloos and other shelters

When the Eskimos first colonised the Polar region they, too, quickly learned the technique of combating the cold and wind by building shelters made from snow (we know them as igloos). Deep inside the shelter, protected from the bitter cold, they were able to live a relatively normal life during the long winter months. When the mild summer came, they used tents for shelter.

Unlike the Mongolians, Eskimos were unable to burrow down into the frozen land or use caves. In their case it was much simpler to use the material to hand – SNOW. Snow cut into blocks and then pressed together proved ideal for their needs, and anyone who has

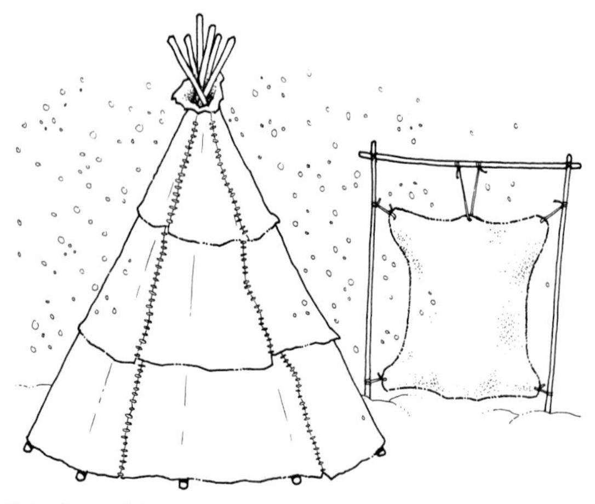
Reindeer skin tent

actually lived in an igloo will tell you it can be extremely comfortable inside.

Providing you are willing to make the effort, there is always an abundance of material to hand for you to work with.

Building an igloo isn't too difficult. Yours may not end up looking as professional as an Eskimo's but providing you work slowly and don't tire yourself there is no reason why you shouldn't make an excellent shelter in a couple of hours. However, it may be better to build yourself a small snow scrape first; this will be less tiring and easier to make than an igloo, and you can use it to fall back on.

As with any shelter, the essential thing is to ensure that it protects you from the elements. Shell scrapes or holes in the ground are intended for overnight stops and to be used in emergencies. Find an area where the snow has drifted to a reasonable thickness – this will save you a lot of hard work. Build yourself a small snow wall by rolling large snowballs and placing them across the front of your snow hole entrance – this will help keep out the driving wind. Now scoop snow from the hillock and continue scooping until you can crawl inside.

Snowhole (*below*) and shellscrape (*bottom*)

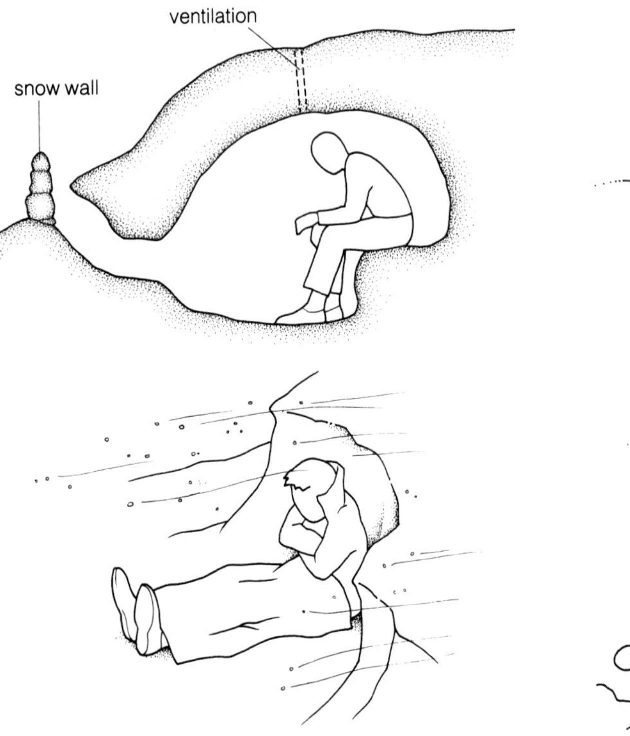

Building a snowhole

Remember, this is simply a quick survival shelter to enable you to rest. Sitting outside in the freezing cold and biting winds will quickly drain your energy. The sooner you are under cover the better. If time allows, inside the shelter build a small platform to sleep on. Smooth off the inner roof but remember to leave yourself enough height at least to sit up. (It isn't necessary to be able to stand up.)

Building a large snow shelter will obviously take a lot longer but if you foresee staying for more than a couple of nights, it might be wise to construct one. Whatever you build, once inside try to insulate yourself from the snow. If there's any old wood or moss lying around, use this. If necessary use your jacket to sit on. If you're not sitting on your jacket, place it over your head and don't let your shoulders or the small of your back come into contact with the walls of the snow hole. The cold will only absorb your body heat.

Heat loss from the head and hands can be very severe. It's better to drape your jacket over your shoulders rather than wear it. This way it will trap the warm air of your body. If the jacket is pulled tight, heat from your body will quickly disperse. If you have a sleeping bag – lucky you – get inside it. Take off your shoes or boots and socks and let them dry inside the sleeping bag. Tie your socks under your arms and around your chest. The heat from your body will help dry them a little. If you leave your boots off and exposed to the

Building an igloo

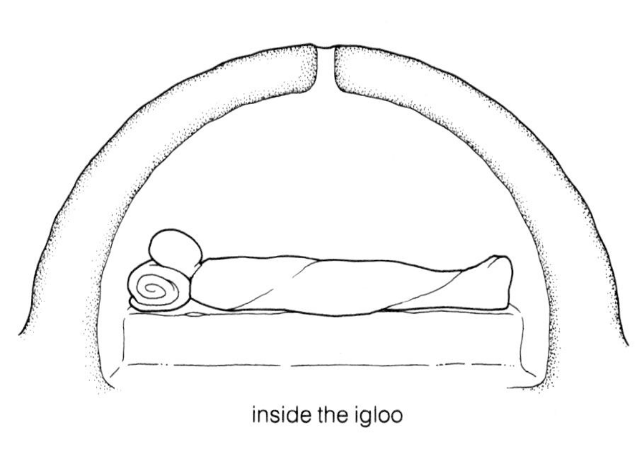

inside the igloo

finished igloo with vent hole, ledge (inside), snow door

cold it may not be possible to get them on again in the morning, because the leather will have frozen solid. Try to keep your mouth and nose clear of your sleeping bag as breathing inside it will cause condensation which will quickly turn to water and make it cold and uncomfortable.

Sleep at first will be very difficult. As you sit there and rest all kinds of thoughts will be running through your head. What with the fear of being lost and alone, you will probably be overwhelmed with the shock and anxiety. As always though, try to get your fears and emotions under control as quickly as possible. Think only of survival – YOUR SURVIVAL!

Building with stone and wood

Not all Arctic regions are covered in snow. Many areas have millions and millions of acres of pine forests and shrubs whilst others are covered in reeds, mosses and lichens. Some are strewn with boulders and stone scree. All are potential building materials. Whatever the terrain it's up to you to improvise with the materials at hand.

If there are stones available build yourself a strong shelter. Use the mosses, lichens and reeds to insulate the shelter floor and for roof protection. In the desert when we were constructing a shelter it was emphasized that you must protect yourself from the scorching sun and try not to cause unnecessary sweating by staying cool and working slowly. Well, the same rule about your work rate applies here. Work at a steady pace; don't remove too much clothing whilst working – it's better to remove only a little at a time. Too much too soon and you'll quickly chill; too little too late and you'll find yourself bathed in perspiration! Only you can judge. As soon as you feel the need to remove some clothing you're probably working too hard. Slow down. If you have to remove anything always remember the chill factor.

Remember those three killers:

COLD . . . WIND . . . WET.

Your feet, hands and face will probably be the first parts of your body to feel the cold. If you haven't any gloves remove the inside liners of your pockets. These will give you some protection. For extra leg warmers tear the lining from your jacket sleeves. Incidentally, these same liners also make excellent water-strainers!

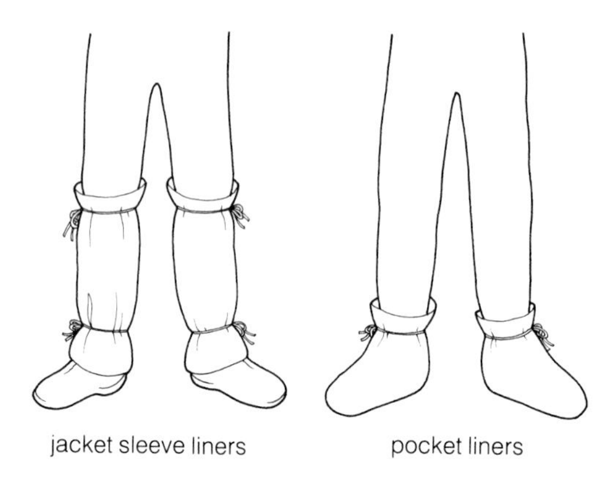

Fallen trees or overhanging rocks often make natural shelters though it's very difficult to heat up rocks without a large fire. During the day when the sun is shining the rock face will be wet and slippery; in the evening as the temperature drops it freezes and will probably be covered in ice.

Wood, on the other hand, is much warmer and easier to handle. If it's very cold and you don't have any gloves, it's unwise to handle cold stones, so if you have a choice, choose the fallen tree. If there are trees around you'll have a better chance of survival because not only do you have something to build your shelter with; you also have fuel for your fire. The ferns and branches may also be used for insulation against the cold. Look for a suitable tree that has been struck by lightning or buckled a little above the ground. These often need very little work to make them suitable for your needs.

Up to the fringe of the Polar Cap the only trees you are likely to find are pine. These are extremely hardy and one of the few living

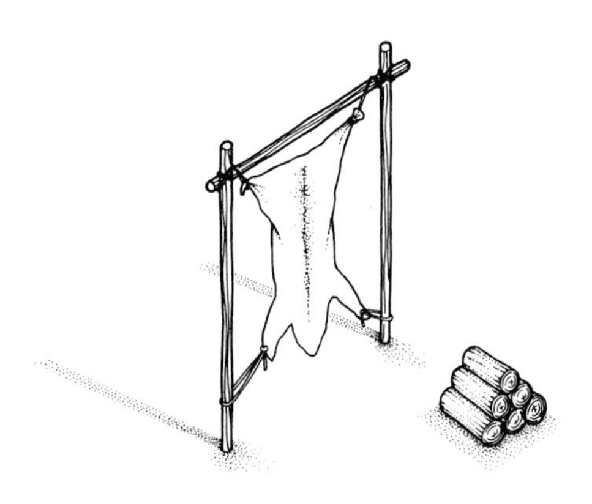

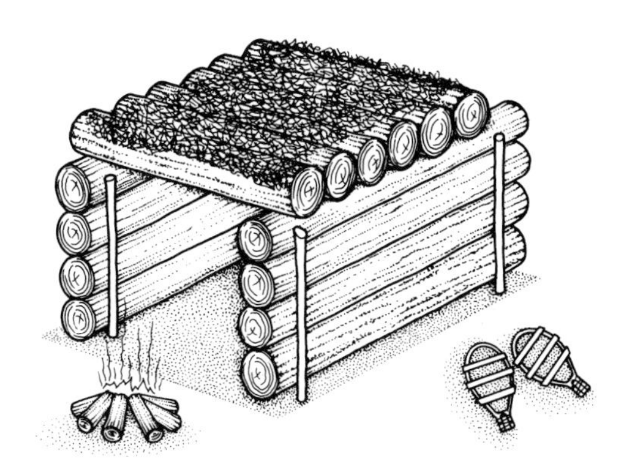

things that can survive in sub-zero temperatures. In some of the remote regions of Canada and Northern Russia, forty to fifty foot high trees are often completely covered in snow for months at a time. Once on exercise whilst serving in the armed forces, I had to dig down alongside a tree to make a shelter. For the best part of a morning my friend and I worked, digging out the snow until we reached the bottom. Eventually when we did break through, at the base of the tree there was a natural shelter ready and waiting for us. On the ground there was a thick covering of dried pine needles. Excellent insulation. Large icicles hung from the tree branches and when these were melted down they gave us a ready-to-use supply of fresh drinking water.

In the desert or jungle it is possible to build a shelter by using a parachute or old blanket, but in the Arctic, whilst they help ward off the wind during the day they do little to keep out the cold at night. However, it's possible to build yourself a teepee shelter and have a small fire burning inside it. Remember to leave a hole at the top for ventilation and escape of smoke. Incidentally, a fire in such a shelter acts like a beacon during the night and for your rescuers this may be the only thing they see.

A log lean-to is easily constructed but the same warning applies here as in the jungle – don't make it too large. Otherwise it will be impossible to heat up and will also take a great deal of materials to build. To waterproof it cover it with moss. Think survival at all times.

Heat loss

This is as good a time as any to mention the heat loss factor. To survive, the body must remain above a certain temperature. While snow itself is an excellent insulator, it can also melt and rapidly absorb your body heat by evaporation.

It's important to keep your hands, face and feet warm and dry. Frostbite, like hypothermia, can creep up on you without your realizing it. As you become weaker and weaker from cold and hunger, so the body demands more and more energy to stay alive. Exposed areas of the skin allow body heat to evaporate, so keep them covered up. Energy will supply your body with the necessary heat and can only be obtained by eating food. Providing you dress sensibly, the body has a natural way of combating heat loss. Think of the body heating system as having two cores; an inner and outer, the outer being your skin. Through glands in the skin, sweating and heat loss is controlled to some degree. The inner core, which includes the blood from various organs, is responsible for returning the energy to re-supply you with body heat. Once the cold begins to get through the inner core, unless quickly stopped, it is almost certain that you will die from hypothermia.

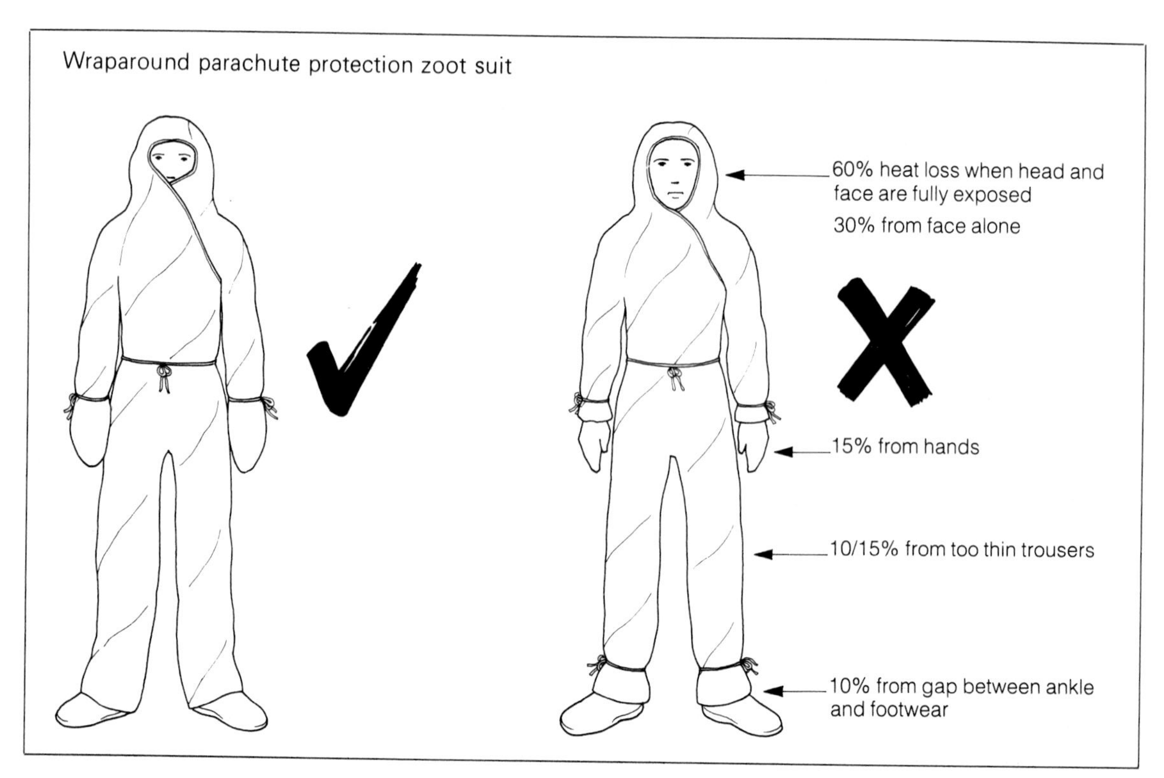

Frostbite symptoms

Like hypothermia, frostbite creeps up on you and the areas of the body most likely to become affected are the exposed parts furthest away from the heart and with the least circulation. For example the finger tips (if uncovered), ears, nose and feet. Prevention is simple: keep all vulnerable areas well protected. Keep warm, dry and out of the biting wind. Also, remember the following rules:

A. If the face has to be exposed it is imperative that you keep wrinkling your face to avoid stiff patches forming.
B. Don't handle bare metal/plastic or petrol cannisters without glove protection. Petrol splashed onto the face or hands evaporates immediately and further lowers the temperature.
C. Clothing that's too tight not only restricts your movements but also restricts air flow between body and clothes. Wear warm, loosely fitting garments.
D. Don't become damp from sweating. If you feel yourself perspiring, stop immediately, wipe the area with a clean dry cloth and cover up.
E. Don't venture outside your shelter area for even a few seconds without adequate protection.
F. Dry any wet clothing, boots or gloves as quickly as possible. Spare socks may be wrapped around the body to prevent them from becoming damp.

Frostbite will be seen as small white or cream-coloured patches on the skin, which when touched feel firm and hard. If you suspect that you may have frostbite, for instance around the face, try making faces or screwing the mouth or eyes tightly. If frostbite is there you'll feel a slight pricking sensation as the skin continues to freeze. If allowed to continue without treatment – by protection, not rubbing – in a few minutes the skin will become too stiff to move. At this stage the condition is dangerous. The longer you leave the area exposed, the deeper the frostbite penetrates the skin. Blood vessels become clotted, both muscles and bone freeze and when this happens the area affected may have to be cut off – be it ear, nose, finger or toe.

When frostbite is severe small blisters and swellings form. If not treated they become ulcerous and infected.

Treatment

No matter how mild the case of frostbite, immediate attention is needed. In less severe cases just moving out of the wind and cold will probably be all that's required. Small areas of affected skin can be defrosted simply by placing a warm hand over it or putting on gloves. Even wrapping a handkerchief over it will ease the pain and prevent the frostbite from spreading further. Frostbitten hands may be tucked inside clothes for a couple of seconds then put directly against the skin. Often just sitting on your hands will ease the pain and in one case I saw in the army, the medical officer made the sufferer push his hands down his pants between his thighs. Rubbing frostbite with snow doesn't ease the pain or prevent further spread. DON'T DO IT.

Never rub vigorously the area affected with frostbite. A warm soft cloth pad may be applied but it must be dry, warm (not hot) and gently held against the skin. In extreme cases you may have to build a fire and heat up some stones, wrap them in spare clothing and lay these against the patient, ideally on the tummy or chest, never directly on the affected area. If you have any pain killers or other medicines such as morphine, use them if necessary. Above all keep the patient warm, dry, comfortable and safe from further injury. Hot drinks can be given when the symptoms are mild or there is definite recovery from a major attack.

Because the blood vessels of the face are close to the surface and easily visible, people tend to think that they are immune from frostbite. This is not so. Any part of the body is susceptible if exposed. Often the first sign of frostbite on the face is when the cheeks become stiff and hard to the touch.

Remember! Frostbite can kill.

Snow blindness

This is very similar to the glare you get from hot desert sand. A powerful reflection from the snow caused by the high intensity of glare from the sun's rays is reflected back into your eyes, causing you to squint. The first symptom of snow blindness is that the eyes become sensitive to the glare and reflection. Blinking and squinting is followed by a slight burning sensation around the eyes which may begin to water. Your vision becomes blurred and the surrounding area appears to have taken on a reddish pink glow. Gradually the burning sensation increases until eventually it becomes impossible to open the eyes because of intense pain, which the slightest amount of glare increases.

Treatment

This consists of rest in a shaded – preferably dark – area and a cool wet compress applied to the eyes at intervals. As a last resort a wet handkerchief will help. Rest and time is the only cure. Ointment doesn't ease the pain; nor do hot compresses – in fact heat will only aggravate it. Make eye protectors, though not from metal, which may cause frostbite. Bark from trees, pages from a book or paper will suffice, as will soot or burnt cork. These will reduce the glare.

Arctic supplies

Water

Sucking on either snow or ice will alleviate your thirst only whilst it is in your mouth. Both old snow and ice tend to taste a little bitter. To get the best results from either it is far better to melt it down slowly in a container. Simply hold a little in your hand and allow it to drip into the container until you have enough to cover the bottom. Now add just a little ice or snow at a time to the boiling water – let the heat of the

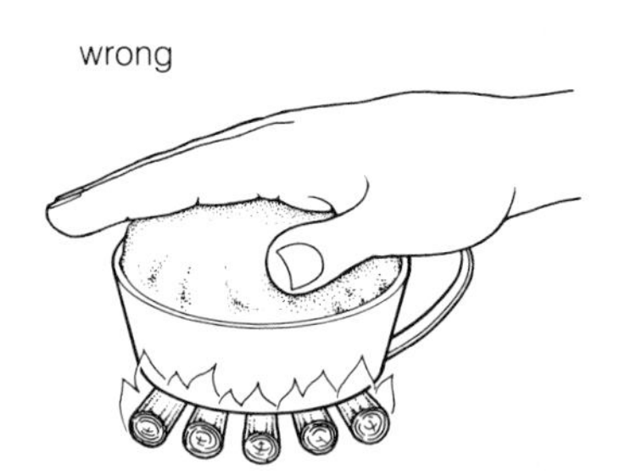

melting snow/ice

water and the fire melt it for you. Once melted it becomes quite palatable, ideal for cooking and washing with. Remember, freshly fallen snow contains a great deal of air and will produce less water, so take snow from below the surface if possible. For more detailed advice on obtaining and purifying water, see Chapter 5.

Catching food

Chapter 4 on 'Fishing' and Chapter 7 on 'Finding Food' contain advice appropriate for the Arctic. Even though it's a bleak and inhospitable place, many birds breed and feed in the region. To the survivor, geese, Arctic ducks and many sea birds can be a good source of food. Here, many birds become flightless for two to three weeks of the year due to moulting and mating. This is the time they become easy prey for the hunter.

A small, simple fish hook that will catch birds, seals and obviously fish can be made by sharpening a section of bone, fastening it to your fishing line then bending it back and covering it with meat as bait. A quick dip in the icy water and it's set. As soon as the animal, fish or bird swallows it the heat of its belly melts the ice and the hook springs back and slits open the creature's stomach. (Cruel, but then Arctic survival is generally pitiless.)

If you manage to see a seal, walrus, ptarmigan or even a polar bear basking on the ice and you want to get closer to kill it, try making a camouflage wind sail. Fasten a piece of white cloth across a couple of sticks (like a kite) and by using this method of camouflage you will be able to get close enough to use your spear or bow and arrow.

Opposite is a series of diagrams showing the variety of Arctic traps you can make, to enable you to catch your dinner from the ice.

Fishing through ice

This is a tried and tested method and one that has been around for centuries. Basically it's the same as when fishing normally except that you first have to find or make a suitable hole through the ice. Many of the trapping techniques used for ordinary fishing can easily be adapted (see Chapter 4), but for obvious reasons foliage and other materials may not be available, so you will have to improvise (see illustration opposite).

If possible, try to find a hole that has already been made rather than make one yourself – it saves energy. But, if you have to make a hole, cut or scour it out rather than knock or stamp through the ice. Either of the latter may weaken the surrounding area and you could end up in serious trouble.

Watch for natural breathing holes used by seals and penguins – these make excellent fishing areas and are generally quite safe. However take care, as the polar bear may have had the same idea.

Remember to mark fishing holes well. During a storm they often become covered with snow and thus become potential death traps. If you do accidently step into one and fall through into the water you must get out as

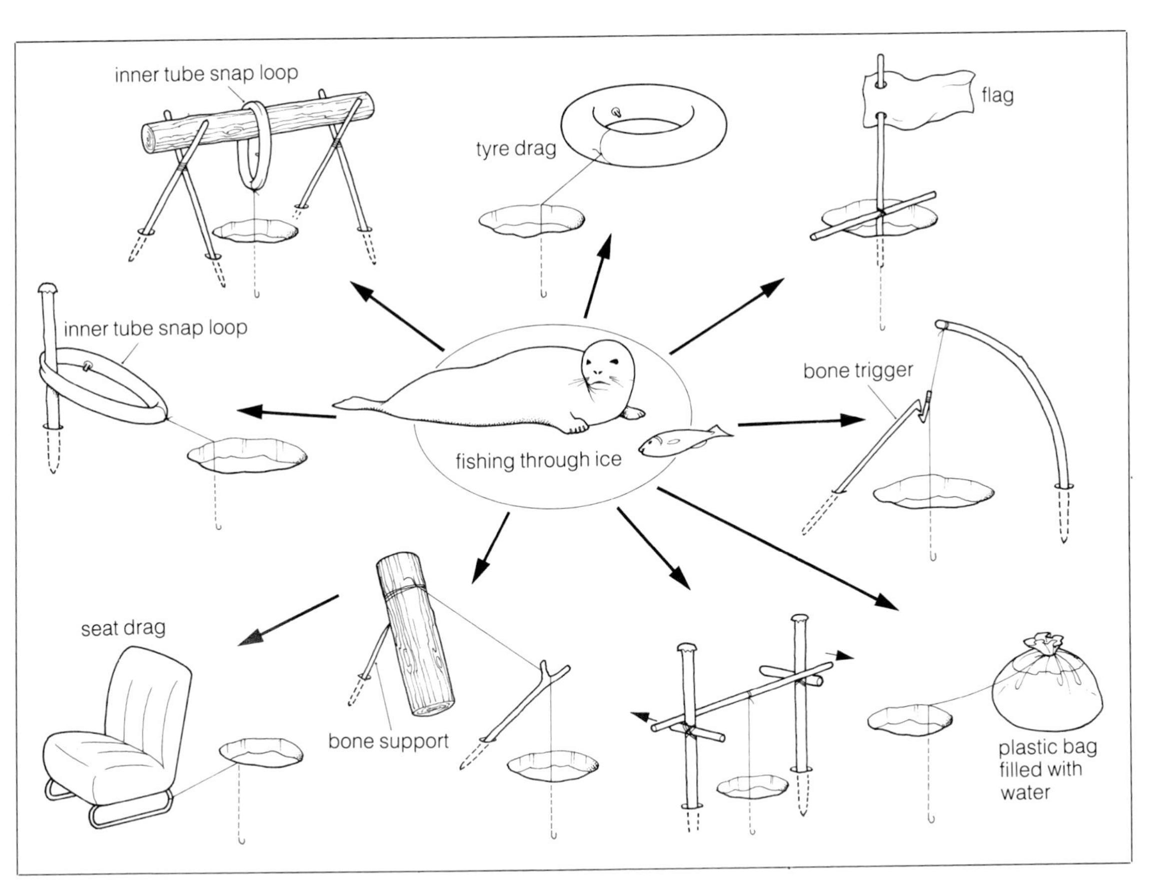

quickly as possible. You literally have but a few seconds to get dry and warm. If necessary remove some of the wet clothing and run around or exercise to get your circulation flowing again. Death by freezing is painless and in just a few minutes you will literally slow down in movement as your brain and reactions dim, and you die.

Traversing ice

For obvious reasons this will require a little more expertise and effort on your part than crossing land. Travelling across flat areas of ice such as a frozen lake, river etc., must be attempted only if there is no other alternative or if you are a hundred per cent sure it is safe to do so. Once you are out in the middle, if the ice has the slightest fracture, it could give way without any warning. If you have to cross remember to carry a rope and keep it handy. Take at least one long, thin, strong pole to help you climb out should you break through.

Animal skin, ice shoes, even branches tied to your feet will give you that little extra security in terms of spreading the load and if you have to take a sledge make sure you pull and not push it. Remember to have a rope long enough to allow you to haul yourself out and scramble clear should the ice shatter. Attach your rope to a tree or similar support before crossing. If the worst happens, let the sledge go and lie flat on your tummy, then pull yourself across. This will take a lot of time and energy but it is better to be safe than sorry. Without some means of helping you to stay on the water surface, e.g. a life jacket, your chances of survival in the water are practically nil. In water even as warm as fifty degrees

Fahrenheit a person of average fitness, and wearing normal clothing, can only expect to remain alive if:

- they tread water – survival possible for about 2 to 2½ hours,
- they swim normally, (breaststroke) – for about 1 to 1½ hours,
- they have some means of floatable aid – for 2½ to 3 hours,
- they adopt the drown-proofing position – 1 to 1½ hours.

Traversing a glacier requires that little bit of extra caution. If you have to cross make sure you have a rope belayed, i.e. secured by winding it round a peg etc. before setting off, especially if the glacier is steep, as many of them are. Ideally an ice axe is needed to stop you from sliding along, with boot crampons (ice shoes). Both are designed for walking across glaciers. You can improvise by pulling a spare pair of socks over your boots – this will help you to get a better grip – or you could fasten some dry grass or reeds to the boots. If you have any spare rope lash this around you loosely. Should you slide, it helps to grip the ice. Remember to keep your rucksack loose on one shoulder, lean into the glacier, face upwards and take each step slowly.

Whatever you use – ice axe, steel stake, knife etc. – to stop you from sliding, remember it will only be effective if you get your whole weight over it, forcing it to dig into the ice. If this fails and you are unable to stop yourself sliding, spreadeagle on the ice and allow your clothes, rope etc. to grip. DO NOT CROUCH UP. Some experts disagree as to whether or not you should be face down on the ice or flat on your back. If you are sliding uncontrollably I'd say you should be on your back with your knees bent and feet flat on the ice. This way at least you can see where you're heading.

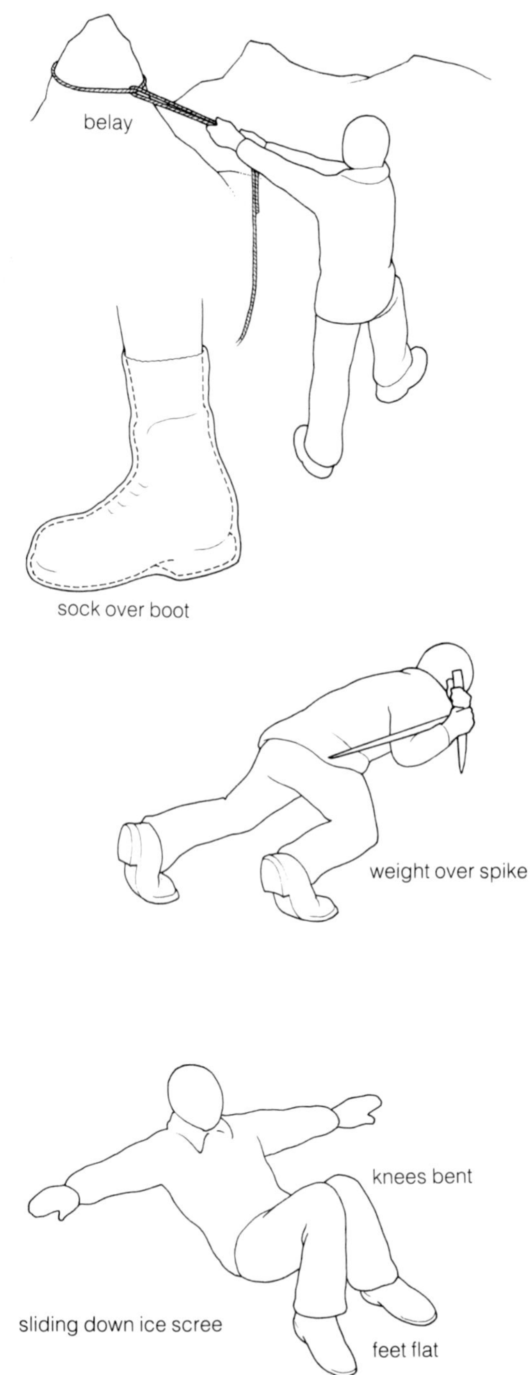

CHAPTER 16

Basic Survival Medicine

Dealing with illness or injury in a critical 'live-or-die' situation may happen to very few of us. But not being prepared is totally irresponsible as the information isn't difficult to get. Many schools, hospitals and voluntary services such as the St John's Ambulance Brigade now run courses that allow the complete novice to gain confidence and experience in dealing with health and injuries.

People today have a great deal more leisure time on their hands and, as one would expect, many want to try the great outdoors, camping and exploring. But in any walk of life and never more so than in a survival situation, it's essential to have some basic knowledge of first aid. A good example of this is the first aid taught to young people who attend outward bound schools and colleges, where quite rightly particular emphasis is always placed on hypothermia, for reasons that should have become clear from this book. Anyone can be a victim of hypothermia, young or old. Another example is the very high standard of first aid taught to our armed forces.

As a result of modern travel, a soldier may be transported to almost any part of the world in a matter of hours, and very often on arrival he has to rely on his own individual survival and military skills to stay alive, and on his basic first aid training.

Basic first aid

Basic first aid is nothing more than common sense. If something is burning you either walk away or remove it. It's as simple as that. If you have a cut and it's bleeding, try to stop it. If you have a broken leg, arm or wrist try to immobilize it (strap it up). Apply the common sense rules first. If it's a major incident involving two or more people always treat the more seriously injured person first. If someone in the group is dead, leave him. Treat only the living and remember to attend to your own injuries if you have any.

Shock may strike hours after the incident and you may be less able to cope later. So do what you can quickly. Remove the wounded, if possible, from any further injury and to safety. Keep them warm, safe, dry and protected from the elements. Above all, look after your own health. If circumstances demand it bury the dead as soon as possible, but only after you are satisfied that they really are dead. Sometimes it's heartbreaking waiting for them to die. I know, I've had soldiers die in my arms. The feeling of helplessness is overwhelming as you hold them or try to stop the flow of blood and ease their pain. But you must be firm. Others may need your help more. Remember you are in a survival situation.

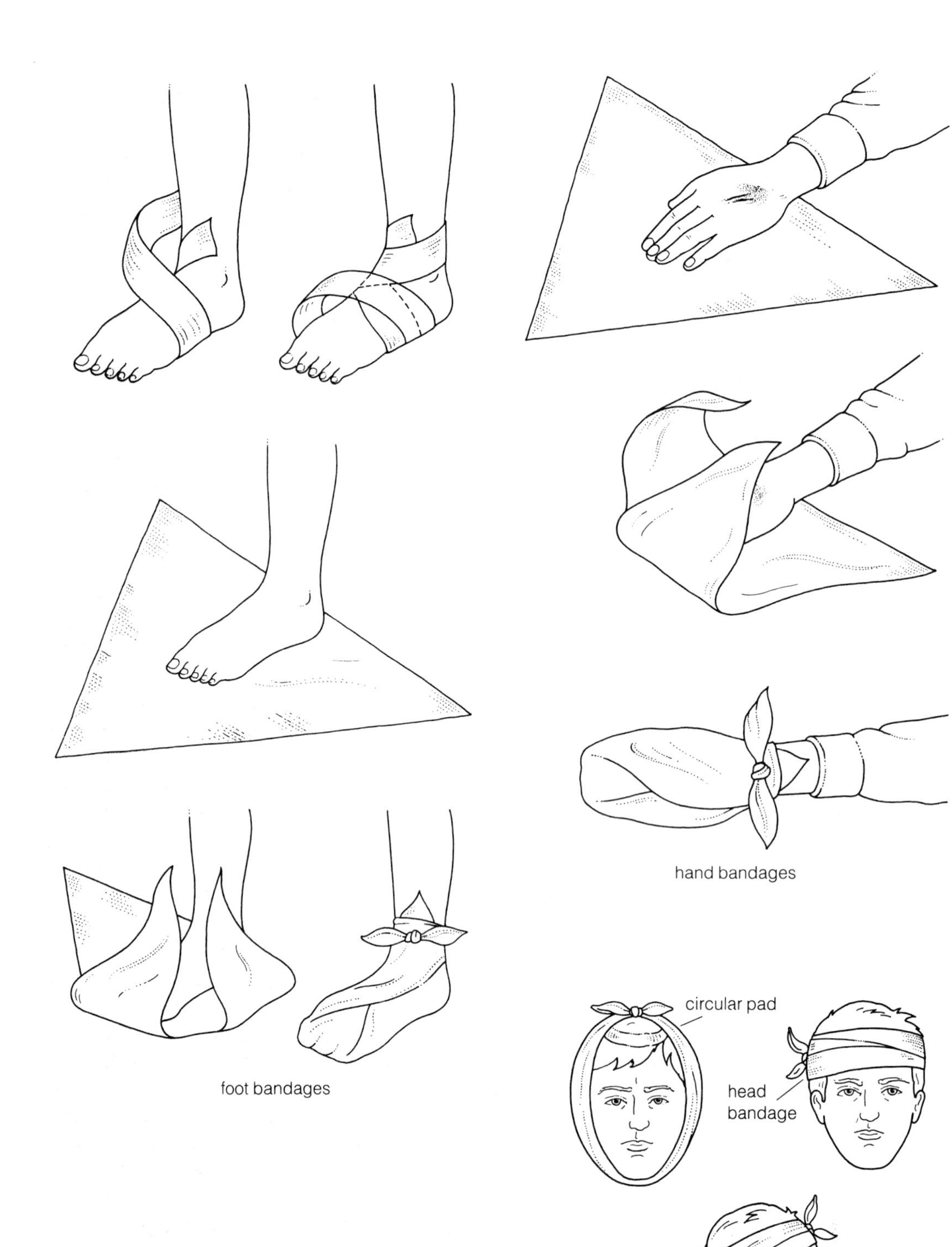
hand bandages
circular pad
head bandage
foot bandages
eye/ear bandage

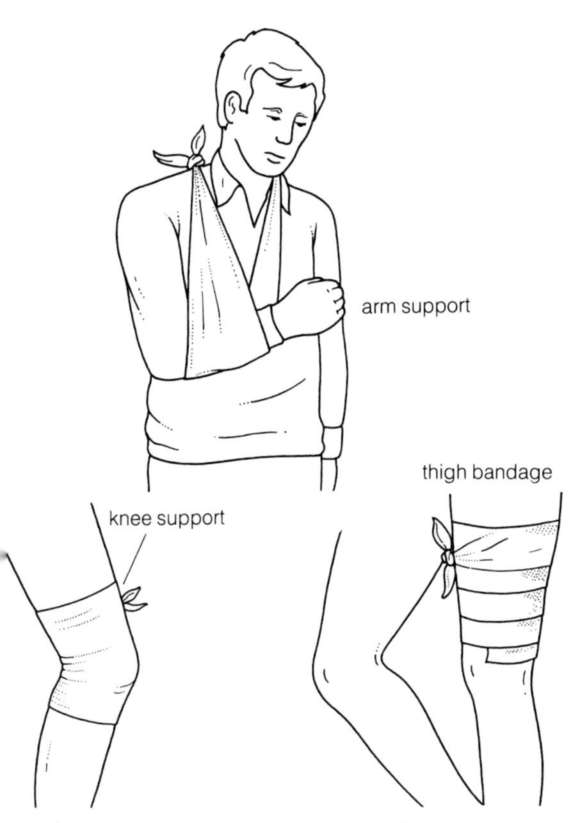

I know of one incident during the war where an aircraft crashed and the pilot was killed. The crew, knowing their survival skills, placed the body inside the plane and cremated him simply by setting alight the aircraft. This way, they eliminated all possible chance of a corpse spreading infection. In hot climates dead bodies quickly decay and smell. This in turn attracts unwanted visitors – for example hyena, rats, and other rodents – as well as being a potential breeding ground for disease.

Burns

Where serious burns have occurred the skin will be severely blistered and life-saving body fluid may be seeping out. Many chemicals will produce skin burn, massive discomfort, bleeding and body fluid loss, petrol being a typical example – when lit it gives off a terrific heat. Remember skin burns can just as easily be inflicted through excessive exposure to the sun, so protection from the elements is essential especially if you've just dragged someone from a burning aircraft or car. The following may inflict or cause burns:
Dry heat (fire, flames, sun, electricity, lightning);
Friction (rope, wire, stones etc.);
Wet heat (chemicals, sulphuric, nitric or hydrochloric acids, quicklime, scalding water, hot fats, etc.).

Insect and animal bites

Injuries from insect and animal bites are quite common in survival situations. However, providing the skin hasn't been broken, there is little danger of any infection, though to be on the safe side a thorough bathing and cleansing of the wound must be carried out. Scratches from an animal's teeth, claws, bird's beak etc. will need the same treatment as for a wound. If the wound is nothing more than a bruise, treat it with a poultice.

Insect bites and stings more often than not are just annoying, though a few obviously can be very dangerous if not treated immediately. Many insect bites cause swelling and irritation (not to mention bruising and pain) and can easily become septic. Try and reduce the swelling and apply an antiseptic. An example of this was brought home to me whilst in Africa. A native in one of the villages I was passing through was so severely stung around the face and neck by a swarm of wasps that he was finding if difficult to breathe. I immediately applied my personal soothing antiseptic – TOOTHPASTE, – then doused his face and neck in cold water. I asked one of the locals to fetch me some fresh limes and a mango. These were quickly pulped and placed on the inflamed area. I kept a close eye on the man's breathing in case it became necessary to clear the air passage but fortunately the swelling began to subside and the pain eased. I instructed the locals to keep watch on him for a while but not to apply anything other than cold water until the swelling had gone down. After a short while he recovered sufficiently to take a long, sweet, cool drink and a few hours later was up and walking about, bruised, a little sore but alive.

Wounds

There are four major types of wounds to the skin surface.

An incised wound

Perhaps from a spear, arrow, knife blade or razor. Expect profuse bleeding.

A lacerated wound

Perhaps from the edge of torn metal, animal claws, scrapes from rocks, etc. Possible slight bleeding.

A bruise or contused wound

Caused by being hit with falling rock, log or some blunt instrument. Generally no external bleeding.

A deep puncture wound

From thorns, knife point, arrow point, etc. Small amount of bleeding.

Other wounds to the skin surface may be caused by burning petrol, oil, chemicals or naked flame. Gunshot wounds or exposure to extreme cold also damage the skin surface. Whatever the cause the treatment is basically the same. Firstly isolate the victim from further injury, treat the wound appropriately and make the patient warm.

Where there is an obvious loss of blood from a gaping wound, your handkerchief, shirt tail, vest or whatever could be used as an improvised bandage. If necessary plug the hole with your finger. Grass, leaves, even bread, clay and moss have all been used to stop the flow. Soldiers are taught to burn clothing and place this on the wound to help dry it. Remember anything that has been through fire can be considered one hundred per cent sterile, provided it is subsequently kept clean.

Natural remedies

Mulched grass and moss make excellent poultices and help ease the pain in bruises. Boiled sea water acts as a mild antiseptic and fresh seaweed, especially the long kelp found on most beaches, is very rich in iodine so it may be used both as an antiseptic and as a bandage. Boiled seaweed mulched into a strainer makes a very good throat gargle. Warm mulched seaweed (or most mosses) applied to the eyes gives almost instant relief from eye bruises or inflammation. These are remedies that go back hundreds of years.

The spoors from the common puffball have been used since early man as a coagulant to slow down the loss of blood from a wound. Everything has its place in nature and with a little effort from you, most things out there can be used to your advantage. When I was a boy my mother would often slap a slice of fresh bread over my grazed knee before applying the bandage and in the army I never went anywhere without a small supply of curry powder in my pack. Sprinkled on an open wound it has extremely good curing potential as well as applying a protective covering. In the tropics I've often seen the white of an egg mixed with curry powder used as a gargle though I must warn you it tends to be a bit strong! Warm fresh lemon juice is an equally effective gargle and much milder. For those who can't stand the bitter taste, try a spoonful of honey with it.

Artificial respiration

If *artificial resuscitation* is necessary it should be done immediately and preferably without having to move the patient. Move him only if he or you are in further danger. Probably the easiest method is mouth-to-mouth. This is the least tiring to you and can be started immediately even if you and the patient are bobbing about in the water. Take up a position preferably to the side of the patient and hold his head in your hands. Tilt it back slightly.

Quickly feel inside the patient's mouth to ensure the air passage is clear and isn't blocked with seaweed or other debris. Check the patient's tongue hasn't rolled back to block the air passage.

Should the casualty have a broken jaw or perhaps have lost his teeth, it may be difficult to administer mouth-to-mouth. Instead, mouth-to-nose could be better. Simply block off the mouth using your thumb and finger, whilst at the same time covering the casualty's nose with your mouth, then blow down the nostrils.

If there is a blockage in the mouth which is difficult to remove to facilitate 'mouth-to-mouth', turn the casualty onto his side and, using the butt of your hand, strike him firmly between the shoulderblades a couple of times. When respirating, if the casualty is a child do not apply as much pressure into the lungs as you would an adult, i.e. no more than a couple of seconds' respiration at the most. If the air passage is blocked, of course you should first attempt to remove the blockage.

Mouth-to-mouth resuscitation

The mouth-to-mouth method

Keeping the head tilted back to allow a clear flow of air to the lungs, place your mouth over the patient's and blow gently but firmly into his or her lungs. It will be necessary to block the nostrils using your cheek or to pinch them with your fingers as you blow. In the first instance give a good half-dozen blows quickly into the lungs and watch for the rise and fall of the chest.

Once breathing has recommenced, place the head gently down onto the ground or support it if you're in water and tilt it to one side. Be ready to clear the mouth if vomiting should suddenly begin. Stay with the casualty until he is breathing evenly and you feel it's safe to rest. Using this method you may help him regain his breathing in seconds; sometimes it may take a good half-hour before you can safely step aside.

Other techniques for artificial respiration

In the past the Holger Neilson and Silvester Broch techniques for artificial respiration were taught and, although they may not be so effective as mouth-to-mouth, it is still a good idea to learn them as there are certain circumstances where they may still have the advantage. They do not involve placing your mouth over the victim's for instance, and they can be used in cases where there is obvious facial damage or burns to the inside of the windpipe. There may of course be occasions, such as when there is an irremovable blockage, when a tracheotomy, awful as it may seem, is the only alternative (a slit in the windpipe, described on page 182).

The Holger Neilson technique

The air passage having been cleared, the patient is placed on the ground face downwards with his head resting on the back of his folded arms. The resuscitator kneels close to his head on one knee, places his hands firmly

The Holger Neilson technique

onto the casualty's back just below the shoulder bone and exerts downward pressure to the count of five. Then slowly, without losing contact with the patient, he sweeps his hands backwards until he takes hold of the patient's elbows and again to the count of five raises the elbows until he feels the resistance in the patient's shoulders. This method works very well but can be a little tiring.

The Silvester Broch technique (above)

This is very similar except that the casualty is placed onto his back and the arms crossed over the tummy. The resuscitator takes up the same kneeling position alongside the head, takes hold of the patient's wrists and with a downward movement proceeds to apply pressure to the tummy again to the count of five. After five the arms are lifted outwards and back until they reach the ground.

Heart massage

If the victim's heart is not beating – check by feeling the pulses in the neck – external heart massage is necessary as well as artificial respiration. This usually requires more than one resuscitator, one for the heart massage and one for the respiration. Kneel by the right-hand side of the victim's chest, place the heel of the left hand over the lower third of the victim's breastbone, place the right hand over the left. Now, with the arms straight, lean your whole body weight onto your hands. You need to squeeze the heart between the breastbone and backbone, so press hard (a few broken ribs are a small price to pay for life). This action should be repeated once a second, and is tiring work! If you are alone, after each six 'heart beats' give one breath of mouth-to-mouth air; if there is more than one resuscitator 'heart beats' and 'breaths' can happen at the same time. The bones of children are softer than adults and will need less force, and their hearts beat more quickly. For a baby, you should use two fingers to press with, and press about twice a second.

Warning! Do not practise heart massage on a healthy person – it could stop the heart beating.

Broken bones

In a survival situation you have to decide whether to try and reset the bone or simply to strap it up and make it immobile. Time may not be on your side.

Resetting the bone does require a certain degree of professional skill as there will be a great deal of pain, probably loss of blood and almost certainly severe swelling and bruising around the break, so it may not be possible for you to reset it on your own (though many people in just such circumstances have managed to do so). It all depends on the victim's pain barrier. Basically there are two types of bone breakages (in modern medical terms these are called fractures):

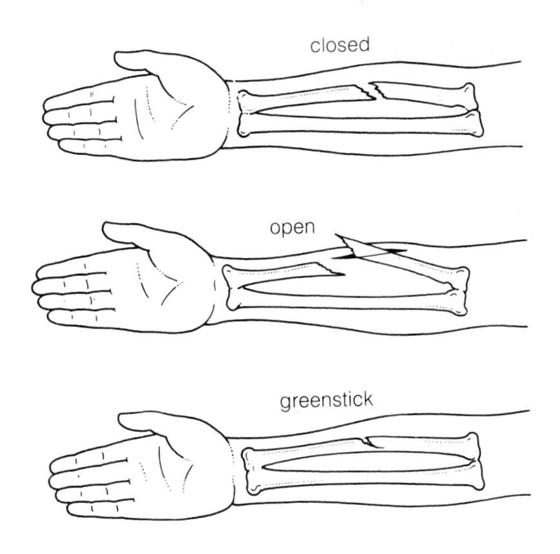

A break where bone penetrates the skin's surface (open).

A break that doesn't penetrate the skin surface (closed).

When the break is incomplete, it is often termed a 'greenstick' break or fracture. If there's any uncertainty or doubt as to the type of injury consider it a fracture and treat accordingly. Because of the obvious pain, self-support or strapping will have to be carried out slowly and with the minimum of movement. For instance, if your arm or wrist is broken and you are lying on the ground on your back, lift the injured arm into your support sling with your other arm, after first placing the sling around your neck. This way you'll only need the minimum of movement to place the broken arm into the sling. Once it is in, roll over slowly onto the elbow of your good arm, get to your knees and slowly stand up, perhaps with the aid of a stick, or pull yourself up on a nearby tree etc. This method works well and I've used it at least twice on myself.

If it's possible (as with resuscitation) try to treat the injury on site without any unnecessary movement. Splints or supports may be made from any of the following:

Sticks
Starting handles
Umbrellas
Magazines
Tie
Strips of cloth
Vines
Strips of aeroplane fuselage
Shoes
Pieces of cardboard
Belt
Shoe laces
Grass
Rolled up newspaper

Even seaweed may be used as a sling, or the injured arm may be slipped into an open shirt, blouse or waistband. If necessary place a small pad beneath the sling to prevent it digging into the shoulder. Soldiers often use their rifles as crutches and splints.

Re-setting broken bones

To apply a plaster cast or splint to a broken limb without re-setting the bone is simply a means of isolating the injury and preventing further movement.

When a bone is broken the surrounding muscles contract causing great pain and swelling as the ends of the bones rub together. If the patient is unconscious and the fracture is easy to reach and set, you could attempt to do so, but I do emphasize, a badly set bone will heal in the position it has been secured in and, once set, it may have to be re-broken at a later date. So, if it's possible to reach medical help within a couple of days, it may be wiser just to strap the injury rather than put it in a cast.

Resetting the bone means placing the broken ends correctly against each other. To do this you need to overcome muscle spasm and literally pull the broken ends apart, then realign them in the correct position. This might be easy for small bones like the fingers or knuckles, but very difficult for large bones with large muscles attached, like the thigh. Once the bone is reset, it needs to be secured in its now correct position.

Making a plaster cast to heal a broken limb is not too difficult if you know your plants and herbs. Gather masses of clover heads, red or white, boil these into a thick syrup, dip your bandages (strips of clothing) into this until they become saturated, wrap the bandages around the wound (not too tightly) and allow to cool.

In Mexico and other areas of South America they use a plant called *Tepeguaje* (a tree belonging to the bean family), or a plant called *Solda-Can-Solda*, a very large tree-climbing lily. To make plaster from them, simply tear off the bark, mix it with water and boil for an hour. Strain off most of the remaining water, and boil again until left with a thick syrup.

To apply

a. Make sure the bones are set correctly.
b. Never apply a cast directly onto the skin. Wrap in a soft dry cloth first.
c. Between each layer of bandage apply cotton or wool packing.
d. Do not apply cast tightly; allow for contraction and injury swelling.
e. Ensure you apply sufficient bandage to keep the injury safe from further movement.
f. Remember if setting a limb in plaster, to leave the fingers and thumb free, or the toes, to ensure you can check on the circulation and colour.

Stitching

Stitching of a wound should be done if there is:

a. A rapid loss of blood from the wound.
b. If stitching is required to prevent further damage being done internally, e.g. organs being exposed or spilling out.
c. If there is no other means of preventing blood or fluid loss, e.g. lack of bandages.

The simplest rule to follow is: if the edges of the wound come together themselves, as with a deep razor-type cut, then stitches may be placed.

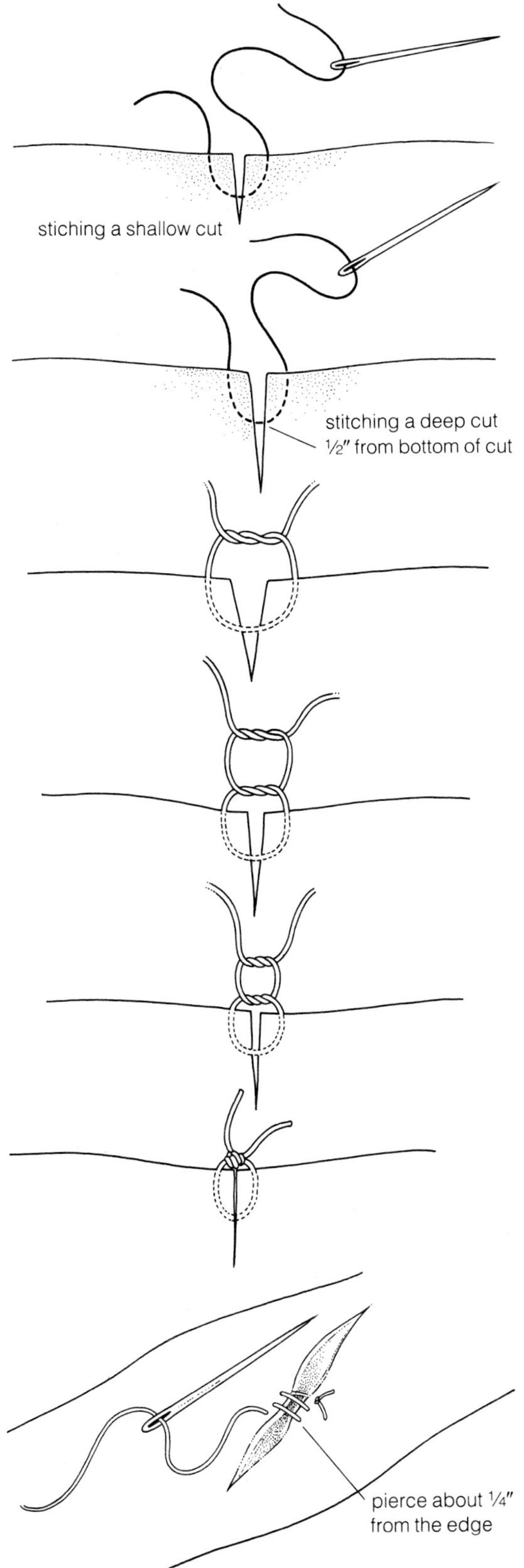

To stitch a wound:

a. Firstly, sterilize your needle and thread for a good ten minutes by boiling them.
b. Wash out the wound with soap and water or any other means of cleansing, e.g. pulped cacti/orange juice/lime etc. The patient's own fresh urine may even be used, but remember the rule – you must only use your own urine on yourself.
c. Wash your hands thoroughly in water and soap.

Begin stitching in the middle of the wound and work outwards each side. Don't overspace your stitches – better too many than too few. If there is no infection leave the stitches in place for eight to fourteen days (on the face, six days only). To remove them, cut into one side of the knot and pull the remainder out.

Splints

You must remember when making a splint that it has to be strong enough to support the injured limb, preferably placed over clothing and not directly next to the skin. Where the bone has broken through the skin's surface, it should be surrounded with a cloth padding to eliminate skin chafing and the entry of germs. Make the patient comfortable and allow him to rest for as long as possible. If it becomes

human crutch

fireman's lift

pick-a-back

four-handed standing position

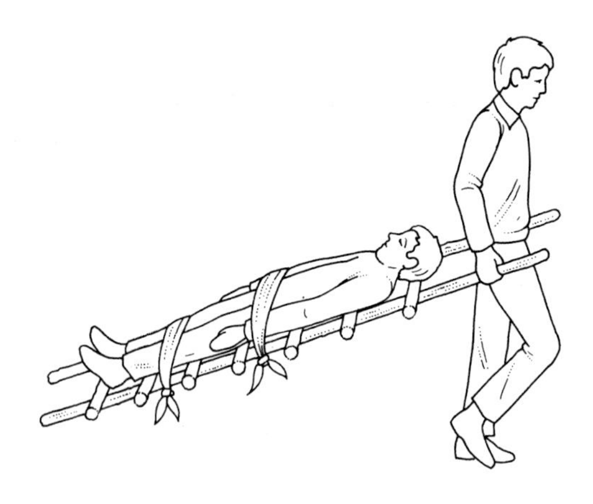

necessary to move the patient and if there's no help available, try the human crutch support or the pick-a-back or, as a last resort, the fireman's lift. If there is help, the four-handed-seat support is a very effective means of transportation, as is the two-handed-seat support. A stretcher is the obvious choice but it will require two of you and can be very tiring. However, if the casualty has a leg or back injury you will probably have to use a stretcher or the drag support – the 'wickiup' as the Indians call it.

four-handed grip

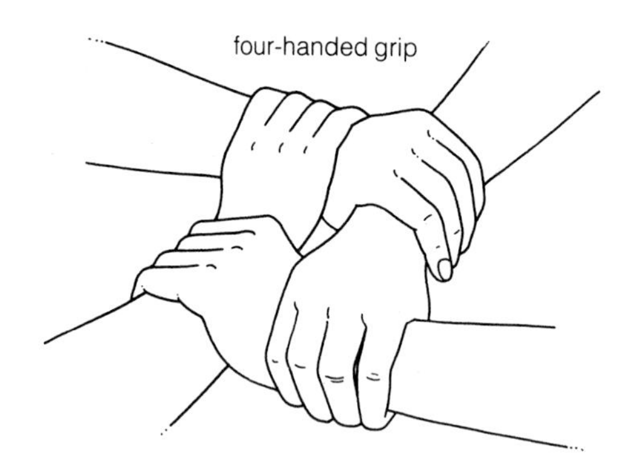

Unconsciousness

If there is no obvious visible injury an unconscious person may be placed carefully into the recovery position (see below), remembering to ensure that the mouth has been checked for possible blockage (tongue turned back, dentures broken, a mouth full of vomit). It may be wise to remove any dentures at this stage. If you have to move him, do so gently, especially if there is a possibility of further injury from falling debris etc. On recovery, a warm sweet drink may be given, but only a little at a time. Above all, to reassure him remain close by or within talking distance. If possible, get professional medical aid as quickly as you can.

two-handed seat

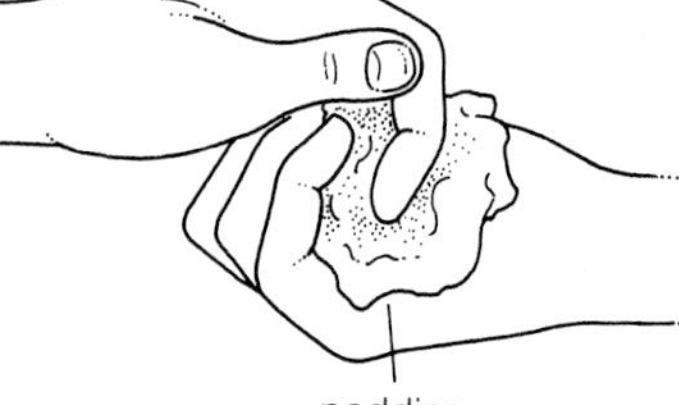

padding

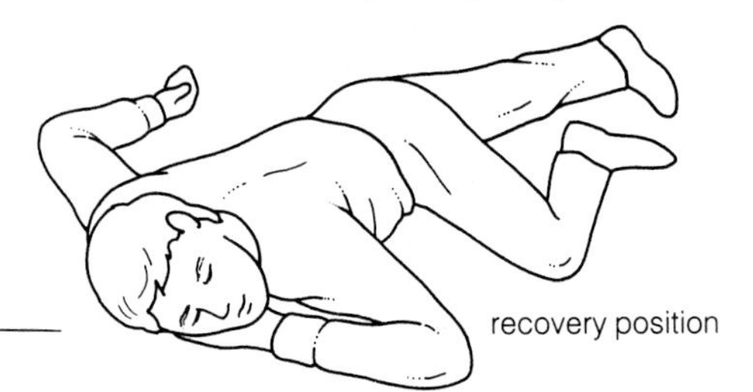

recovery position

Lifting an unconscious person

Often after an accident and in the interest of safety it becomes necessary for you to remove an unconscious person from the area, and to do this you may have to carry him off without any assistance, so it's worth learning how to lift a person off the ground and carry him using the fireman's lift. Firstly you must gently roll him over onto his stomach, placing one arm extended above the head, the other down beside the body and bring both legs together.

Kneel on one knee close to the patient's head and place your hands under his shoulders. Lifting gently, walk him back onto his knees, then support him with the side of your body.

Place one hand between his thighs, holding to the rear of the thigh. Place one arm over your shoulder and gently lift whilst walking him back onto his feet. When he is fully standing, gently lower him over your shoulders and pick him up in the normal manner for the fireman's lift.

This method of lifting should only be carried out if circumstances demand it and the person being lifted has no obvious injury, e.g. broken bones. If internal bleeding is suspected (this is very difficult to diagnose) leave the patient where he is. You also need to be sure that his back has not been broken, because moving him may cause permanent paralysis.

As soon as you have the patient safe, gently put him back down onto the ground and carry out your normal first aid drill. Keep him warm, dry and, if necessary, in the recovery position.

Quite recently whilst serving in Northern Ireland a young medical sergeant carried out a tracheotomy in the field on a soldier who'd been shot in the throat, and in doing so saved

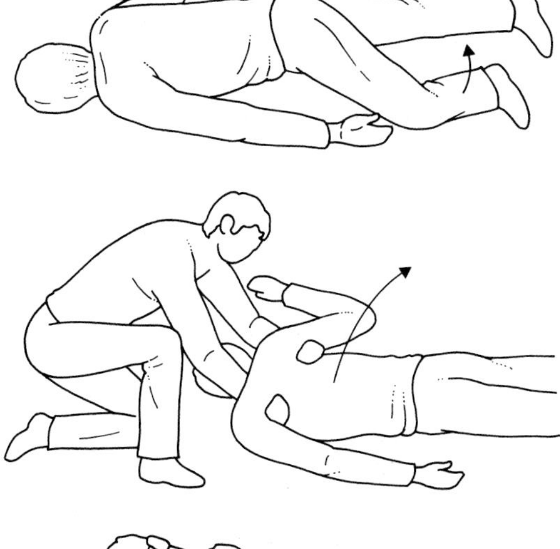

the soldier's life. He took the decision to operate there and then. Any delay at all would have been fatal. That soldier is alive and well today, thanks to the speed, skill and confidence of that sergeant. Obviously if there is professional advice and help available you use it, but in an emergency it could be you who has to make the final decision. Be prepared; confidence comes with knowledge and training. Be like the sergeant. Just as Mother Nature provides us with all our food, shelter and tools, she can also provide most things we need to help overcome sickness and injury.

For you, lost in some remote desert, pushing your way through an impenetrable jungle, or adrift at sea on a life raft, the odds aren't in your favour. The chances of being rescued, probably for a few days anyway, are pretty slim even with today's 'high tec' travel. No, it's more likely that you'll have to go it alone, and if there's any bone mending or surgical stitching to be done, then it's you who must do it. Many people have died unnecessarily because they didn't have the knowledge to treat themselves, or their friends didn't have the confidence to do so. As in most survival situations, it's a matter of getting your priorities right. Remember the rules of survival: Inspection (see to yourself and/or the injured) and needs; Protection; Location; then Food.

Early man wasn't as fortunate as you or I – he learnt the hard way through trial and error. Often the most primitive of medicine and treatment can save a life. For instance, in an emergency an ideal substitute for cleaning out wounds is your own urine. Fresh urine, and I emphasize fresh, is very rich in salts and if applied immediately to the wound before it cools acts as a mild astringent. I've used this method time and time again.

Once whilst travelling across Africa I came to a village where a man had been badly attacked by a crocodile. The whole bottom half of his body was covered in scratches and lacerations from the crocodile's teeth; fortunately only a few needed stitching. This I did by closing the wounds with sellotape and used fishing line to stitch them. However, before I did any of this I managed to get the man to urinate into a container and quickly began washing out the wounds. To prevent infection I then washed them with hot water and eventually covered them with warm fresh ash from the fire. I had been taught in the army that anything that has been burnt to ash must be a hundred per cent sterile. Primitive, you'd agree; effective, extremely. After a few days the man was up and about as normal.

No matter where you are in the world the same rules apply for basic field medicine as they would in your own back yard.

Three ways of dying are:

Asphyxia	(stoppage of breath)
Haemmorhage	(loss of blood)
Shock	(poor circulation)

These three may be induced by drowning, poisoning, contact with hot metal etc., electricity/burns, as well as severe lacerations to the body or simply death through starvation or exposure. Whatever the circumstances under survival conditions your quick thinking, basic first aid knowledge and practical ability will be taxed to the full.

Infections

In modern times we forget about the dangers of infections. Not so many years ago germs were *the* major cause of death, and may be so again in survival situations. The great scourges of the past (plague, dysentery etc.) were diseases of overcrowding and poor hygiene; in survival situations overcrowding is an unlikely problem, but good hygiene must be kept (see also page 133). In particular, stools must be disposed of safely (in a pit), away from drinking water and away from the camp (if you are lucky enough to have one). Because it is so important it bears repeating: water should be sterilized before drinking.

Unfortunately, the scourges of western man – colds, the 'flu, sore throats etc. – will remain problems in survival situations. In patients with a lower resistance (through shock and injury etc.) these may become killers, leading to pneumonia and kidney disease. Because the symptoms are so familiar, I won't repeat them here – but beware, they can kill! Instead I will describe some more unusual infections that might be met in some of the vast, under-populated areas of our globe.

But before this, consider the motto of a medical friend of mine: PREVENTION IS BETTER THAN CURE. BE PREPARED! Vaccinations exist to combat typhoid, cholera, tetanus, polio, diphtheria, 'flu, measles, hepatitis, yellow fever . . . and more! Tablets can be taken to prevent malaria. Good hygiene can prevent some types of dysentery. Food poisoning can be avoided by careful cooking of food. So, get wise to the hazards of the places you will be visiting and ask your doctor about prevention before you travel.

Three day or sandfly fever

Location: Found throughout the world, but especially in the Americas and sub-tropics.

Incubation (time from infection to symptoms): Two to six days normally.

Cause: A virus infection (very like 'flu) passed on in the bite of the sandfly. The sandfly (a fly-like midge) lives in grasslands and occasionally sandy areas and bites the ankles and wrist, passing the virus into the bloodstream.

Symptoms: After the initial symptom of itching at the site of the bite, headache, fever and muscle soreness develop. This passes in three days (hence the name) and causes no lasting harm.

Cure: Rest, a light diet and plenty of fluids. There is no specific cure.

Prevention: In areas where you suspect the midge might live – cover up and prevent bites.

Cholera

Location: Worldwide in human habitations; remember cholera was once the cause of an epidemic in London.

Cause: A bacterium (a germ) that lives in the faeces of man and passes on through contaminated water.

Symptoms: Sudden onset of copious, very watery stools ('rice-water diarrhoea') with little or no fever and abdominal pain. Unless treated, the loss of water and salts in the stools will rapidly cause dehydration (thirst, sunken eyes, lax skin, cold and blue hands and feet) and kidney failure (lack of urine). If dehydration sets in and enough fluids cannot be given, the patient may die. The illness lasts from twelve hours to one week. Recovery is shown by a reduction in the watery stools.

Cure: The infection cannot be cured, but the dehydration can. Large amounts (up to twelve pints per day) of fluid with added salt and sugar must be given. A typical rehydration fluid would be one litre of boiled water plus twenty grammes of sugar plus five grammes of salt. Give one litre of this in small amounts with each loose stool.

Prevention: Good hygiene. Vaccination also exists – BE PREPARED.

Malaria

Location: Africa, Asia and Latin America in general, but local variation exists.

Incubation: About two weeks from being bitten by the mosquito to the onset of symptoms.

Cause: The female Anopheles mosquito carries the protozoon (a kind of germ) that causes malaria. If you are bitten by the germ-carrying mosquito, the germs get into the bloodstream and pass to the liver where they multiply. Once proliferated the germs are released back into the bloodstream and enter the red blood cells. There they grow and eventually burst the red blood cell releasing fresh germs to attack new cells. It is at this stage that fever occurs.

Symptoms: Fever is the main symptom of malaria, indeed malaria should be suspected in any person with fever in an area where malaria occurs or who has just returned from such an area. Although fever can be continuous, more commonly it occurs in paroxysms consisting of three stages:

Cold stage (shivering)
Hot stage (high fever)
Sweating stage (sweating and loss of fever)
These stages occur immediately after each other. They may then fade away for a short while until the next attack, usually the next day. Malaria may also recur at a much later date. In severe attacks there may be anaemia, kidney failure ('blackwater fever'), liver failure, and, most serious, brain complications (cerebral malaria).

Cure: There are many drugs that can cure malaria. One of the oldest of these is quinine; in South America the Indians have for centuries used the bark of the tree called the Cinchona or Jesuit's tree which contains quinine. As well as being used to cure malaria, these drugs can be taken to prevent attacks. If drugs are not available (and they should be if you plan to go to a malarious region) there are still things you can do to help the patient. Every effort should be made to reduce the fever. When the fever is at its height it may cause delirium, so keep the patient (or yourself) from getting lost or injured. Once the fever has abated warm soup or milk should be taken in small amounts. A lot of body fluid is lost by sweating, so plenty of fresh, clean water should be given.

Prevention: No vaccine yet exists to combat malaria; instead drugs active against the germ can be taken regularly (once a week for some) to prevent the disease. Ask your doctor if you intend to go to a malarious area. If you are unfortunate (or unlucky) enough to be stranded in a malarious area without a supply of these drugs, you should try to prevent mosquito bites. Smoke drives away mosquitoes, nets prevent their entry; they do not like wind. In order to survive, mosquito larvae (the babies) need water, stagnant water in particular. They can't stand oils or insecticides of any description. If either of these are poured onto their breeding areas they quickly kill off any new larvae.

Dysentery

Location: Worldwide but all forms are more common in the tropics; most cases are found in human habitation and are due to overcrowding or poor hygiene.

Incubation: From one to two days to some weeks, depending upon the cause.

Cause: Dysentery can be caused by bacteria (bacillary dysentery – a germ), amoebae (amoebic dysentery – a single cell animal similar to the malaria protozoon) and schistosoma (schistosomial dysentery – a worm like germ). Bacillary and amoebic dysentery are passed on through poor sanitation and hygiene; especially when human excreta contaminates drinking water. Schistosomial dysentery can occur without contact with other humans.

Symptoms: Dysentery is the medical word for bloody diarrhoea. The disease usually starts off with the sudden onset of diarrhoea (with blood in the stools) and fever; there may be stomach cramps. The illness may last for a few days to a week, and can be fatal. In times past, many large armies were wiped out by bacillary dysentery.

Cure: Effective antibiotics exist for all forms of dysentery, but are usually only necessary for amoebic and schistosomial dysentery (where the infection is chronic). In general, fluids and soft, nutritious food should be given. Rest and isolation are necessary. To prevent further spread, stools should be disposed of by burning.

Prevention: Is simple, GOOD HYGIENE AND CLEAN WATER (remember, boil all water for at least five minutes before use).

Diarrhoea

Diarrhoea (passing frequent, loose stools) is a symptom of many diseases (commonly food-poisoning). When it occurs, replacement of fluids is the most important treatment and frequent drinks should be given.

In a survival situation you could try boiling the bark from trees, especially the oak as this is very rich in tannin. Boil for at least twelve to fourteen hours and keep adding water until it ends up in a mulch. You may have to force yourself to take it, but it's worth the effort. Strong tea, also rich in tannin, will help ease both diarrhoea and dysentery. Try chewing a tea bag wrapped in a damp cloth. (Incidentally, both tea leaves and boiled bark make excellent pain relievers for bruises and cuts.) There are, of course, many other roots, plants and leaves too numerous to mention that will also help. Again, you must read up on the medical properties of plants, as Nature in different parts of the world will provide you with a wide variety of natural remedies.

Snake bites

The possibility of being bitten by a snake is very slim indeed, unless you intentionally set out to seek and annoy them. Only once in all my years of travel and survival training have I ever been bitten by a snake, and that was in England! I foolishly began toying around with a small adder and it bit me. At first it felt as if I'd stood on a wasp or sharp nail, but a few minutes later the area around the bite began to swell and became very painful. Fortunately I managed to get myself to a doctor who placed a cooling antiseptic on the wound and covered it with a light dry bandage. After a couple of days rest I was as good as new, but I'd learnt my lesson, and that was to leave well alone. (See colour section for some of the more common poisonous snakes.)

If you are bitten by a snake there are certain survival rules that you must follow for your own safety, especially if there's no doctor available. Firstly, try not to panic. If you do decide to go for help – WALK, don't run. Keep calm and try not to move the injured area unnecessarily.

Some snake experts advise never to use a tourniquet on a bite as this often is counter-productive. Others are quick to point out that hundreds, if not thousands, of lives have been saved by applying a tourniquet immediately. Applied correctly I personally find tourniquets very effective. Their basic function is to stop the flow of lymph in one direction. In the case of a snake bite the idea is to stop the poison injected into the wound from travelling further and into the bloodstream. The tourniquet may easily be improvised from a strip of cloth or a shoe lace. The tourniquet should not be too tight, and if the area around it swells should be loosened or moved closer to the centre of the body, at no time should a limb go blue or lose its pulses. In any case, many snake venoms do not disperse into the bloodstream, so you will do more harm than good. The area around the bite may, as a result of the constriction, become gangrenous and could result in the loss of a limb, or at worst, your life.

If applying a tourniquet for the first time remember to do so *above* the wound and as a precaution it may be better to apply two broad bands rather than a single thin one.

Incisions into the skin to draw out the venom by sucking or using a hot piece of wood or metal have no value at all. They will only inflict more unnecessary pain and could cause further infection. Keep the infected area around the wound cool and dry. If you should be fortunate enough to have some anti-snake bite serum with you, you must follow the written instructions carefully. Early attention by a specialist is obviously essential, especially where the victim has been bitten by a highly poisonous snake. So until help is available give the casualty plenty of liquids, preferably with a little added salt or sugar. Make him comfortable and safe.

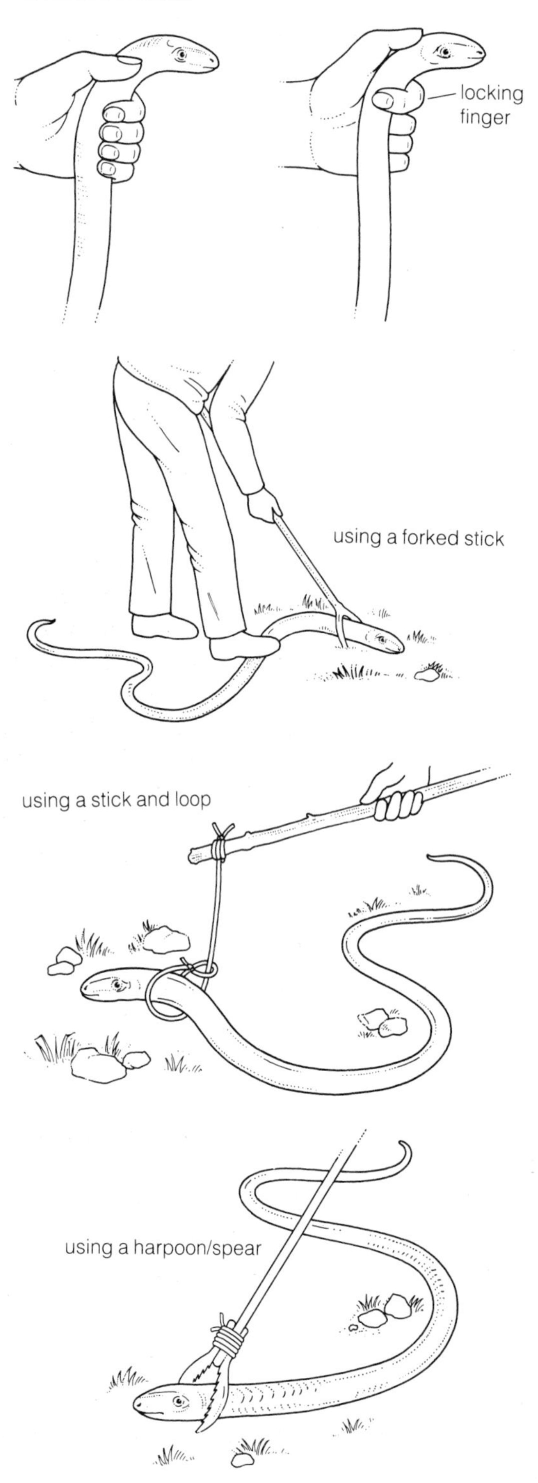

Serum

If possible try to identify the type of snake responsible for a bite. If you have to apply anti-snake bite serum, read the instructions carefully and use the serum only as a last resort – quite often snakes only bruise the skin surface and don't puncture. Anti-snake bite serum is carried in a sealed container in most modern aircraft for just such emergencies.

Where the venom has been spat into the eyes – by a spitting Cobra for instance – bathe the eyes as quickly as possible in water, milk, tea or anything that will dilute the venom quickly without causing further inflammation. Most soft drinks have a high sugar content and application may cause some of the venom to stick, but it's better than nothing. Mango, coconut and even water melon juices have been used as well as snow and melted ice. Urine must only be used as a last resort and as you don't have a great deal of time, speedy action is necessary. In a civilized region proper medical treatment generally sees us safely through. Out there in the wilds without the correct expertise and facilities, it's a different story.

Sores and ulcers

Whenever and wherever a sore appears on the body it should be treated immediately. Sores leave the body open to infection. They are a constant source of irritation and may, if not treated, refuse to heal. Sores around the lips, eyes and genitals may be very painful indeed. A sore may be due to nothing more serious than chafing or something very serious such as venereal diseases, e.g. syphilis!

Antibiotics generally clear most sores quickly, but some may need thorough medical treatment under supervision of a doctor. Generally in a survival situation, once you settle down into a routine, take regular meals and attend to your hygiene correctly, they soon go. There are many creams for healing sores but they may just dry up themselves by the body's natural healing system.

Keep all sores dry and free from infection. If necessary cover them lightly with bandages. The Kalahari bushmen and the Australian Aborigine cover sores with hot ash from the fire. A species of common puffball fungus (Lycoperdales) produces a crude antibiotic when dried. The spores are pressed into the wound along with fresh cobwebs (all cobwebs are sterile). Both help to speed up the body's natural healing process.

Foreign body in the eye

Very often it may be necessary to remove dirt, sand, grit etc. from the eye. Travelling in the desert you must expect sand blown up by the winds to get into your clothes, hair and eyes. When this happens, if possible, try to remove it immediately otherwise it will inflame the eyes and could do serious damage. More often than not the mere action of lifting the top lid and gently pulling it down over the eye will remove anything on the surface. Dirt caught in the corner may be removed either by bathing the eye in clean warm water or by very gently using the corner of a clean cloth or the tip of a matchstick wrapped in moist cotton wool.

Sore eyes, especially in the desert or Arctic where they are subject to intense glare, must not be left unattended. Rubbing the eyes with your hands or bathing them in salt/sea water will only worsen the inflammation. If it becomes very bad, but you aren't able to treat it with eye ointment or get medical help, covering the eyes with a clean, soft, damp pad will help ease the irritation. Eskimos, who suffer a great deal from eye strain due to the glare from the snow, regularly place lumps of clean, fresh ice on their eyes. As the ice melts it helps wash away any foreign bodies.

Trachoma

This is an infection similar to conjunctivitis that gets steadily worse if left unattended. It may be contagious (spread by contact) or, in areas where people live in poor, crowded conditions, by flies.

Symptoms/signs

1st Stage: As with conjunctivitus, red watery eyes.

2nd Stage: After a month or so, small pinkish lumps form inside the upper lids. These lumps (follicles) may take on a grey colour.

3rd Stage: The whites of the eyes become inflamed and the top of the cornea begins to look greyish.

4th Stage: Eventually, if left untreated, both the follicles and conjunctiva (the covering skin of the eyes) scar, gradually covering the whole of the eye and causing blindness by drawing down the eyelid and the lashes.

Making a simple crutch

Made properly, a crutch can alleviate a lot of pain and increase mobility simply by giving support. To make one, choose a branch of fresh green wood, as shown in the illustrations on the next page, strong enough to support the injured person's weight. Remove the leaves and other small branches and give added support by strapping two small logs across. To give extra comfort bind the top support with cloth, seat padding or a split hosepipe from a car radiator.

Using a hot compress/soak

1. Boil some water and allow it to cool until you can bear to hold your hand in it without pain. Drop a piece of clean cloth into the water.

2. Remove the cloth and squeeze out any excess water. Prepare your compress by folding the cloth and if knowledgeable filling with selected herbs, grass etc.

3. Gently place the compress on the infected/bruised area.

4. Secure the cloth with strips of material.

5. Rest the injured limb. After the compress cools, remove and re-apply using the same process.

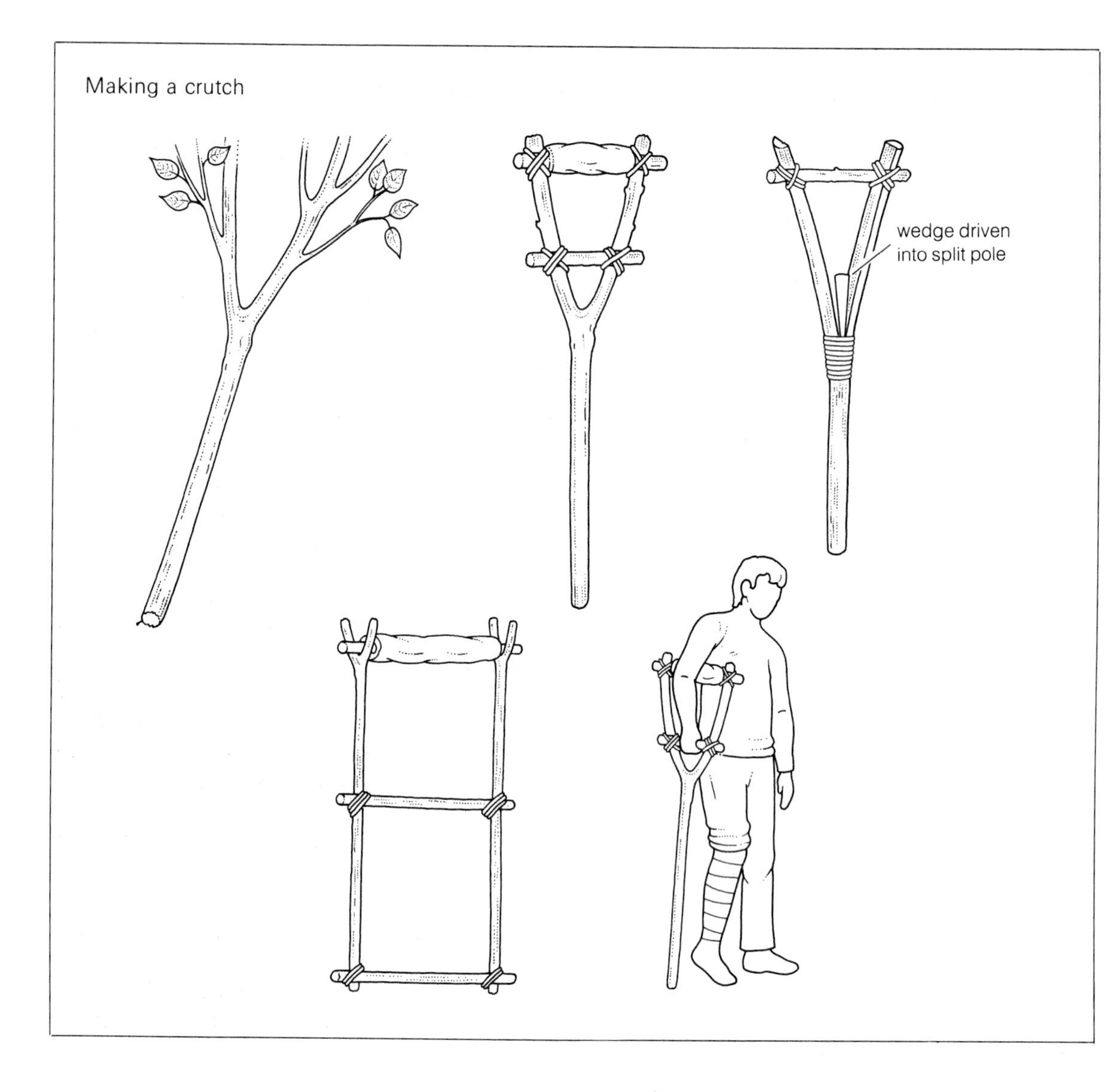

Infection

Recognition – a wound is infected when it:

a. Becomes swollen, is red hot to the touch and painful.
b. Produces pus.
c. Begins to smell.

Infection is spreading through the body when:

a. It causes fever and soreness.
b. A red line (poison in the lymph vessel) is seen above the wound.
c. Any of the lymph nodes (the body's early warning glands) become swollen and tender. Lymph nodes/glands are areas where germs collect under the skin causing lumps as they become infected.

For example: Swollen nodes in the groin indicate infection in the legs, feet, genitals etc. Swollen nodes under the armpits indicate infection of the arm, head or breast. Swollen nodes in the neck indicate infection in the head, neck, ear etc.

Gangrene

If, even after treatment, an infected wound begins to smell bad (a decaying/rotting garbage-type smell), or if it turns a mushy brown or grey, or if smelly pus oozes from it or if the skin turns black and air bubbles start to appear, this may be gangrene. Professional medical advice is needed *immediately*.

Delivering a baby

As a survivor you may be called upon to help deliver a baby, as I have on two occasions. Providing you work slowly and methodically, and remember your basic first aid, delivering a baby isn't too difficult. All the hard work is done by the expectant mother.

In many parts of the world childbirth is still carried out in what seems to us a very primitive way. Many nomadic women simply squat on the ground, hold onto a tree branch and give birth without help from anyone else. Giving birth however may require your help. If this is the case then here is what you should do.

First make sure the woman is lying down comfortably, preferably on something soft and warm such as a carpet, bed of ferns etc., or ideally a plastic or rubber sheet covered with other clean sheets. Any available tissues or cotton wool need to be on hand, along with jugs or bowls of hot water. A sharp knife or scissors will be needed to cut through the umbilical cord (if possible leave these in a separate container of hot water to sterilize). You may also need some cotton thread and a needle.

The mother will let you know when she thinks the baby is on its way. This she will recognize by the intervals between contractions. As the doctor-come-midwife you must prepare her for delivery. If she hasn't already done so, remove her pants, tights or slacks etc., as they will restrict the baby's passage. Ensure that she is lying back, her knees pulled up and her legs wide apart. In this position her genital area can be washed with clean tissues/cotton wool soaked in the warm water, providing the baby's head hasn't appeared.

As soon as the head begins to show through the vulva, before attempting to touch the baby remember to thoroughly wash your hands to prevent any infection to both the mother and her newborn child. In addition, place a firm pad of tissues against the anal opening just below the vulval outlet to avoid any faecal contamination of the area.

As the mother increases her pushing action the baby's head will push through. At this stage she may need a little reassurance and encouragement (a wet cloth placed on the forehead can be very reassuring). As the baby's head clears the vulva check that the cord is not around the baby's neck. If clear, gently ease the baby out as the mother continues to push using her stomach muscles. If the cord *is* round the neck it can usually be looped over the child's head or shoulders. If the cord can't be freed, cut it there and then and tie off both ends. Continue to ease the baby out with the mother's pushes until it is safely delivered.

When clear of the mother sever the cord cleanly *after* tying it with the cotton or nylon cord, five to ten cm from the baby's abdomen and 15 to 20 cm from the mother. In an emergency, you may have to use a strip of cloth or your shoe lace to tie off the cord. Once the cord has been severed and the baby begins to dry, wrap it in a clean sheet or towel and give it to the mother.

If, on delivery, the baby didn't cry out and begin breathing immediately, even before the cord has been cut, the airway must be checked and cleaned out. Then, holding it upside down by the ankles, give it a sharp smack on the buttocks. If after a couple of smacks the baby still isn't breathing you may have to apply mouth-to-mouth resuscitation. This must be performed very gently – use only mouthfuls of air.

The mother, meanwhile, will begin to expel the afterbirth which may be accompanied by blood clots and fluid. This is normal. Once clear of all the afterbirth the mother may be washed, dried and wrapped up in a warm blanket, parachute, jacket etc. and given a warm sweet drink. She will obviously have used a great deal of energy in giving birth and will need some time to recover. After a brief rest place the baby in the mother's arms and wrap both up safely.

Breech delivery

If the baby begins to emerge buttocks first, do nothing until the child's limbs have been born. Keep both mother and baby warm using a light clean cloth. As soon as the head appears continue as before: check umbilical cord, breathing etc.

Surgery

In survival situations there are times when a person wishes he was a skilled engineer, shipwright, animal trainer, herbalist . . . and surgeon. Although I have personally helped a medical sergeant to amputate a wounded man's foot whilst in the Middle East, I have learned that situations where *your* decision may kill a fellow survivor because of a lack of skill are best left to experts in ethics. For this reason, I will not describe such operations except to say that if your fellow survivor's life is in *certain* jeopardy, and if good pain relief is available, then major surgery by the unskilled may be the only life-line.

There is however one operation that should be known to everyone; it will save life and has few complications – a tracheotomy.

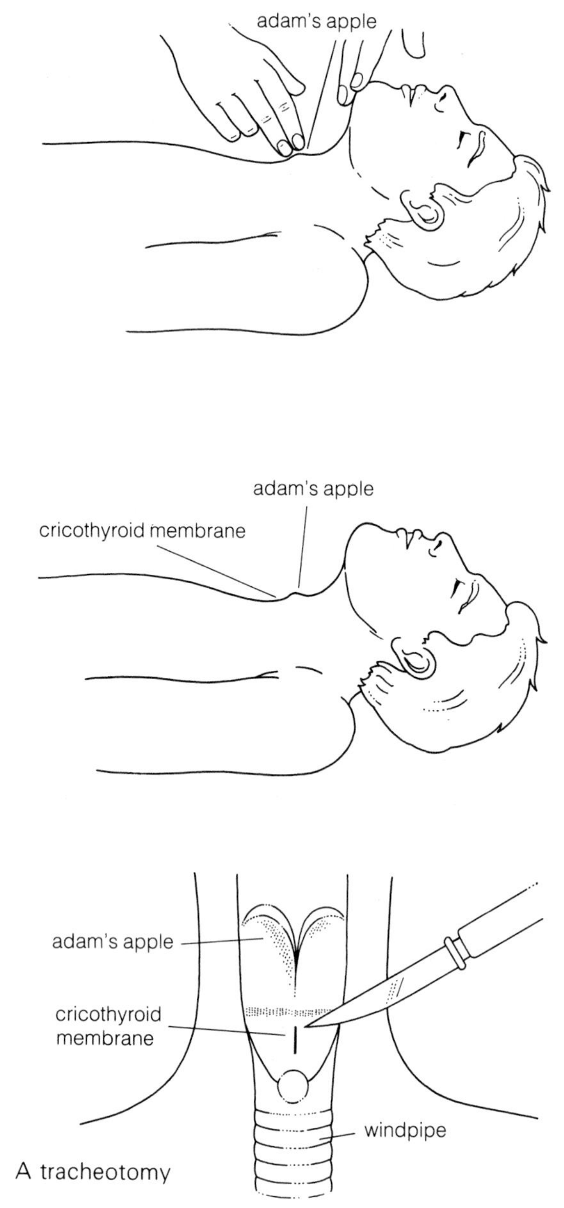

A tracheotomy

Tracheotomy

This involves making a hole in the windpipe through which a patient can breathe. To the survivor this is a true life-saving emergency. Blockages of the windpipe that cannot be easily removed via the patient's mouth are found in cases of severe facial injury, burns to the windpipe and inhalation of foreign bodies such as food, vomit and even blood. The symptoms are: a choking noise, restricted breathing and a blueness of the face. If this has happened, quickly try to relieve the blockage using conventional first aid: clearing the throat, slapping the back etc. If this fails, the patient is now literally choking to death, and *you* must make an immediate decision. The chances of life now depend on your quick thinking, skill and ability to do the operation.

Before starting make sure you have an improvised air tube available, a quill or plastic biro tube or hollow length of bamboo, with as large a bore as possible, and a sharp knife. Then, kneeling on the patient's right-hand side, place the left hand under the chin and tilt the head back. With your right hand feel for the Adam's apple (the thyroid cartilage); immediately below this is a thin, bloodless membrane (the cricothyroid membrane) and it is this membrane that once punctured will give access to the windpipe. With a very sharp knife or sharp, large needle puncture the skin over the membrane and the membrane itself. You are now into the windpipe (see illustration opposite). Remove the knife or needle, enlarge the hole if necessary and insert your air tube (to keep the hole open). The patient's breathing should now be easy.

Because you cannot observe sterility in such an emergency, you will need to keep a close watch for infection and you must try to get the patient to expert medical help as soon as possible. If it isn't possible to get the patient to a hospital or any qualified medical help, after six to twenty-four hours it may be possible to remove the improvised air tube and allow him to breathe normally. The longer the tube is left in, the more chance you have of infection setting in.

CHAPTER 17

Making Your Own Survival Pack

A great deal of mythology is written about what you should put in your survival pack. Personally, I think it all depends on your individual preference, but when I'm putting a pack together I always try to include items that will have as many uses as possible.

For instance, a needle can obviously be used for sewing but it will also double up as a fish hook, can be used for removing splinters and, when rubbed vigorously across man-made fibres, it collects static electricity and so can be used as a compass. Simply press it through a matchstick or similar piece of wood, lay it gently in water and as it settles the magnetized end of the needle will spin and point north. It can also be used for removing the edible flesh from various shellfish, snails etc. If one end is heated up and flattened out, then honed to a razor sharp edge, it makes an excellent scalpel, ideal for minor surgery.

Uses of a needle

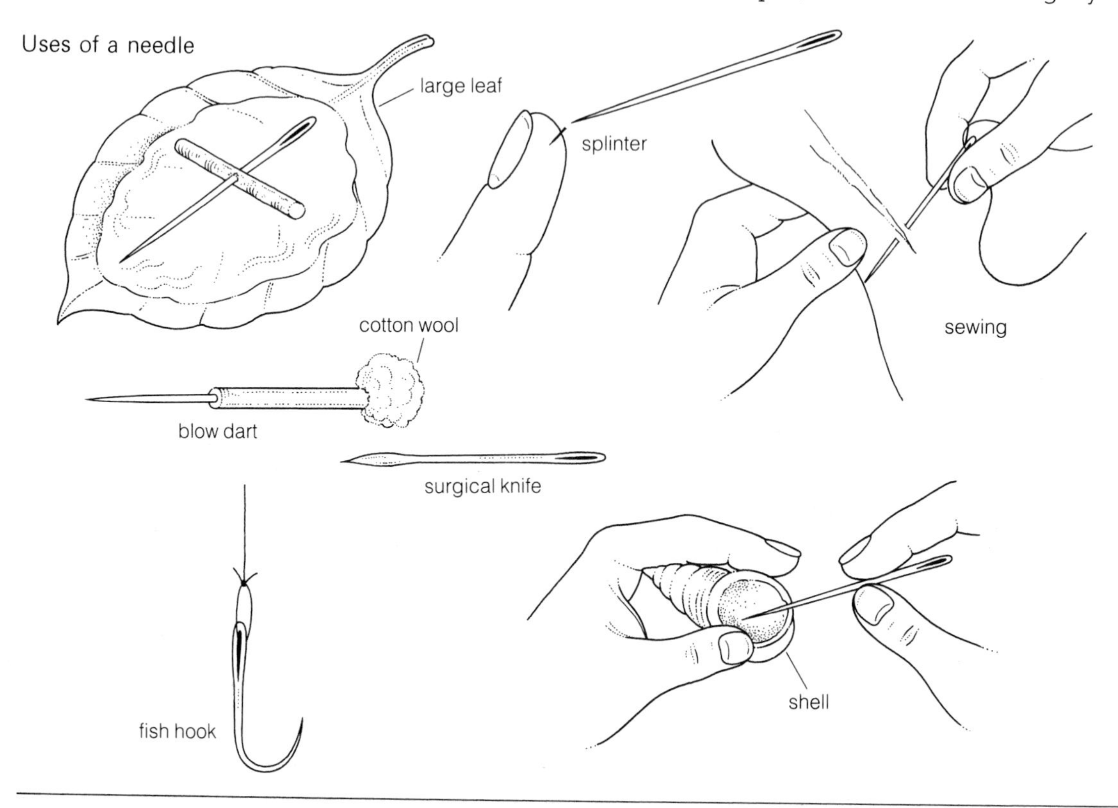

Similarly, multiple uses can be made of a matchstick. Once finished for its intended purpose it can serve as a scalpel blade holder, a dart for a blow gun or a fishing float – either pushed through a dried oak apple, or pressed into the quill of a feather. Linked together, several matches can make a fish trap. Or with the end flattened out and shaped one can be used to write or paint with. Twisted into cotton wool it makes a very good medical swab and if great care is taken it can be split and made into four matches instead of one. If the heads of several matches are removed and pressed into the core of a straw or dried length of corn, it becomes an excellent firelighter. So you can see it's important when choosing items to put into your survival pack to pick things that have multiple purposes.

When instructing at my survival centre I ask my students to make up their own individual packs and then we sit around in groups and discuss each other's efforts. I explain that it's very easy to cram a lot of useless items into your pack, items that can be obtained out in the wilds. Cotton, for instance, can easily be improvised from many species of plants. Depending on your ability to recognize many of the natural medicinal plants and fruits available to you, I strongly recommend that you include a few first aid items such as plasters, a small amount of antiseptic, a couple of aspirins etc., and if room allows some

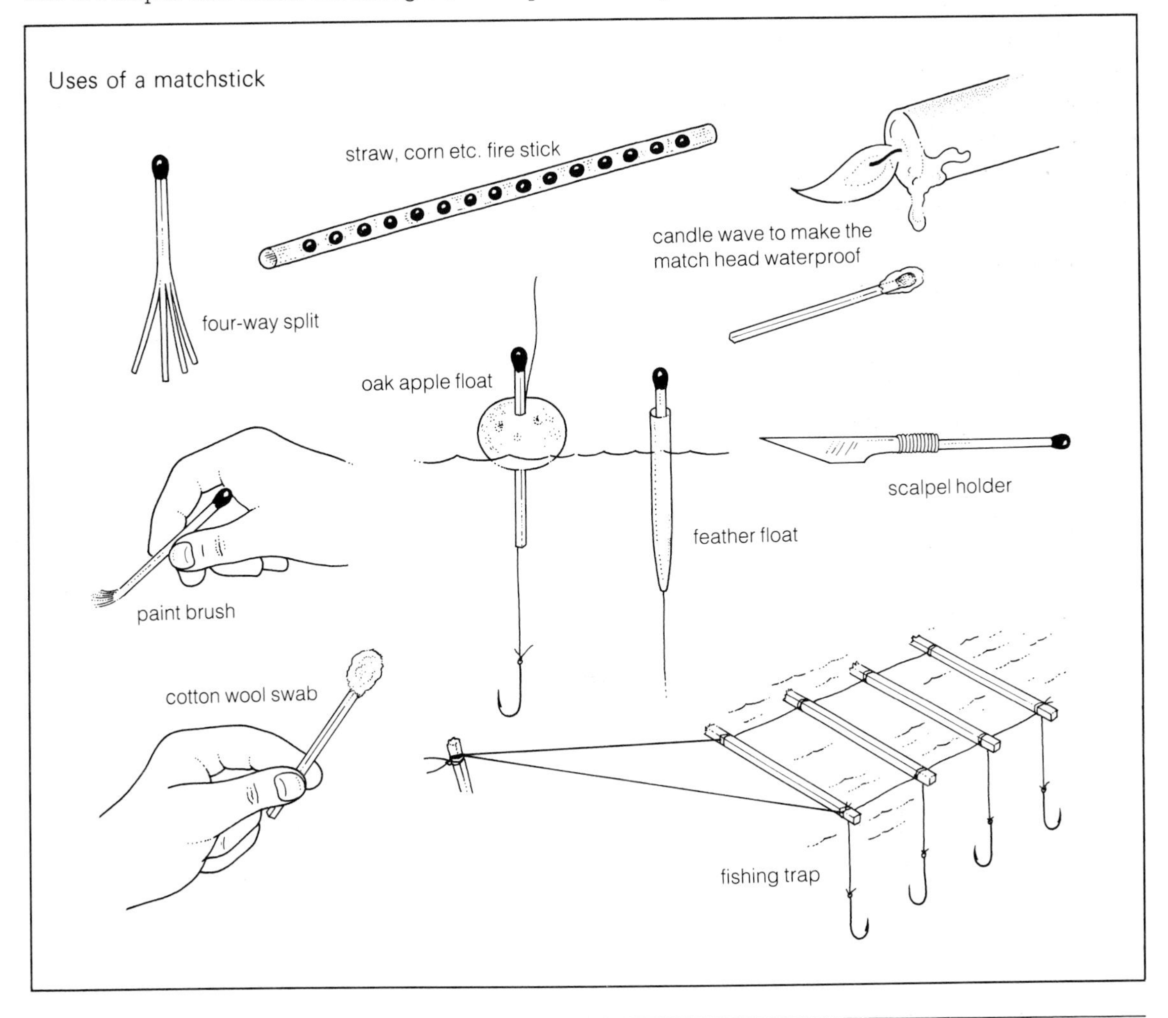

bandage, preferably the stretchy type or one soaked in some form of antiseptic Vaseline. The latter isn't just an excellent bandage but it makes very good tinder for starting your fire, especially if all around you is damp and wet. Many times I've used my army bandages for just such emergencies. The problem with bandages is that they tend to be a bit bulky, but if space allows pack one. Incidentally, an unwound bandage will provide you with unlimited cotton for sewing and for making fishing line or nets. Knotted and twisted together, bandage is exceptionally strong and an improvised rope can be made for your stretcher or sling. It can also be used as a filter, strainer, or eye-protector.

The market is flooded with many variations of survival kits. A great deal of them, I have to say, are filled with useless, cheap items and are often very expensive to buy. With a little thought and for only a few pence you can provide yourself with all your essential needs quite easily, and as you put your pack together you begin to discover more and more how adaptable many of the items become. Listed below is a series of items that I personally include in my own survival packs.

First you have to decide what size of pack and how many you want to carry with you. As I've explained, I always carry three, one sewn into my clothing, another in a container strapped to my rucksack or belt and a third either in the handle of my knife or simply in a small tin or matchbox kept inside my rucksack. An old cigar container or film canister is ideal. Some people even carry them in an old empty fountain pen. If travelling by vehicle you can of course include a great deal more. A spare blanket, flask, water bottle, spare water container, spare rations and a comprehensive medical kit, as well as spare clothing, a torch, whistle and even a fishing rod.

Eddie McGee's Personal Survival Pack

Assorted fish hooks
Waterproof/windproof matches
Needles/pins/safety pins
Two balloons/contraceptives (for water storage)
Pencil/paper/chalk
Aspirins
Small compass/magnet
Razor blades/scalpel
Snare wire
Six inches by six of tin foil
One Oxo cube or food pellets
Half a dozen carbide pellets
Spare match striker
Three assorted sticking plasters
Assorted rubber bands
Length of hacksaw blade
Small pair of tweezers or scissors.

All of these items chosen carefully will pack into a matchbox or small cigarette tin. I also usually carry a length of plastic or rubber tubing.

Survival tools

It may be necessary through circumstances forced upon you to improvise and make yourself some crude tools to supplement your survival pack. This isn't too difficult and apart from the obvious practical use, occupying your mind and hands is therapeutic and a great morale booster.

Initially probably the most useful tool will be a knife, spear or bow and arrow. All of these are simple to make. A knife, for instance, can be fashioned out of parts of your crashed aircraft/car/boat, or simply from a sharp rock, slate or even a shell. Many excellent knives can be made from old bones. On the next page are some examples of ones that I have actually made:

Turning a washing line into a climbing rope

An excellent use of rope and knots is in making an escape ladder. This is a trick we used to use in the armed services. Done properly you can turn a simple washing line into a safety ladder strong enough for you to climb down from your bedroom window if, for

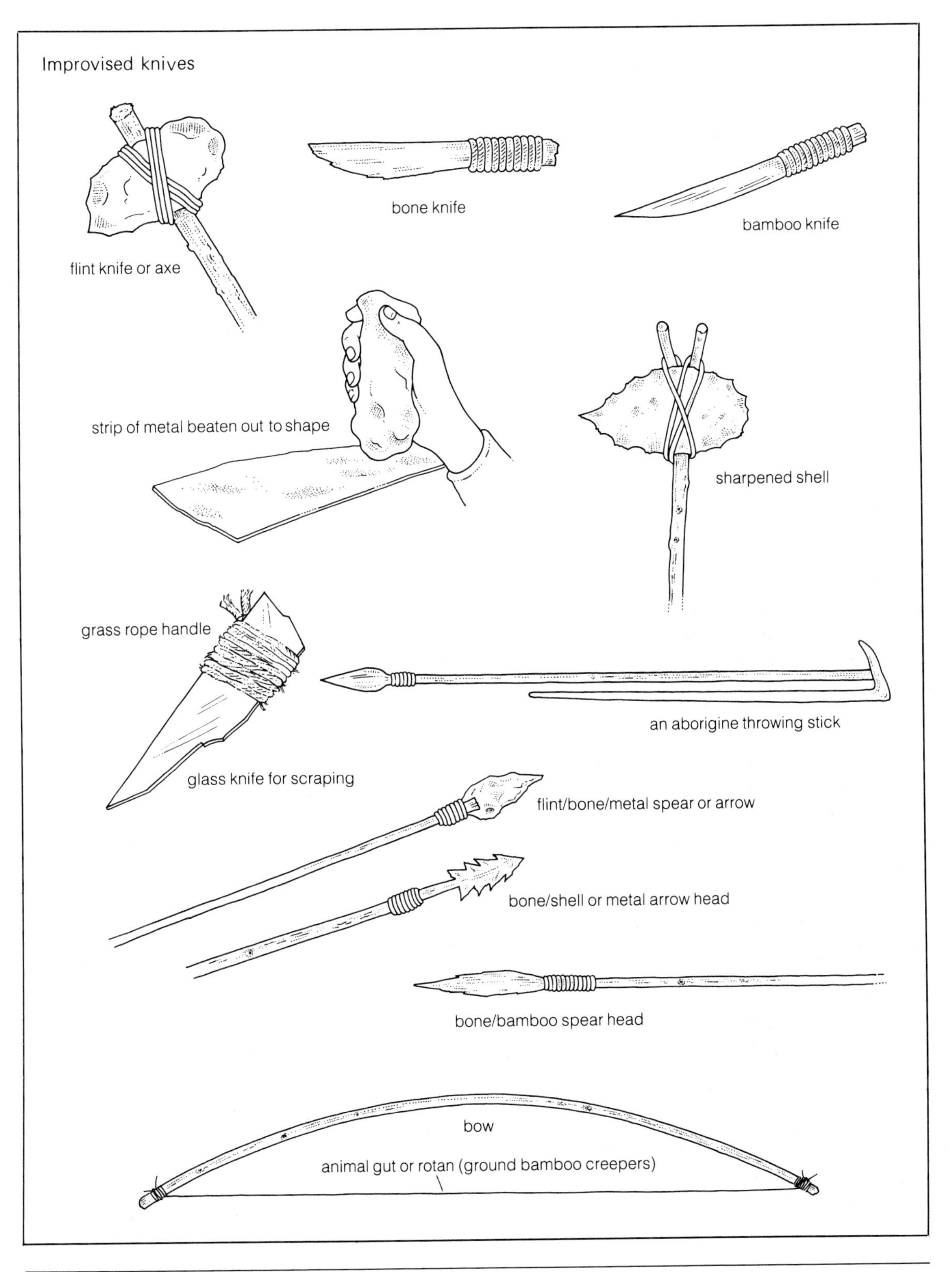
Improvised knives
flint knife or axe
bone knife
bamboo knife
strip of metal beaten out to shape
sharpened shell
grass rope handle
an aborigine throwing stick
glass knife for scraping
flint/bone/metal spear or arrow
bone/shell or metal arrow head
bone/bamboo spear head
bow
animal gut or rotan (ground bamboo creepers)

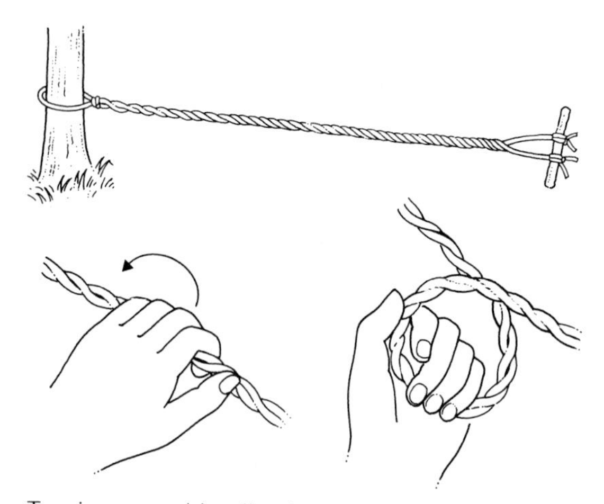

Turning a washing line into a strong rope

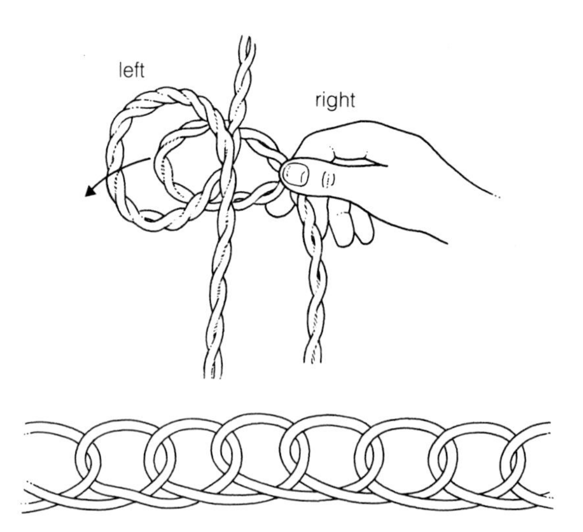

example, you're escaping from a house fire.

Firstly, choose a reasonably strong washing line – rope rather than nylon – then double it. As shown above fix it to a tree and run it out. Tie a bit of wood to the two ends and twist it until the two lengths are joined together.

Leaving it fastened to the tree, lay the free end on the ground still tied to the wood.

Take hold of the rope close to the tree in your left hand (as shown) and simply make a loop by rotating your wrist outwards. Holding this loop in your left hand, take hold of the rope with your right and push a second loop through the one in your left hand. Take hold of the second loop with your left and simply repeat this process until you run out of rope. In no time at all you will have quadrupled the strength of your domestic washing line into an exceptionally strong rope.

Practice makes perfect

Remember, your survival pack will only be as good as the items you put into it and there is no point in having a pack strapped to your belt, rucksack or stowed away in your car if you don't use it.

It's good practice for you to go off one weekend to the nearest forest or park and see just how useful the items in your pack are. Choose a nice warm, sunny day, seek permission from the landowner or park ranger, and try to survive for the weekend living off your pack. You will be amazed how quickly you begin to depend on that fishing hook or match, and how important that needle and cotton become.

Don't just pack items because they look good or you feel you ought to need them. If possible practice with every single individual item to see how many uses you can get from it.

There is a lot to be said for that old adage:

Practice makes perfect.

If nothing else it certainly instills confidence.

Photographic Acknowledgements

The author and publishers are grateful to the following for permission to reproduce photographs.

Colour section

Poisonous snakes: M K & I M Morcombe/NHPA, common death adder; E Hanumantha Rao/NHPA, king cobra; Alan G Nelson/OSF, green mamba; Alan Root/Survival Anglia, spitting cobra; Stephen Dalton/NHPA, adder, western diamond-back rattlesnake

Poisonous mushrooms: John & Irene Palmer/ Survival Anglia, death cap (above) destroying angel (below); David Thompson/OSF, fly agaric (above); Alastair Shay/OSF, fly agaric (below); Brian Hawkes/NHPA, destroying angel (above)

Poisonous plants: E A Jones/NHPA, privet in bloom; Dennis Green/Survival Anglia, deadly nightshade; David Woodfall/NHPA, hemlock; Ton Myssen/Survival Anglia, henbane; Jany Sauveanet/ NHPA, black nightshade; L Campbell/NHPA, monkshood, yew berries; John & Irene Palmer/Survival Anglia, mistletoe; Jack Dermio/OSF, poison ivy

Poisonous fish: W Gregory Brown/OSF, slender filefish; Rod & Moira Borland/OSF, zebra fish; Zig Leszczynski/OSF, porcupine fish, oyster toadfish; John Paling/OSF, sting ray; Jen & Des Bartlett/Survival Anglia, scorpion fish; Seaphot Ltd, stonefish

Black and white

N Elkins, cumulonimbus (above) page 27; C S Broomfield, cumulonimbus (below) page 27; K H Switak/NHPA, barrel cactus page 48, fucus & rockweed page 91; M J Coe/OSF, prickly pear page 49; Keith Penn, Eddie eating coconut, Eddie spiking fruit page 49, crocodile trap page 75, smoking fish page 87, corn fibres page 117, shelter page 131; E R Watts/Survival Anglia, cassava tree page 66; S R Morris/OSF, cassava root page 66, coconut palm grove page 117; John & Irene Palmer/Survival Anglia, shaggy ink cap page 69, summer truffle page 70, oyster fungus page 70; Stephen Dalton/NHPA, common field mushroom page 69; H L Fox/OSF, morel page 69; Tim Shepherd/OSF, wood blewitt page 69, female anopheles mosquito page 125; L Campbell/NHPA, cep page 70, green laver page 91; Brian Hawkes/NHPA, boletus elegans page 70, boletus luteus page 70; Barrie E Watts/OSF, beef-steak fungus page 70; G A Maclean/OSF, giant puffballs page 70, parasol mushroom page 70; Dieter & Mary Plage/Survival Anglia, figs page 71, wild bananas page 72; G I Bernard/NHPA, papaya tree page 71, saw wrack & kelp page 90; P K Sharpe/OSF, mangoes page 71; J B Free/NHPA, bread fruit page 71; Peter Davey/Bruce Colman Ltd, chimpanzee page 90; Rodger Jackman/OSF, bladder wrack page 90; Dr C E Jeffree/OSF, egg or knotted wrack page 91; Ivan Polumin/NHPA, pandanus palm page 91; Gamma, amazon (left) page 115, river from air page 128; Rob Cousins/Susan Griggs Agency, amazon (right) page 115; Richard Packwood/OSF, rubber plantation page 116; Annie Price/Survival Anglia, bamboo plantation page 122; Deni Bown/OSF, jack fruit page 72, bamboo page 122; Kathie Atkinson/OSF, blood sucking leech page 125; Heinz Stucke/Frank Spooner Pictures, an approaching sandstorm page 136; David Curl/OSF, desert scorpion page 138

Index